THE COIN OF THE ISLAMIC REALM

INSURGENCIES & THE OTTOMAN EMPIRE, 1416-1916

Timothy R. Furnish, Ph.D.

The COIN of the Islamic Realm: Insurgencies & The Ottoman
Empire, 1416-1916

ACKNOWLEDGEMENTS

I started this book a few years ago, but new course preps and sons in high school football and wrestling tossed it in the back seat. Still, my wife, Davina—despite being a very busy attorney—encouraged me to finish it. So once again, I thank her for that loving support. I am also extremely grateful for her superb editing skills, since she knows the secret of putting manuscripts up on Amazon. My gratitude goes, as well, to Joel Langford, the head librarian at Reinhardt University, where I teach history. As I was scrambling to finish the manuscript this summer (2020), Joel's ability and willingness to find even the most obscure secondary source on the Ottomans was an enormous help. Finally, I must once again thank my old friend and artist extraordinaire, Tony Arrasmith. While running his business, Arrasmith & Associates, in Cincinnati, he made time to create this book's covers—as he did for two of my previous tomes.

In 2013, my older son's fifth grade class was studying World War I. When I looked at that section in his history textbook, I was surprised to see that it didn't even mention the Ottoman Empire—which of course fought on the side of the Central Powers. Neglect of the Ottomans is not limited to elementary school textbooks, however. Modern Middle East analysts often ignore them, as well. I've lost track of how many articles I've read on the Israeli-Palestinian issue which skip from Biblical times to 1948, as if the Turks had not ruled Jerusalem and environs for centuries. Likewise, one would look mostly in vain for mention of the 159 years the Ottoman army and administrators spent trying to pacify Yemen—which might be rather important to understanding the war currently raging there. Dark references to Turkish President Recep Erdoğan's alleged "Neo-Ottomanism" are about as deep as current affairs research into that Empire's 500-year Middle Eastern reign goes.

This observation holds true, in particular, for studies of insurgency and counterinsurgency (COIN). The field is rife with articles and papers on the French (Napoleonic) in Spain or Algeria (modern), the Brits in Malaya or Ireland, and of course the Americans in Vietnam, Iraq and Afghanistan. The subject matter is treated, almost without exception, as a Western issue. (Remember that even the Arab Revolt of World War I was instigated, and led by, a Brit: T.E. Lawrence "of Arabia.") But Western powers have not been the only ones, across space and time, fighting challenges to their rule. In the Middle East and Africa, the Ottomans did so, repeatedly. This neglect is probably not intentional. I chalk it up to the fact that most analysts know little about the Middle East prior to the 20th century; while historians of the Ottoman Empire are rarely well-versed in military or COIN studies. (The few exceptions are noted later in this book.) Nonetheless, a real gap in both historical studies and COIN inquiry exists—and this book is a preliminary attempt to rectify it by examining the Ottoman experience.

I am a historian of the Islamic world, not of the Ottoman Empire specifically. While I have studied the latter, as well as the Ottoman Turkish language, I have neither the time nor the level of expertise required to mine the extensive Ottoman archives in Istanbul. This book, then, relies on secondary sources—albeit, the best and most relevant ones I could find. It is an attempt at applied history: looking at the past for guidance to the present, and future. As such, it's aimed mainly at military and government professionals for whom studying warfare, particularly COIN, is part of their jobs. Its secondary audience is the general public, who can learn about Ottoman political and military history but don't need to worry about the extensive footnotes (unless they want to). This is definitely not a work intended to please (other) academics—who would no doubt scorn a book published on Amazon, in any event. In that vein, I have tried to keep the transliteration of Ottoman and Arabic terms as simple as possible, often deviating from standard academic systems for doing so.

Also, let me acknowledge that the cover illustration for this book comes from Wikimedia Commons, and is entitled "Nizami-cedid-ordusu"—the Ottoman "New Order Army."

Finally: I welcome feedback on this book and its topic. I can be reached through my website, www.occidentaljihadist.com or via email, jinnandtonic@yahoo.com.

CHAPTER ONE—INTRODUCTION

The world is currently bedeviled by a legion of terrorist groups, among which Islamic State and al-Qa`idah are the most powerful, but far from the sum total. Indeed, it is not a stretch to say that "political violence and instability in the Middle East has become not only a topic of great interest but also arguably the most important political issue in the world today."[1] Whether we choose to call ISIS, AQ and that ilk "Islamist," "Islamic extremist," "radical Muslim" or just plain "jihadist," the ideology remains the same. It is, make no mistake, the religion of Islam—via a brutally literalist, if anachronistic, understanding and application of that faith's 7th century AD norms. This does not mean that all, or even most, Muslims are terrorists—far from it; in fact, the vast majority clearly are not. What it does mean is that this belief system, in its rigid, archaic form, is disproportionately responsible for worldwide terrorism and violence. As of spring 2020, there were 69 total groups on the U.S. Department of State's list of foreign terrorist organizations [FTO].[2] Fifty-three of those, or 77%, self-identify as Islamic in ideology, motivation and goals. All other ideologies combined—mostly nationalism, Marxism, or some combination

---

[1] Barry Rubin, "Introduction" to *Conflict and Insurgency in the Contemporary Middle East*, Barry Rubin, ed. (London and New York: Routledge, 2009), p. 1.

[2] "Foreign Terrorist Organizations," *state.gov/foreign-terrorist-organizations/*; accessed June 3, 2020.

thereof—were the *raison d'être* for only 16, or 23%. In real numbers, these were: six nationalist, six Marxist, and one each Maoist, anarchist, syncretic,[3] and Jewish.[4] Notably, not one terrorist organization adduces Christianity, Hinduism or Buddhism as its inspiration.

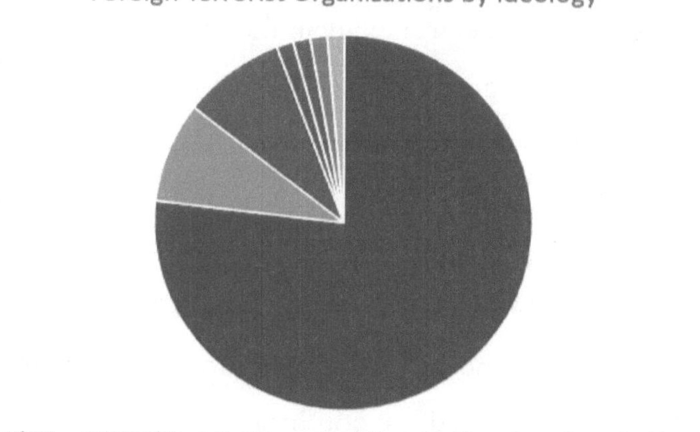

[Source: US State Department FTO List]

Furthermore, 81 of 82 organizations deemed terrorist by the Muslim government of the United Arab Emirates in 2014 were Islamic.[5] Back in 2016, a study by the U.S. Senate Judiciary Subcommittee on

---

[3] This is Aum Shinrikyo of Japan, which is a weird mélange of Buddhism and apocalypticism but never overtly trumpeted its allegiance to the former.

[4] Why Kahane Chai/Kach is still on the list is frankly baffling. The group is moribund, and last engaged in any terrorist activity 20 years ago. One suspects the US government gets political mileage, or at least cover, out of having at least one ostensibly Jewish group on the list.

[5] Staff Writer, "UAE Blacklists 82 Groups as 'Terrorist,'" *al Arabiya News*, November 15, 2014; accessed June 3, 2020.

Immigration and the National Interest[6] empirically demolished claims by the former (Obama) administration[7] and the media[8] that "right-wing" terrorism is as rampant as the Islamic kind. Between 9/11 and summer 2016 attempted terrorists in the U.S. pledged their loyalties to some 24 different groups—21 of which were Islamic. From the time of the destruction of the World Trade Center and for the following 13 years, AQ was the overwhelming favorite inspiration for such. Then ISIS has moved into the lead of a pack every member of which claims to be Muslim. Whether one wishes to call the former caliphate created by Abu Bakr al-Baghdadi ISIS (Islamic State in Iraq and Syria), ISIL (Islamic State in the Levant), or even the allegedly-insulting and delegitimizing "Da`ish,"[9] the group is profoundly, albeit brutally, Islamic (as I have explained on TV[10]). The same holds, *mutatis mutandis*, for AQ, Boko Haram, the Taliban, al-Shabab, each and every group with *jihad* in its name, and the other legion of groups on the aforementioned lists. As I write this, a number of US cities are wracked by riots, fires and looting,

---

[6] See the summary and analysis thereof by Judson Berger, "Anatomy of the Terror Threat: Files Show Hundreds of US Plots, Refugee Connection," *Fox News*, June 22, 2016; accessed June 3, 202o.

[7] Peter Hasson, "DHS Secretary: Right Wingers Pose Same Threat as Islamic Extremists," *Daily Caller*, June 14, 2016; accessed June 3, 2020.

[8] As, for example: Kurt Eichenwald, "Right-Wing Extremists Are a Bigger Threat to America than ISIS," *Newsweek*, February 4, 2016; accessed June 3, 2020.

[9] As per Faisal Irshaid, "Isis, Isil, IS or Daesh? One Group, Many Names," *BBC News*, December 2, 2015; accessed June 9, 2020. The Arabic verb *dawasha*, "to irritate," might also be an etymological inspiration. Whether this term has had any actual deleterious effect on ISIS is questionable at best.

[10] See "War Stories: Fighting ISIS," *Fox News*, April 20, 2016; accessed June 3, 2020.

following Antifa thugs hijacking any peaceful protests over the killing of George Floyd by cops in Minneapolis. The Trump Administration says, as a result, it will start treating Antifa as a domestic terrorist organization.[11] Many commentators, opposed to this, are still convinced that "white supremacists" pose the greatest threat, both domestically and abroad.[12] However, Islamic terrorism's reach and lethality still easily outstrip that of both the Left and Right.[13] The best deconstruction of Islamic terrorist apologetics demonstrates clearly that terrorism in the name of Islam is a much greater threat both abroad and inside the US than is any other kind.[14]

There are indeed sects of Islam that eschew jihad-as-violence and do not preach the need to subjugate non-Muslims. These include, at a minimum, the Ahmadis, Isma'ili Shi`is and several Sufi orders.[15] These groups avoid jihadist terrorism by allowing non-literal interpretations of the Qur'an's violent passages, and by disavowing some of the more odious Hadiths (putative sayings of

---

[11] Robert Jonathan, "Trump Announces Designation of Antifa as a Terrorist Organization," *BPR*, May 31, 2020; accessed online June 4, 2020.

[12] For a pre-Trump example, see Julia Craven, "White Supremacists More Dangerous to America than Foreign Terrorists, Study Says," *Huffpost*, June 24, 2015. For one since his election: Siobhan Neela-Stock, "'Time' Magazine's Powerful New Cover Calls Out White Nationalist Terrorism," *Mashable*, August 8, 2019. On "white nationalism" and its alleged international scope: Art Jipson and Paul J. Becker, "White Nationalism, Born in the USA, is Now a Global Terror Threat," *theconversation*, March 29, 2019. All were accessed June 4, 2020.

[13] As I explained in my article "White Terrorists vs. the Sultans of Slaughter," *The Stream*, August 13, 2019; accessed June 4, 2020.

[14] Damion Daniels, "No, You're Not More Likely to be Killed by a Right-wing Extremist than an Islamic Terrorist," *Areo*, May 28, 2017; accessed June 3, 2020..

[15] As I explained in my article "Sectsploitation: How to Win Hearts and Minds in the Islamic World," *History News Network*, May 31, 2009; accessed June 3, 2020.

the Islamic prophet Muhammad).[16]   But unfortunately, Sunni Islam—comprising some 85% of all Muslims and which thus, by definition, is mainstream—has for centuries maintained that the Qur'an and Hadiths should be taken at face value; and that, in particular, their sections promoting violent jihad against non-Muslims must be followed slavishly.[17] Would that these sectarian positions were more influential among the world's 1.6 billion Muslims. Until they are, or until mainstream Islam itself adopts a more flexible and less absolutist exegetical paradigm, ISIS, AQ and their brethren will be almost impossible to completely delegitimize.

Former President Obama,[18] his official spokesman,[19] and his Director of Central Intelligence[20]—just as, almost comically, his first

---

[16] See, for example, "Permissibility of killing women and children [of polytheists] in night raids," from "The Book of Jihad and Expeditions," *Sahih Muslim*, available at *Sunnah.com*; accessed June 7, 2020. That searchable site—which deals only with one of the six major Hadith collections—allows one to research Muhammad's opinion (usually approving) on topics such as drinking camel urine, beheading those who turn away from Islam, or the 263 entries on his clarifications about jihad.

[17] Here are some recent examples: "Kuwaiti Islamic Scholar: The Quran Encourages Offensive Jihad by Means of Force," *Middle East Media Research Institutes* [MEMRI] *TV*, December 6, 2019; "Al-Aqsa Mosque Address: Job of Muslims is to Bring 'Hateful Infidels' to Islam through Jihad," *MEMRI TV*, April 15, 2019; "Kuwaiti Cleric Salaam at-Taweel: Jihad for the Sake of Allah Means Fighting the Infidels to Make Them Convert to Islam; Enslaving Infidels is One of the Virtues of Islam," *MEMRI TV*, November 7, 2017; and "Egyptian Al-Azhar Cleric Muhammad Zaki: Ramadhan is the Month of Jihad, Not of Sleep," June 26, 2015. All were accessed June 7, 2020.

[18] Charles Spiering, "President Obama: 'No Religion is Responsible for Violence and Terrorism,'" *Breitbart*, February 18, 2015; accessed June 3, 2020.

[19] Susan Jones, "Obama Spokesman on Islam: 'It's a Peaceful Religion,'" *CNSNews*, January 7, 2015; accessed June 3, 2020.

[20] "Obama Advisor John Brennan Speaks about the Beauty of Islam," *Youtube*, May 19, 2010; accessed June 3, 2020.

Attorney General[21]—could not bring themselves to admit the obvious connection between Islam and violence. To the contrary: they deemed Islam entirely peaceful and the very idea of *jihad*—which Muhammad himself waged, and which is enshrined in the Qur'an[22]—was portrayed as some sort of aberrant interjection into the world's second-largest faith, rather than an intrinsic part thereof whenever the theology is followed literally. Such willful blindness about Islam was not just a phenomenon of Obama's first term, either; his National Security Advisor was doubling down on such duplicitous declarations even in late 2017.[23] This Muslim apologetics approach was enshrined in Obama's 2011 National Strategy for Counterterrorism,[24] which mentioned the world "Islam" a grand total of once.

Things have changed since the election of Donald J. Trump. The 45th President, to his credit, put out a new counterterrorism agenda in fall 2018, in which "radical Islamist[25] terrorism" is

---

[21] "Attorney General Eric Holder Won't Say 'Radical Islam,'" *Youtube,* May 17, 2010; accessed June 3, 2020.

[22] For those lacking the time or energy to scour the Qur'an on this topic for themselves, utilize Yoel Natan, "164 Jihad Verses in the Koran [sic]," *answering-islam.org,* 2004; accessed June 4, 2020. The concept of jihad is explored most fully by Rudolph Peters, *Jihad: A History in Documents* (Princeton: Markus Wiener Publishers, 2016).

[23] "Video—H.R. McMaster: Muslim Terrorist Groups Are 'Really UnIslamic,' 'Irreligious,'" *Youtube,* August 15, 2017; accessed June 3, 2020.

[24] "National Strategy for Counterterrorism," June 2011; accessed June 3, 2020.

[25] The term "Islamist" is, at this point (much like "radical" or "extremist Islam") enshrined in national security discourse—unfortunately. "Islamist" is most often used to differentiate followers of political Islam from everyday Muslims. The problem is that Islam is probably the most political religion on Earth, and has been so going back to its founder Muhammad being made the leader of the

adduced some 16 times.[26]   While terrorism in Islam is far from

"radical,"[27] the Trump Administration view at least has one eye

open—unlike Obama's, which had both slammed tightly shut.

Trump's National Strategy for Counterterrorism [NSCT] stresses the

need to "do more than merely kill or capture terrorists. We must

dismantle…networks and sever the sources…that sustain them."[28]

This report highlights threats such as ISIS, AQ and the Islamic

Republic of Iran (the world's foremost state sponsor of terrorism),

Boko Haram, Tehrik-e Taliban Pakistan and Lashkar-e Tayyiba

(which operates in India and Pakistan) But it also notes that some

non-Islamic entities might be potentially dangerous, such as the

---

city of Yathrib (later Medina) in 622 AD. This was quite unlike Christianity. As
Bernard Lewis points out, particularly in *The Political Language of Islam* (Chicago:
University of Chicago Press, 1988), "[i]n classical Islam there was no distinction
between Church [that is, religion] and state. In Christendom the existence of
two authorities goes back to the founder, who enjoined his followers to render
unto Caesar the things which are Caesar's and to God the things which are
God's. Throughout the history of Christendom there have been two powers:
God and Caesar…or, in modern terms, church and state…. In pre-westernized
Islam, there were not two powers but one, and the question of separation,
therefore, could not arise" (p. 2). Lewis continues, next page: "the very notion
of a secular jurisdiction and authority" in the Islamic world "is seen as an
impiety, indeed as the ultimate betrayal of Islam. The righting of this wrong is
the principal aim of Islamic revolutionaries and…those described as Islamic
fundamentalists." However "[t]**his definition of political identity and loyalty
by religious belief…is not limited to the revolutionaries**" (emphasis added).
An "Islamist," then, is actually a Muslim literalist—or fundamentalist.

[26] See "National Strategy for Counterterrorism of the United States of
America,"[NSCT 2018] October 2018, accessed June 3, 2020—as well as my
explicatory blogpost, "Trump's New Counter-terrorism Strategy: The One-Eyed
Man is Still King," October 12, 2018, accessed online June 3, 2020.

[27] A point which I must make repeatedly, since the term has become not just a
staple of conventional wisdom but a virtual shibboleth of the media and even
government policy makers.

[28] NSCT 2018, p. I, Executive Summary.

Nordic Resistance Movement [NRM], UK's National Action Group [NAG] and India's Sikh Babbar Khalsa.[29] Still, the Trump Administration focuses, much more than did either of its 21st century predecessors, on those 53 Islam-oriented organizations which wage, as they see it, *jihad fi sabil Allah*: "holy war in the path of Allah." ISIS, which supplanted AQ as the West's main enemy from 2014 by conquering and declaring a territorial caliphate, is no more—at least as a polity.[30] But it lives on in its former incarnation as a terrorist group.[31] This despite the death of its founding caliph, Abu Bakr al-Baghdadi, at the hands of US forces.[32] ISIS' devolution back to a (mere) terrorist organization from a territorial state was not unexpected,[33] although the power of its eschatological beliefs in holding the organization together even at that level should not be underestimated.[34]

---

[29] *Ibid.*, p. 9. Of the latter three, only Babbar Khalsa has killed anyone, and that in an airliner bombing back in 1985. NAG has fewer than 100 members and, while odious, has done little besides stage marches and some fights. The NRM is mostly known for listening to Middle-earth-themed death metal bands, albeit quite loudly.

[30] Mark Katkov, "Analysis: The End of the 'Caliphate' Doesn't Mean the End of ISIS," *NPR*, March 22, 2019; accessed June 4, 2020.

[31] As per "U.S. Report: ISIS Regrouping in Syria and Iraq," *Wilson Center*, November 20, 2019; accessed June 4, 2020.

[32] "Donald Trump Announces ISIS Leader Abu Bakr al-Baghdadi is Dead," *Youtube*, October 27, 2019; accessed June 4, 2020.

[33] Most clearly predicted by Paul Staniland, "Whither ISIS? Insights from Insurgent Responses to Decline," *The Washington Quarterly* (Fall 2017), pp. 29-43; accessed June 4,2020.

[34] See "Wikistrat Special Report on Abu Bakr al-Baghdadi's Death," *Wikistrat*, November 25, 2019—especially my section, toward the end, on ISIS' apocalyptic ideology; accessed June 4, 2020.

So an accurate *description* of the main terrorist threats facing the world must acknowledge the overwhelming Islamic nature of such. But what about *prescription* for dealing with them? Since 9/11, churning out studies and policy recommendations purporting to tell us how to defeat these enemies has become something of a cottage industry. "Defeating Islamic terrorism" yields 15.8 million Google hits, even more than "defeating Al Qaeda (4.8 million) or "defeating ISIS" (1.3 million). The list of significant, and sound, policy analyses that shed light on how to actually do so grows quite thin, however. I examined a number of them and hereby render the following verdicts.

In late 2014, after ISIS had just recently declared its caliphate, the Institute for the Study of War put out "A Strategy to Defeat the Islamic State," authored by Kimberly Kagan, Frederic W. Kagan, and Jessica D. Lewis.[35] This publication identified strategic objectives as: destroying ISIS and Jabhat al-Nusra, AQ's Syrian branch; reconstituting Iraq and Syria as territorial states; keeping Iran from regional hegemon status; and protecting Lebanon and Jordan, the other two countries most at risk from ISIS.[36] The authors laid out some rather vague military objectives such as "prevent genocide,"[37] the implementation of which would have required as many as 25,000 men as ground forces.[38] As for political efforts, this

---

[35] Available online at "Middle East Security Report 23" (September 2014), Institute for the Study of War; accessed June 5, 2020.
[36] Kagan, *et al.*, p. 21.
[37] *Ibid.*, p. 23.
[38] *Ibid.*, p. 26.

particular study recommended working closely with Iraqi Sunni leaders, creating a parallel replacement government for al-Assad in Syria, leaning on unspecified regional states supporting ISIS (probably led by Saudi Arabia), and, most importantly, "helping a moderate opposition defeat Assad"[39]—although the definition of "moderate" and identifying of such, is lacking (a constant problem with such assessments). Furthermore, as it turned out, the Obama Administration program to empower a "moderate opposition" in Syria, wound up costing $500 million and was a total failure.[40] Ironically, that Administration then pursued "a strategy that only disrupts without defeating or destroying ISIS"—a policy which "A Strategy to Defeat" warned against as a recipe for perpetual U.S. military operations in Iraq and Syria."[41] While some of its ideas would have benefitted the US had we pursued them at the height of ISIS' power, this ISW policy paper's major flaws were that it promoted and depended upon the aforementioned chimera of the moderate (Sunni Muslim) opposition[42] in places such as Syria; rejected working with the al-Assad government;[43] and reinforced the World War I-era betrayal of the Kurds' legitimate and pressing

---

[39] *Ibid.,* p. 25.

[40] Jonah Goldberg, "Team Obama Has Spent $500M to Train 'Four or Five' Syrian Rebels," *New York Post*, September 18, 2015; accessed June 6, 2020.

[41] Kagan, *et al.,* p. 28.

[42] Gareth Porter, "Obama's 'Moderate' Syrian Deception," *Common Dreams*, February 17, 2016; accessed June 6, 2020.

[43] Which ultimately won the conflict (although at the cost of ruling over a rump Syrian state). See Gil Barndollar, "Assad Has Won and America Must Go," *The National Interest*, September 17, 2018; accessed June 10, 2020.

demands for their own independent state.[44] Overall, too, it was aimed at eroding the ISIS territorial caliphate—which is no longer an issue (at least as of summer 2020). The larger problem of the ideological and, yes, religious legitimacy of Islamic literalism/fundamentalism in the eyes of a substantial minority of the world's 1.6 billion Muslims—whence ISIS drew, and draws, its strength—was never addressed.

In 2015 media documentary film-maker and author Joseph V. Micallef published *Islamic State: Its History, Ideology & Challenge.*[45] His book is quite well-done for a non-specialist, particularly in pointing out ISIS' weaknesses and strengths.[46] In terms of the former, ISIS had no access to the sea, no air forces, little access to above-board international trade, and is surrounded by enemies. On the other hand, ISIS was opposed by a shaky alliance headed up by two nations whose governments detest one another—the US and Iran. While its territory might be taken away, the organization would likely simply devolve back into a non-geographic terrorist group. In this Micallef proved accurately, if not singularly, prescient. But beyond speculating about whether the Kurdish Pershmerga or the Iraqi Army, assisted by Iraq's Sunnis, should have been more capable of "rolling back" ISIS, Micallef's slim volume identified some of the issues facing the anti-ISIS front. However, he never really laid out an agenda to degrade, much less destroy, ISIS; it was

---

[44] Kagan, *et al.,* p. 28.
[45] Put out by Antioch Downs Press of Vancouver and Portland.
[46] Micallef, pp. 98-100.

all description, no prescription. And he touched not at all on the Islamic ideology of the Islamic State.

That same year former Speaker of the US House of Representatives, and ex-college history professor, Newt Gingrich published an article entitled "Why We're Losing to Radical Islam."[47] It outlined steps to defeat "radical Islam" which the US Congress should take: compile detailed data on this "nihilistic global movement;" hold hearings on specific countries, especially Nigeria, Somalia, Yemen, Syria, Afghanistan and Pakistan; investigate the Muslim Brotherhood; look into sources of "radical Islamist funding," to include Saudi Arabia, Qatar and Iran; examine how and why Egypt, Jordan, Morocco, Tunisia and Algeria have "successfully contained and minimized radical Islamists;" investigate "radicalization in mosques and on social media;" and help prepare the US for the "Islamist cyberthreat." Even (allegedly) arch-conservative Gingrich apparently accepts the inaccurate and indeed misleading phrase "radical Islam." He compounds this mistake by categorizing the legion of global Islamic fundamentalist movements as "nihilistic," when in fact they have a concrete and, to them, rational agenda: establishment of Islamic law and, for the many Sunni ones, reestablishment of a legitimate caliphate. Gingrich is on much more solid ground in suggesting we look at how friendly Islamic nations have dealt with such groups—even if the assertion

---

[47] Behind the firewall at *The Wall Street Journal*, the piece can now be found at *Gingrich 360*; accessed June 6, 2020.

that Egypt and those other four countries have actually countered Islamic fundamentalism is probably overstated. Perhaps the former Speaker would have had better luck analyzing a topic which in which he has expertise—such as post-World War II colonial European educational policies in sub-Saharan Africa.[48]

One of the few book-length treatments of the issue at hand by a Muslim writer is *Refuting ISIS: A Rebuttal of its Religious and Ideological Foundations* by the Syrian Shaykh Muhammad al-Yaqoubi.[49] The author, a Syrian Islamic scholar, opposed both the al-Assad government (for which he was exiled to Morocco) and ISIS.[50] As might be expected, al-Yaqoubi claims adamantly that ISIS is not Islamic and lumps the group in with the ancient *Khawarij*, the "dissidents" who were the fundamentalist outliers of early Islamic history. He also blames Fox News,[51] "nefarious strategists,"[52] and (of course) former President George W. Bush[53] for ISIS, as well as the lack of a constraining central religious authority in Sunni Islam. Shaykh al-Yaqoubi presents a litany of allegedly unIslamic atrocities carried out by ISIS;[54] but many of those are actions that Islamic

---

[48] Gingrich's entire Tulane University doctoral dissertation, entitled "Belgian Education Policy in the Congo, 1945-1960," can be read at *Global Black History*; accessed June 6, 2020.

[49] The complete subtitle on the publication page is *Destroying Its Religious Foundations and Proving That It Has Strayed from Islam and That Fighting It Is An Obligation* (Sacred Knowledge, 2015).

[50] "Muhammad al-Yaqoubi," *Wikipedia*; accessed June 6, 2020.

[51] Al-Yaqoubi, p. xvii.

[52] *Ibid.*, pp. xviii, xix.

[53] *Ibid.* p. 3.

[54] *Ibid.*, pp. 10-17.

states have done in the past: "exacting revenge upon the public;" putting ulama to death; "expelling Muslims and non-Muslims from their towns and villages;" destroying churches; "enslaving non-Muslims; and "considering themselves the only saved group of Muslims." The Ottomans, medieval North African Almohads and Egyptian Fatimids each did some or all of those—so it's hard to see how such are beyond the Islamic pale. In his conclusion, the Shaykh spells out recommended policies:[55] Iraq's government must stop oppressing Sunnis; al-Assad must step down in Syria; Muslim minorities' rights must be respected around the world; "Western countries must respect Muslim values and sacred figures and reconsider the boundaries of free speech."[56] Specifically he asks the West, in effect, to stop being the West: "[p]ersisting in offending the Prophet of Islam…will…exacerbate the feeling of anger among Muslims."[57] Former President Obama said the same thing in his address to the United Nations in 2012.[58] Ironically, the Shaykh even criticizes both ISIS and Obama: "ISIS is using us to give it what it wants: wide Islamic mobilization, the de-legitimization of allied Arab leaders, and an inchoate 'war' with no strategy or 'end game'—a process Obama is in fact facilitating."[59] Shaykh al-Yaqoubi's book, alas, ultimately amounts to a long series of *ad hominem* attacks against

---

[55] *Ibid.*, pp. 36-38.
[56] *Ibid.*, p. 36.
[57] *Ibid.*, p. 37.
[58] "Obama: 'The Future Must Not Belong to Those Who Slander the Prophet of Islam,'" *Youtube*, September 25, 2012; accessed June 6, 2020.
[59] al-Yaqoubi, p. 39, footnote 1.

ISIS and its then-leader, al-Baghdadi. Nowhere does the learned author wrestle with, or even admit, the massive problem that Islam's founder himself sanctioned beheadings,[60] led armies in battle,[61] and sometimes ordered opponents tortured.[62] Until those aspects of Islam are addressed, ISIS and its ilk will remain at least tacitly legitimate within the world's second-largest religion.

In 2016 Malcolm Nance and Richard Engel published the 500-page tome *Defeating ISIS: Who They Are, How They Fight, What They Believe*.[63] Nance is a former Navy senior enlisted cryptologist with a BA[64] whose credentials and career, however, have been questioned by fellow veterans.[65] Engel is a journalist who covered the Iraq and Syria wars, speaks Arabic, and holds a B.A. in International Relations.[66] The latter is a more credible analyst, although not exactly politically objective.[67] Their lengthy book, while chock-full of tactical recommendations for "taking ISIS offline," suffers from a strategic lack of understanding and ludicrously ahistorical contentions which amount to factual errors.

---

[60] See my article "Beheading in the Name of Islam," *Middle East Quarterly* (Spring 2005), pp. 51-57; accessed June 6, 2020.

[61] Richard A. Gabriel, "Muhammad: The Warrior Prophet," *historynet,* n.d.; accessed June 6, 2020.

[62] Samuel Green, "Muhammad's Use of Torture," *answering-islam.org* (2005); accessed June 6, 2020.

[63] Put out by Skyhorse Publishing of New York.

[64] "Malcolm Nance," *Wikipedia*; accessed June 6, 2020.

[65] Most openly Peter Morlock, "Opinion: A Matter of Honor and the Fiction of Malcolm Nance," *SOFREP*, June 1, 2018; accessed June 6, 2020.

[66] "Richard Engel," *Wikipedia*; accessed June 6, 2020.

[67] Engel has, for example, compared President Trump to Joseph Stalin. Sam Dorman, "NBC Reporter Compares Trump to Stalin after He Suggests Kurds Should Leave Syria," *Fox News*, October 24, 2019; accessed June 6, 2020.

For example, the authors claim that Muslims "lived for fourteen centuries with relative peacefulness in their own world" and that ISIS only "mimick[s] the religion's outward form."[68] Nance and Engel also accuse ISIS of having a "cult of jihad"[69]—a description that proves their ignorance, willful or otherwise, of 14 centuries of Islamic conquests fueled precisely by that concept.[70] The authors do lay out a coherent prescriptive strategy for defeating groups like ISIS[71]— or at least as coherent as can be achieved when their descriptive analysis is riddled with presentism, taking little or no note of Islam's past. Said strategy would include 1) dispatching small (100-150 member) Special Operations teams to cut lines of communications, electricity, water, etc.; 2) drumming up "Pan Arab humanitarian intervention" against terrorists; 3) having Muslims take the lead in the fight; 4) unleashing the full diplomatic power of the US State Department to get rid of dictators like al-Assad while also devising and implementing a "Middle East Marshall Plan;" and 5) engaging in "counter-ideological warfare." This last point is the most problematic, working from Nance's and Engel's perspective— which assumes that ISIS's brand of Islam is a "gyrating, heretical and hypocritical" one, constituting a "thrill-kill death cult" and that its supporters are "rare." While I love the authors' verbiage, very little

---

[68] Nance and Engels, p. 410.

[69] *Ibid.*, p. 440.

[70] See almost any reputable book on Islamic history. The most recent example thereof is Raymond Ibrahim, *Sword and Scimitar: Fourteen Centuries of War between Islam and the West* (New York: Da Capo Press, 2018).

[71] Nance and Engels, pp. 412ff.

of that is clear or accurate. I have no idea how an ideology can "gyrate" or be "hypocritical." In addition, it's clear that ISIS, while ruthless and enamored of death, is—again—within the Sunni mainstream of Islamic theology and history, as well as in terms of modern support among Muslims (according to both empirical[72] and self-reporting[73] polls). Nance's and Engel's detailed and useful book is undermined by this lack of in-depth understanding and slavish adherence to modern, politically correct shibboleths.

The most well-known work on this topic is probably former LTG Michael T. Flynn's *The Field of Fight: How We Can Win the Global War against Radical Islam and its Allies.*[74] Co-written with Michael Ledeen,[75] it's rather obvious which sections each man did. Flynn opines from his experience on fighting terrorists in Iraq and Afghanistan, streamlining intelligence collection and exploitation methods, and the problems of "cooking" intell to please higher-ups. The tirades against Iran[76] are almost certainly Ledeen's. The authors

---

[72] See "Chapter 1: Beliefs about Sharia," *Pew Research Center*, April 30, 2013; accessed June 6, 2020. Large minorities and often even majorities in many Muslim-majority countries favor making sharia the law of the land, support stoning as a punishment for adultery and favor executing "apostates" from Islam. All those are ISIS positions.

[73] According to a poll run by Aljazeera, 81% of respondents said they support ISIS. That original is no longer available, but a screen shot of the Arabic question and its responses can be found in Jordan Schachtel, "Shock Poll: 81% of AlJazeera Arabic Poll Respondents Support Islamic State," *Breitbart*, May 25, 2015; accessed June 6, 2020.

[74] Published by St. Martin's Griffin, NY, 2016.

[75] Who is, despite his longtime anti-Iran writings and maneuvering, not a Middle East expert—as several glaring factual errors in this book demonstrate. See "Michael Ledeen," *Wikipedia*; accessed June 7, 2020.

[76] Flynn and Ledeen, pp. 79ff.

are largely correct that "we don't know our enemy and are not prepared to fight effectively. Fewer still have any idea how to win."[77] And that defeating jihadists "includes attacking their evil doctrines and detailing their many failures."[78] Flynn in particular must be given credit for calling a spade a spade; that is, his willingness to confront, and discuss, the inconvenient truth that America is in a global conflict with Islamic opponents—which I maintain is the major reason he was targeted for investigation by the outgoing Obama Administration.[79] However, even the good General and his bellicose co-author cannot bring themselves to be totally honest. Forty-one times, in just 180 pages of text, they refer to "Radical Islamists." Again, this is unhelpful because jihad is anything but "radical." In addition, as explained earlier,[80] the term "Islamist" sets up a false dichotomy between allegedly "political" and regular Islam. Sometimes Flynn and Ledeen are just flat-out wrong, as when they blame the Iranians for the 1979 occupation of the Grand Mosque in Mecca and the concomitant attempt to overthrow the Saudi regime.[81] In point of fact, the militants were all Arab Sunnis, led by Sunni Muslim malcontent Juhayman al-`Utaybi who had convinced them that his brother-in-law, one Muhammad al-Qahtani, was the messianic Mahdi.[82] These authors are so eager to crown Iran as the

---

[77] *Ibid.*, p. 7.

[78] *Ibid.*, p. 9.

[79] See my article "Out Like Flynn," *The Stream*, May 2, 2020; accessed June 7, 2020.

[80] Footnote 25, above.

[81] Flynn and Ledeen, p. 80.

[82] As per Yaroslav Trofimov, *The Siege of Mecca: The Forgotten Uprising in Islam's Holiest Shrine and the Birth of Al Qaeda* [sic] (New York: Doubleday, 2007. See

"heart of the alliance"[83] against us that they blame the Islamic Republic—which was listed as a state sponsor of terror back in Reagan's first term[84]—for things it didn't actually do. These authors, to their credit, recommend that the US learn from the experiences of Israel, Jordan and Egypt.[85] One wonders, however: why not Saudi Arabia, which successfully fended off a Mahdist insurgency in the very heart of Islam?

Perhaps the most thorough and useful book, both descriptively and prescriptively, in this realm is Sebastian Gorka's *Defeating Jihad: The Winnable War*.[86] It's almost certainly the most acclaimed—if not most heeded. Gorka was briefly a deputy assistant on national security to President Trump, later moving on to Fox News and now hosting his own radio program.[87] He and I both lectured at Joint Special Operations University in Tampa in 2010 and 2011, on the history of terrorism. The Trump Administration in general, and Gorka in particular, is a breath of fresh air in the otherwise torpid miasma of conventional "wisdom" on countering groups like ISIS. For example, Trump's first national security advisor, H.R. McMaster, maintained that "terrorist organizations like ISIS represent a perversion of Islam, and thus are unIslamic."[88]

---

also Rif at Sayyid Ahmad, *Rasa'il Juhayman al-`Utaybi: Qa'id al-Muqtahimin lil-Masjid al-Haram bi-Makkah* [*The Letters of Juhayman al-`Utaybi: Commander of the Invaders of the Sacred Mosque in Mecca*] (Cairo: Maktabat Madbuli, 1988).

[83] Flynn and Ledeen, p. 175.

[84] "State Sponsors of Terrorism," *State.gov*; accessed June 7, 2020.

[85] Flynn and Ledeen, p. 177.

[86] Published by Regnery, NY, 2016.

[87] "America First with Sebastian Gorka;" accessed June 6, 2020.

Gorka recognized that while "Russia may be a spoiler on the international stage and China may be our economic rival and cyber-adversary…neither is driven by an immanent vision of apocalypse based upon a historic and theological idyll familiar to more than a billion people in the world today."[89] (Islamic apocalyptic beliefs have been a hugely influential and dangerous subset of that faith for centuries—and remain so in the modern world.[90]) He thus recognizes that our fight is not just with ISIS or any similar group, but with a historical concept and movement: jihad.

Gorka analogizes and adapts, mostly (but not entirely), the approach we took to win the Cold War to the global struggle against reified jihad, recognizing that "our enemy is not a monolithic nation-state but a global movement of fanatical believers."[91] His policy recommendations are as follows: speak the truth about the religious aspects of global terrorism and engage in strategic communications to counter such; help our (especially Muslim) allies via "[f]ewer drones, more psychological operations" as well as judicious deployment of our special operators to help them win the "war within Islam" themselves; and "establish a nationwide program of

---

88 Louis Sarkozy, "Political Correctness Shuts Down Any Reasonable Critiques of Islam," *Washington Examiner*, March 19, 2018; accessed June 6, 2020.

89 Gorka, p. 120.

90 End of Time beliefs in Islam—whether we call them apocalyptic or employ the less-fiery term "eschatological"—have been my primary area of research since my 2001 Ohio State doctoral dissertation, "Eschatology as Politics, Eschatology as Theory: Modern Sunni Arab Mahdism in Historical Perspective." See also my relevant books on Amazon, as well as the commentary on my website, *The Occidental Jihadist*.

91 Gorka, p. 126.

education and training in the enemy threat doctrine of global jihadism" not just in our armed forces but in the intelligence community and law enforcement. In the final analysis, we and our Muslim allies must "delegitimize the message of holy war against the infidel and bolster modern interpretations of Islam."[92]

I agree with most, but not all, of this book. For example, it's simply untrue that "the Islamic State is the world's first trans-regional insurgency."[93] Islamic history is rife with similar movements based in Islam that spanned vast distances and fought against extant governments: the 11th century AD *al-Murabitun* (Almoravids) and their supplanters, the 12th and 13th century *al-Muwahhidun* (Almohads). Various and sundry Sufi groups who fought against the Sunni Ottoman Empire, 13th through 17th centuries. And the Wahhabis, who before they helped the House of Sa`ud created the state of that name in the early 20th century served as a fundamentalist thorn in the side of the less-literalist Ottomans—and indeed afterwards, in the 20th and early 21st centuries, in their non-state versions have caused problems for Muslim governments in both Africa and Asia. Furthermore, ISIS is far from the first group to be driven by a vision of the apocalypse, whether immanent or imminent, in its agenda and actions. The aforementioned Almohad movement, later caliphate or empire, was created by a man who believed himself the Mahdi, Abu Abd Allah

---

[92] *Ibid.*, pp. 129-144. Gorka's policy prescriptions are very similar to those of Flynn and Ledeen, especially as the latter lay such out, pp. 119ff of that book.
[93] *Ibid.*, p. 112.

Ibn Tumart. The Mahdi is Islamic eschatology's "divinely-guided" leader, who will come to take over the world for Islam. A number of Sufi leaders believed the same, convinced that they had been ordained to overthrow rule their parts of the *umma* and perhaps even to overthrow the Sultan in Istanbul. One of the most notable of these was Muhammad Ahmad, the 19th century Sudanese Mahdi of *Khartoum* movie fame.[94] Much more recently, a Wahhabi-Salafi Mahdist movement, the aforementioned 1979 one led by Juhayman al-Utaybi that tried but failed to displace the Saudis, fits this bill. So eschatological, violent transnational Islamic movements are nothing new under the sun. Such have arisen and threatened less-fanatical (or, at least, already-established) Muslim states and forced them to combat their vicious brethren.

But one would search in vain for useful historical data about previous Islamic polities' defeats of such violent Islamic rebellions. The aforementioned seven proposals, where they do wax prescriptive, adduce the same historical analogies for countering ISIS and similar modern Muslim movements: previous US experience; strategically, in World War II and/or the Cold War; tactically, American asymmetric warfare in Iraq and Afghanistan. Some mention is made of looking at the examples of a few modern Sunni Arab states in beating back co-religionist-based violent opposition.

---

[94] Starring Charlton Heston as General Charles Gordon, the British officer hired by the Ottomans to fight the Mahdi; and Sir Laurence Olivier as the latter. "Khartoum (1966)," *IMDb*; accessed June 8, 2020.

But none lays out how to delegitimize groups like ISIS *as* an Islamic movement. The lone Muslim foray in that regard surveyed does attempt (albeit unsuccessfully) to undermine the religious bases of the main terrorist group. But it grapples not at all with the military side of the coin. What we need is a wholistic approach for defeating such organizations that encompasses both kinetic and inform and influence activities, or ideological warfare—what used to be known as psychological operations. Yet the US has, to date, not yet successfully engaged in both these sides of the COIN struggle against enemies operating from within the Islamic fold. So that is why we need to ***look at the historical record of Islamic states that have contended with ISIS-like challenges to their rule. <u>That</u> is the purpose of this work.***

Two shorter works have touched on this topic. One is a book chapter by Norvell B. DeAtkine, who over a decade ago wrote about "The Arab as Insurgent and Counterinsurgent."[95] Colonel DeAtkine touches briefly on Lawrence "of Arabia" and the Arab Revolt against the Ottomans in World War I, but spends most of his essay on 20th century insurgencies in Iraq, Syria, Yemen and North Africa and how the extant Arab regimes suppressed them. I submit, however, that we should look further back into history, and outside the narrow purview of the Arab world, for an even better example

---

[95] Found in Rubin, ed., *Conflict and Insurgency in the Contemporary Middle East,* pp. 24-45.

of an Islamic polity grappling with violent and ideological challenges to its rule: the Ottoman Empire.

The longest-tenured, and most successful, Islamic state in history was the Ottoman Empire, which arose in the 15th century and lasted until the early 20th. The Ottomans were officially and, at times, harshly Islamic but were also far too large, populous and religiously diverse to be ruled solely by strict *shari`ah*. In their five centuries they faced domestic uprisings on a number of fronts, both geographical and religious-ideological, from: Islamic fundamentalists (Kadizadelis, Wahhabis) in Anatolia and Arabia; eschatological Mahdists, both  Shi`i (Zaydis of Yemen) and Sunni (Sufis and Sudanese Mahdists); and new religious expressions of Islam (the Druze of Lebanon). I will thus focus on the Ottoman Empire and how that vast, powerful and legitimate Islamic state dealt with such challenges to its rule.

There has been only one previous study even nominally along these lines. Seven years ago Nicholas Warndorf completed a thesis on Ottoman unconventional warfare.[96] But it only covers that Empire's experience in World War I, and then deals solely with the Armenian issue. He does point out, however, that "internal security threats were not unknown in the Ottoman Empire prior to the First World War. Quite the opposite is true; they were experts in dealing

---

[96] Nicholas Warndorf (2013), "Unconventional Warfare in the Ottoman Empire: Turkish Counterinsurgency and their [sic] Western Inspiration" (Master's thesis, University of Louisville). Retrieved from core.ac.uk/reader/143834852; accessed August 6, 2020.

with insurgency, both politically and militarily."[97] Warndorf also notes that "research into Ottoman counterinsurgency has been virtually non-existent."[98]

This book, then, will seek to rectify that omission. As such, it will cover not just relevant aspects of the history of terrorism, but also Middle Eastern and military history—in particular the latter, in terms of how the Ottomans countered the aforementioned challenges. History, including the military subfield, has oscillated between adherence to "Great Man" and "contingent" schools of thought.[99] The former focuses on leadership: Alexander, Julius Caesar, Muhammad, Napoleon, Grant. The latter, on the contrary, view "the actions of leaders as virtually irrelevant to the course of a battle."[100] In recent decades another perspective has developed, and come to predominate, among the professional military ranks in the West: the "art of war" studies, which strives to distill "universal military principles" based on "a 'rational' model of the past, that is, a model that sees rationality as something common to human analysis of military...challenges and **assumes that rational analysis will therefore produce similar results in similar situations through time and across cultures**"[101] [emphasis added]. The problem is that this "universal rationalist model has often led to military history

---

[97] *Ibid.*, pp. 32, 33.

[98] *Ibid.*, p. 98.

[99] See the pithy explanation thereof in Stephen Morillo with Michael F. Pavkovic, *What Is Military History? 2nd Edition* (Cambridge, UK: Polity Press, 2013), pp. 46-49.

[100] *Ibid.*, p. 47.

[101] *Ibid.*, p. 50.

that **ignores social and cultural factors** separating the military art and military organization from its historical context"[102] [emphasis added].

As a devotee of the great Middle Eastern scholar Bernard Lewis, who emphasized that any true student of that region and its civilizations must know the relevant history as investigated through the primary languages,[103] I subscribe, rather, to the constructionist view. This methodology "places military decisions and systems in their social and cultural context, and then tries to assess them in their own historicized terms...."[104] A constructionist would take religion seriously as a factor, even when and where some might find it "irrational."[105] The relevant religion would, of course, change across space and time. For the Sassanians, it would have been Zoroastrianism. For the Romans, paganism and then, later, Christianity. Any honest examination of the conflict between those two competing empires must take into account, for example, the Sassanian rulers' distrust of Christians in their domains as potential fifth columnists for Rome. The Thirty Years War cannot begin to be understood unless the respective roles of the Catholic and Lutheran polities in, and around, the Holy Roman Empire are considered. Likewise, in the subject at hand, Islam is key to understanding both the non-state challengers to Ottoman rule, and the Empire's state

---

[102] *Ibid.*, p. 51.
[103] Arabic, Persian and Turkish—whether Ottoman or modern.
[104] Morillo, p. 52.
[105] *Ibid.*

responses. This approach "has the additional benefit of offering potentially better 'lessons' for modern policy makers faced with conflict against non-traditional enemies including terrorists and guerilla insurgencies."[106]

Besides the Ottomans, this work will examine one other example of an Islamic polity facing an internal, co-religionist threat—but one that, unlike the Turkish empire, did not rise to meet the challenge. As a counter-example, I will examine a much older conflict but one that turned the other way: the aforementioned North African state ruled by the Almoravids who tried, ultimately in vain, to stave off the insurgent, Islamic Almohad movement. Adjusted across space and time, the Almoravids' failure can also shed valuable light on current attempts to de-legitimize and defeat ISIS and similar groups.

Specifically, one area of application of this book's research is to Turkey— logically enough, considering the Turkish Republic was established on the edifice (or ruins) of the Ottoman Empire. After the failed coup against him in July 2016, many feared that Turkish President Recep Erdoğan would become an Islamic fundamentalist. But that misreads Turkish politics, culture and people, all of which are light-years away from accepting an Iranian- or even Pakistani-style agenda, much less any one modeled on ISIS. Rather, Erdoğan is following the lead of his imperial Islamic predecessors—whether that should be described as "neo-Ottoman"[107] or not.[108] And as this

---

[106] *Ibid.*, p. 53.

work will show, sultans of the Ottoman state had little tolerance for Islamic fundamentalist movements that challenged their political supremacy. Whether that, and other, Ottoman predilections have resurfaced in Turkey's current government will be examined in the final chapter.

ISIS's territorial caliphate may be gone, but the organization is still active in many locales: the Syrian heartland,[109] a new home in Libya,[110] and even Afghanistan, where it utilizes Indian recruits to leverage the Kashmir issue and attempts to outstrip the Taliban.[111] However, ISIS is but *one* of a legion (at least 53, remember) of similar Islamic jihadist groups dedicated to creating a caliphate and imposing Islamic law therein—when not staging attacks on non-Muslims at every opportunity. AQ, the other major jihadist organization, may very well now be (yet again) the terrorist top guns,[112] not ISIS. However, there is very little under the sun that is truly

---

[107] See Giancarlo Elia Valori, "The Neo-Ottoman Issue," *moderndiplomacy.eu*, January 24, 2019; and even more pointedly, Asya Akca, "Neo-Ottomanism: Turkey's Foreign Policy Approach to Africa," *csis.org*, April 8, 2019. Both accessed August 4, 2020.

[108] Nicholas Danforth, "The Nonsense of 'Neo-Ottomanism,'" *warontherocks.com*, May 29, 2020; accessed August 4, 2020.

[109] Gregory Waters, "ISIS Redux—the Central Syria Insurgency—April & May 2020," *Counterextremism Project*, June 3 2020; accessed June 8, 2020.

[110] See the many posts on ISIS activity there at *eyeonisisinlibya.com*; accessed June 8, 2020. I predicted ISIS' *hijrah* to Libya four years ago: "Dousing ISIS' Apocalyptic Spark in Syria—Analysis," *Eurasia Review*, July 11, 2016; accessed June 8, 2020.

[111] OpIndia Staff, "ISIS Terrorist Who Attacked Gurudwara in Kabul was from India, Killed Afghan Sikhs to 'Avenge' Plight of Kashmiri Muslims," *OpIndia.com*, March 27, 2020; accessed June 8, 2020.

[112] Katherine Zimmerman, "Al-Qaeda is Rising Again, and No One Seems to Give a Damn," *The National Interest*, June 8, 2020; accessed June 8, 2020.

new. ISIS and its breed are no exception. Islamic fundamentalist and/or apocalyptic movements have plagued the Islamic (and the Christian) world in the past, and we should learn from how such were successfully defeated—or unsuccessfully countered. We in the West, and Americans in particular, have a tendency to impose our civilizational examples and experience on others, and then to look only to them for guidance going forward. Witness the incessant push (by both the Right and the Left) to make every evil dictator a new Hitler[113] or the automatic assumption that Islam needs a Reformation modeled on the Christian world's Protestant one.[114]

Likewise for the case at hand. Americans grappling with formulating a response to Islamic terrorist movements accept as axiomatic that what worked for us in World War II against the Nazis, and/or the Cold War against the Marxist-Leninist USSR, translates into a program for defeating Islam-based movements, jihadist or political. But the differences between those two repugnant 20th century ideologies, on the one hand, and Islam, on the other, are profound. Nazism was truly an aberrant ideology, despite its attempts to transform into a religion. Communism has proved more durable, but despite its similarities to Christianity is not a faith in the same way as Islam. Violent movements and groups claiming Islamic

---

[113] Ted Galen Carpenter, "Stop Comparing Every Angry Dictator to Hitler," *The National Interest*, June 29, 2016; accessed August 4, 2020.

[114] Theo Hobson, "Why Calling for an 'Islamic Reformation' is Lazy and Historically Illiterate," *The Spectator*, February 7, 2015; accessed June 8, 2020.

cover for their activities cannot be thwarted, much less defeated, in the same way as were German Nazism and Soviet Communism.

There are no doubt lessons to be learned from our previous global conflicts which could apply to this current struggle. But limiting ourselves to 20th century examples for guidance on this important issue makes us blind to the wealth of Islamic experience, going back almost a millennium, which we could fruitfully draw upon in order to formulate plans for defeating today's pervasive militant movements in the Islamic world. My contention is that we can learn important lessons from how Islamic polities such as the Ottoman and Almoravid empires dealt with that civilization's very own history of violence. In his first overseas visit, to the Kingdom of Saudi Arabia in May 2017, President Trump laid down the challenge that Muslim-majority countries, and thus Muslims themselves, must "honestly confront… the crisis of Islamist extremism and the Islamist terror groups it inspires."[115] The bad news is that Islamic governments have been fighting such groups for centuries. But the good news is that the more temperate Muslims have often won. Let us see what the Muslim Ottomans, in particular, have to teach us about this, operating from the premise that "the road to the future lies through the past."[116]

---

[115] "Full Transcript of Trump's Speech to the Muslim World from Saudi Arabia," *Haaretz*, May 21, 2017; accessed June 8, 2020.

[116] Thomas R. Mockaitis, "The COIN Conundrum: The Future of Counterinsurgency and U.S. Land Power," (Department of the Army, 2017), p. 83.

CHAPTER TWO—POLITICS AND GEOPOLITICS

Political disputes within Islamic civilization almost always have revolved around questions of religious authority—that is, whether rulers are legitimate, according to Islamic norms, or not. In fact, "it is characteristic of Islamic society that social, economic and political questions often take on the guise of religious problems and are fought out using the rhetoric of religion...."[117] Those who would deem a monarch deficient in Islamic *bona fide*s have been the ones most likely to resort to jihad against him (and for reasons both theological and historical the leader has always been male). Of course after the passing of Islam's founder, (traditionally said to have been in 632 AD), a *khalifah*, or "successor," to Muhammad was chosen—at first by consensus among the inner circle of the former "prophet;" and later by virtue of political maneuvering and rank military power. Dozens (at least) of caliphates have been proclaimed across space and time throughout Islamic history, but only the most prominent need be mentioned here: the Umayyads of Syria (and later Iberia); the Abbasids of Iraq and the central Middle East; the Fatimids of North Africa and Egypt; the Almoravids and Almohads of the medieval Maghrib; the Ottomans, who supplanted the

---

[117] Norman Itzkowitz, *Ottoman Empire and Islamic Tradition* (Chicago and London: University of Chicago Press, 1972), p. 69. Patricia Crone and Martin Hinds put it this way: "[t]here is no point in Islamic history at which the caliphate can be said to have been entirely devoid of religious meaning." *God's Caliph: Religious Authority in the First Centuries of Islam* (Cambridge: Cambridge University Press, 1986), p. 97.

Christian Byzantine Empire; the Sokoto Caliphate of west Africa; and of course the Islamic State of Iraq and al-Sham—ISIS or, more recently, simply IS. The caliphate has been almost exclusively a Sunni institution despite fact that a few Shi`i states, most notably the Sevener, or Isma'ili, Fatimids used the term as well. Shi`is were the subgroup of the early Islamic community which believed that Muhammad's closest male relative—Ali, his much younger cousin and, eventually, son-in-law—should have succeeded to leadership. Ali did become the fourth caliph, but was murdered after five years in office and neither of his sons, Hassan and Husayn, ever became caliph. (The latter, in fact, led an uprising against the Umayyads and was killed in 680 AD.) Shi`is ever after have wanted a descendant of Muhammad via Ali to be the Muslim ruler, and the three major subdivisions of this branch take their designations from the number of imams, or rightful leaders, they trace post-Muhammad as well as (in the case of two branches) from the name of the final one. Thus, the Twelver Shi`is (the largest group) count 12 imams, the last of whom disappeared in the 9th century AD and will return before the end of time as the Mahdi, Allah's "rightly-guided" eschatological agent. The Seveners enumerate seven true imams and split the line off at Isma'il—hence Isma'ilis. The Fivers, for their part, truncate the line of leadership at the fifth imam, Zayd.[118] All of the bloodline

---

[118] Twelvers, the largest branch of Shi`ism, predominate in Iran, Iraq, Azerbaijan, Bahrain and almost certainly Lebanon (despite lack of official demographic data). Isma'ilis are second-largest and divided into a number of subsects, mainly in south and central Asia, although the leader of the largest group (the Nizaris),

descendants of Muhammad via Ali and his wife Fatimah (Muhammad's daughter) are known to the Shi`is, collectively, as *ahl al-bayt*: "people of the house [of Muhammad]."

Both Sunni and Shi`i caliphates were, in effect, theocracies and the ruler was expected to enforce *shari`ah*;[119] caliphs (Sunni) as well as caliph-imams (Shi`i) ruled by divine right, of course. The major difference, besides alleged descent from Islam's founder, was that the Sunni caliphs were no longer receiving direct guidance from Allah, whereas the Shi`i caliphs-imams were deemed still in divine contact.[120] Neither type of rulership was as utopian as is often claimed by respective adherents, however (to put it mildly); and after many defeats by the majority Sunnis, the Shi`is "retreated into otherworldliness, especially with their doctrine of the Mahdi"[121]

---

the Aga Khan, lives in France. Zaydis comprise about 40% of the population of Yemen and their branch of Shi`ism is considered to be the closest, in many ways, to Sunni Islam. See Pew Research Center, "Mapping the Global Muslim Population," subsection on "Sunni and Shia [sic] Populations" (2009), accessed June 15, 2020, as well as Fuad I. Khuri, *Imams and Emirs: State, Religion and Sects in Islam* (London: Saqi, 1990), pp. 113-130.

[119] Andrea M. Farsakh, "A Comparison of the Sunni Caliphate and the Shi`i Imamate (Conclusion)," *Muslim World*, Vol. 59, No. 2 (1969), pp. 127-144; specific data is from p. 138.

[120] Farsakh, "A Comparison of the Sunni Caliphate and the Shi`i Imamate," *Muslim World*, Volume 59, No. 1 (1969), pp. 50-63; specific information is from p. 52.

[121] This is the "divinely-guided one" who according to Hadiths (but not the Qur'an) will emerge onto the stage of history and, along with the returned prophet `Isa (Jesus), conquer the world for Islam. Both Sunnis and Shi`is (particularly Twelvers) have this belief. But whereas for the former the Mahdi will turn out to be a fantastically successful Muslim military leader whose true identity will only gradually be recognized, Twelver Shi`is believe that he has already been on earth as the 12th descendant of Muhammad via Ali; that he went into *ghaybah*, or "occultation," in the 9th century AD; and that this Muhammad

while even triumphant Sunni caliphates often came to be seen as "instrument[s] of political suppression" no matter how much they "satisfied the needs of rulers, jurists and theologians."[122] Even the Sunni caliphate, then, has proved a two-edged sword for Muslims themselves—and not just their opponents. It "has given Islam extraordinary powers of survival; but at the same time it has always interfered with the capacity of Muslims to organize themselves"[123]— insofar as rival claimants to that position have often squared off, violently.

What were the qualifications for the caliphate? According to the famous and influential medieval Muslim historian Ibn Khaldun, they were: 1) knowledge of Islam; 2) honesty; 3) competence in governing and leading jihad; 4) lack of bodily defects or shortcomings (such as deafness, blindness or missing limbs); and, ideally, 5) Qurayshite lineage—that is, being from the same tribe as Muhammad.[124] Ibn Khaldun was writing in the 14th century AD, and his summary of caliphal prerequisites was already becoming merely an idealized abstraction even by his time. The real

---

al-Mahdi will return from his mystical concealment to make the world safe for Twelver Shi`ism. Many jihads have been waged in the name of self-proclaimed Mahdis across the centuries, some so successful that they established states. See my books *Holiest Wars: Islamic Mahdis, their Jihads, and Osama bin Laden* (Westport, CT: Praeger, 2005) and *Ten Years' Captivation with the Mahdis' Camps: Essays on Muslim Eschatology, 2005-2015* (Timothy R. Furnish, 2015).

[122] Farsakh, No. 2, p. 140.

[123] Crone & Hinds, p. 110.

[124] *The Muqaddimah: An Introduction to History*, trans. Franz Rosenthal, ed. N.J. Dawood (Princeton: Princeton University Press, 1967), pp. 158-9.

requirements, by the Middle Ages, were in effect only two rather utilitarian ones: being Muslim, and having sufficient military assets to seize and hold power.[125] And the Muslim leaders who exemplified these two characteristics from the late medieval period until the 20th century were of course the Ottomans, who not only disposed—at long last, from the Islamic perspective—of the stubborn Byzantine Empire, but whose massive military power[126] was legitimized by rulership of Mecca and Medina[127] as well as by the mythology that the last of the Abbasid "shadow caliphs" in Cairo had bestowed his office on Ottoman Sultan Selim I when the latter conquered Egypt in 1517.[128]

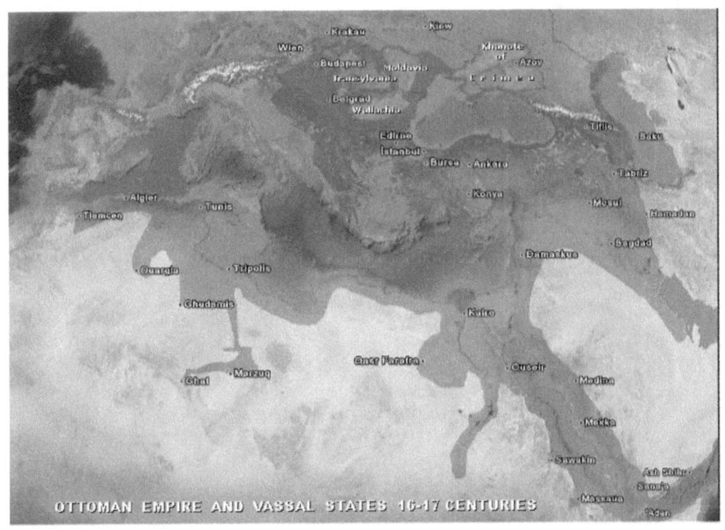

---

125 Bernard Lewis, *The Political Language of Islam* (Chicago and London: University of Chicago Press, 1988), p. 99.
126 *Ibid.*, p. 49.
127 Crone & Hinds, p. 100, footnote 18.
128 Lewis, pp. 48-9.

The Ottoman Empire c. 1600 AD.[129]

Caliphates were, however, not the only form of Islamic government—although they were certainly the most prestigious ones. Islamic states could also be ruled by an *amir* ("commander" or "leader"), *sultan* ("authority"), *malik* ("king") or *za'im* (literally "alleged leader," often used of someone whose legitimacy was recognized, but suspect; or a man who held *de jure*, rather than *de facto*, power).[130]   *Amir al-mu`minin* meant "commander of the faithful" and was tantamount to caliph, which was why the more modest (or perhaps realistic) medieval al-Murabitun rulers, for example, took the less grandiose title *amir al-muslimin*: "commander of the Muslims."[131] The leaders of the movement which supplanted them, the al-Muwahhids, did style themselves, rather, *amir[s] al-mu`minin*, however; and even, at times, caliphs[132]—but in the sense of "vicar" to their founder Ibn Tumart, who had proclaimed himself the ultimate authority: the Mahdi! Many Islamic leaders of course used the term *sultan*—most notably the Ottomans, whose aforementioned assumption of the caliphate was not regularly trumpeted until Sultan Abdül Hamid II's reign in the late 19th century. In the 20th and 21st centuries, a number of Arab Muslim

---

[129] From "Map of the Ottoman Empire at its Greatest Extent, at the End of the 16th century (1600)," *commons.wikimedia.org*; accessed June 13, 2020.

[130] Lewis, pp. 50-60.

[131] Jamil M. Abun-Nasr, *A History of the Maghrib in the Islamic Period* (Cambridge: Cambridge University Press, 1987), p. 83.

[132] *Ibid.*, p. 94.

leaders—the Saudis and Jordanians, in particular—have called themselves kings, a term implying merely "local sovereignty"[133] rather than the more expansive power of a sultan or caliph.

Rebelling against any of these established authorities has regularly been deemed an upsetting of the Allah-ordained order, and fighting against a caliph, with his political and religious role, the most grievous political sin—tantamount to *fitnah*, which was (and still is) "sedition" or "civil strife." Arab Muslim rulers referred to such as engaging in `*isyan*: "disobedience, insurrection, revolt, rebellion, sedition."[134] This passed almost verbatim, and with the same meaning, into Ottoman Turkish; and *isyan etmek* meant "to rebel against."[135] Some modern scholars prefer the term "mutiny" for such;[136] and although this term does encompass resisting or fighting against lawful authority, it's also safe to say that most Westerners (or at least certainly Americans) who hear or read that term associate it solely with uprisings against naval commanders. Whatever we call them, such were a regular occurrence in Ottoman

---

[133] Lewis, p. 56.

[134] Hans Wehr, *A Dictionary of Modern Written Arabic (Arabic-English)*, J. M. Cowarn, ed., 4th edition (Urbana, IL: Spoken Language Services, Inc., 1994 [1979]), *s.v.* `*asa* [p. 723].

[135] *New Redhouse [Ottoman] Turkish-English Dictionary* (Istanbul: Redhouse Press, 1984 [1968; 1890]), *s.v. isyan* [p. 560].

[136] Notably Jane Hathaway, ed., *Mutiny and Rebellion in the Ottoman Empire* (Madison, WI: University of Wisconsin-Madison, 2002); and Palmira Brummett, "Classifying Ottoman Mutiny: The Act and Vision of Rebellion," *The Turkish Studies Association Bulletin*, Vol. 22, No. 1 (Spring 1998), pp. 91-107. See also Dick Douwes, *The Ottomans in Syria: A History of Justice and Oppression* (London and New York: I.B. Tauris, 2000), pp. 153-154.

history—in fact, rebellions were chronic in that empire.[137] While some of these were aimed at redressing grievances (whether real, such as lack of army pay; or perceived, such as relative lack of social status), or breaking away outlying provinces (Sudan or Yemen, for example), others did intend on replacing the entire regime and the ruling sultan in the name of repristinating Islam or ushering in the Mahdi's eschatological regime. In order to quell such challenges, the Ottomans (and other Islamic regimes) often dealt with political, military and social challenges to their rule as if they were religious ones (which they frequently were): when **toleration** had reached its end and **assimilation** proved untenable or impossible, then the **persecution** and/or **expulsion** cards were played.[138]

What sort of rebellious movements, specifically, did the Ottomans face? One major type came from the Sufi orders.[139] Sufis are often deemed a third branch of Islam, over against both Sunnis and Shi`is. But Sufism is really a mystical tendency that can manifest

---

[137] Brummett, p. 106.

[138] See Karen Barkey, *Empire of Difference: The Ottomans in Comparative Perspective* (Cambridge: Cambridge University Press, 2008), p. 113.

[139] On Sufism *per se* the list of sources is legion, but at a minimum one should consult J. Spencer Trimingham, *The Sufi Orders in Islam* (Oxford: Oxford University Press, 1998 [1971]); Frederick De Jong and Bern Radtke, eds., *Islamic Mysticism Contested: Thirteen Centuries of Controversies and Polemics* (Leiden: Brill, 1999); Kamil Mustafa al-Shaibi, *Sufism and Shi`ism* (Surrey, UK: LAAM Ltd., 1991); Itzchak Weismann, *The Naqshbandiyya: Orthodoxy and Activism in a Worldwide Sufi Tradition* (London and New York: Routledge, 2007); Julian Baldick, *Mystical Islam: An Introduction to Sufism* (New York: NYU Press, 1989); and "Sufi Orders," Pew Research Center, September 15, 2010; accessed June 15, 2020. An excellent source on Sufism in the Ottoman Empire is the podcast by John Curry, "Sufism and Society in the Ottoman Empire," August 9, 2013; accessed June 15, 2020.

among either of those two (although more often found in the former), historically comprising Muslims who feel that adherence to the Qur'an, hadiths, and *shari`ah* is necessary but not sufficient for true piety and that some sort of direct communion with Allah can be achieved through intense prayer. Sufism developed within Islam by the 10th century AD and differentiated over the years into hundreds of orders,[140] usually named after their founders. Some of the major ones across space and time have been the Suhrawardiyah, Rifa`iyah, Qadiriyah, Mawlawiyah, Naqshbandiyah, Tijaniyah and Chishtiyah. Besides being mystical, Sufi orders were, and are, often characterized by hierarchical organization and strong, bordering on slavish, adherence to their particular shaykhs, or leaders.

While perhaps only 10% or fewer of Muslims today admit to membership in a Sufi order,[141] the number was likely much greater in the past—particularly in the Ottoman Empire.[142] Some of these were establishment—a tradition that pre-existed the Ottomans, going back to the time of the Seljuq Turks. The Bektaşis, for example, provided many of the Ottoman military's chaplains; while

---

[140] Singular *tariqah*; plural *tariqat* or *turuq*.

[141] See "Chapter 1: Religious Affiliation" of "The World's Muslims: Unity and Diversity," Pew Research Center, August 9, 2012; accessed June 15, 2020.

[142] As per Barkey, in particular pp. 160-175; and Ahmet Yaşar Ocak, "Sufi Milieux and Political Authority in Turkish History: A General Overview (Thirteenth-Seventeenth Centuries)," in Paul L. Heck, ed., *Sufism and Politics: The Power of Spirituality* (Princeton, NJ: Markus Wiener, 2007), pp. 165-195. Trimingham points out that even as late as 1921, when the Ottoman Empire was being dissolved in favor of the Turkish Republic, Istanbul alone was home to 17 "officially recognized" *tariqat* and 258 Sufi meeting houses! (p. 253).

the Mevlevis and in particular Naqshbandis (the latter of whom have always been fond of jihad, down to this day[143]) often served, at every level, in the Sultans' ranks. On the other hand, many other Sufis were "at the center of dissent."[144] One such order was the Qalandariyah, who by even mystical Muslim standards were a bit weird: members wore their piety proudly, in outward practices such as shaving the head and all facial hair except for a luxuriant mustache, and piercing not only their ears but their hands, aiming to scandalize. This was in contradistinction to the Malamatis, who hid their devotion and kept it between themselves and Allah—at least in theory.[145] The Wafa`is, of Egyptian origin, also were often at loggerheads with the Ottoman government.

Whatever the particular Sufi order, political (and military) opposition to the establishment usually followed this pattern: "a *zawiya*[146] leader might react against established authority out of personal or factional interest or ambition, or he might be a channel for the expression of social discontent, especially where connected with a guild organization. The blind obedience accorded a shaikh

---

[143] This order has been involved in or with ISIS, whether fighting with that group (Abudlrahman al-Rashed, "The Sufist [sic] Izzat al-Douri and the Extremist ISIS," "al-Arabiya English," April 20, 2015) or incurring its wrath (Abdelhak Mamoun, "ISIS Executes Four Members of Naqshbandi Order in Central Mosul," "Iraqi News," January 27, 2016. Both the latter accessed June 15, 2020.

[144] Barkey, p. 160.

[145] On these groups see Trimingham, Appendix B, "Sufis, Malamatis, and Qalandaris," pp. 264-269.

[146] A Sufi establishment/meeting house, or lodge. Such is also known as a *tekke*, *khanqah* or *dargah*, depending on which part of the Islamic world is at issue. See "Zawiya (Institution)," *Wikipedia*, accessed June 15, 2020.

assured him of a nucleus of potentially fanatical followers. The most remarkable example of such a movement was that which led to the foundation of the Safawi [Safavid] dynasty in Persia"[147] (that latter point which shall be elaborated upon, below). "Fanatical followers" exhibiting "blind obedience" to a Sufi leader, along with the movement's inherent mystical proclivities, are the main reasons why self-proclaimed Mahdis—men claiming to be the eschatological "divinely-guided one" of both Sunni and Shi`i Islam—are most likely to emerge from Sufi contexts. This was true in the Ottoman Empire of a number of Sufi orders and leaders, who would openly advocate, and sometimes take up arms, for one of their shaykhs as the End Times Mahdi whose ambit would encompass both spiritual and temporal power, thus supplanting the illegitimate sultan.[148] From the 1200s to the 1700s, the Ottomans and their predecessors the Seljuks faced a number of these apocalyptic threats.[149] In a precursor uprising, c. 1240 AD, two Turkmen Wafa'i Sufis, Baba Ilyas-i Khurasani and Baba Ishaq, led armed Turkmen against the extant Seljuq Turkish state. The first major Sufi rebellion recorded was that in 1416, which took place in the wake of Timurlane's conquests and depredations. This was initially led by two Qaladari shaykhs, Torlaq Kamal and Borkluğe Mustafa, who were soon replaced by Badr al-Din, or Şeyh Bedreddin; all three were supported

---

[147] Trimingham, p. 239.
[148] See especially Ocak, pp. 183ff.
[149] *Ibid.*, pp. 186ff.

by Byzantine Christians unhappy with living under Ottoman Muslim rule, as well as by disenchanted *sipahis* (Ottoman cavalry).

Bedreddin was perhaps the major rebellious figure of this period. He was a devotee of the Hurufiyyah, a mystical methodology employed by Sufis and Isma'ili Shi`is of interpreting the Qur'an that was similar to Jewish Kabbalistic ways of interpreting the Hebrew Scriptures. In the wake of Tamerlane's defeat and dismemberment of the first Ottoman state in the early years of the 15th century, Bedreddin was made a judge in the re-forming Ottoman army by Musa Çelebi, one of the surviving Ottoman princes. But Mehmet I became sultan in 1413, killing Musa and removing anyone he had appointed from their positions.[150] Eventually, this humiliation as well as Bedreddin's contact with disenchanted individuals and groups in Asia Minor and southeastern Europe—"Turcoman nomads, *gazis,*[151] *sipahis,* Christian peasants, and others, mostly those with local grievances, the importance of which is not to be underestimated given the post-1402 chaos"[152]--led him to revolt. Bedreddin seems to have preached a syncretistic Islamo-Christian creed that was decidedly anti-Ottoman. He was not just another dangerous dervish[153] to the Ottomans, however: his religious syncretism greatly appealed to the marginal, both Muslim

---

[150] Barkey, p. 172.

[151] Or *ghazi(s)*, referring to a Turkish holy warrior for Islam—analogous to today's *jihadi[s]*.

[152] Barkey, p. 173.

[153] The Turkish for the Persian *darwish*, referring originally to an ascetic mystic but eventually coming to mean any Sufi.

and Christian, in western Anatolia and his networks, formed by years of wandering, provided him with ready-made ranks to command. The Ottomans eventually crushed Bedreddin and his followers with overwhelming military power, executing thousands in doing so. Interestingly, the judge who sentenced Bedreddin to death, after his capture, "asked the sultan for private time with the Şeyh in order to benefit from his wisdom before he was put to death. Therein lay the duality of **a state that both punished and learned from dissent**"[154] [emphasis added].

More revolts followed in 1511 and 1512, led by Shah Qulu and Nur Ali Khalifa, respectively. In 1520 one Shah Wali also rebelled. All three of these were Sufis (of unknown orders) who put themselves forward as either Mahdi or *sahib al-zaman*, "Lord of Time"—an equivalent eschatological title. In the reign of Sultan Murad I (r. 1623-40), two different Naqshbandi shaykhs each claimed to be the Mahdi.[155] Another quasi-Mahdist uprising led by Sayyid Abd Allah broke out in 1665. Some of these apocalyptic pretenders were almost certainly supported, if not instigated, by the Ottomans' major state rival: the Twelver Shi`i Safavid Empire in neighboring Persia (Iran), which had itself begun as an eschatological Sufi movement, albeit not a Sunni one.[156] The Safavids tried to use Sufi orders, especially those with Shi`i tendencies—such as the

---

[154] Barkey, p. 174.

[155] Ocak, p. 178.

[156] On which see Colin P. Mitchell, *The Practice of Politics in Safavid Iran: Power, Religion and Rhetoric* (London and New York: Tauris Academic Studies, 2009).

Qalandaris and Malamatis—as fifth columns against the Ottomans, often successfully.[157] In particular, the Safavids "agitated, provoked, and subsidized"[158] Turcoman Shi`is known as *kizilbaş*;[159] the formers' agents were dispatched to Ottoman territories in order to "feed, clothe, convert, and politicize these poorer nomadic populations."[160] This was an especially dangerous threat to the Ottomans, in that, these kizilbaş had a state benefactor, unlike many similar non-state rebellions against the sultans' rule —and one that was not only politically, but theologically, diametrically opposed to the Sunni Ottoman state. Ultimately, the Safavids were defeated by the Ottomans at the Battle of Chaldiran in 1514, effectively ending any hope the former might have had of defeating the latter on the conventional battlefield; nonetheless, the Safavids continuously engaged in asymmetric warfare against their Sunni antagonists by stirring up amenable Sufis and Shi`is, throughout the Ottoman realms, against the Sunni sultan in Istanbul. This anti-Ottoman agitation persisted until the collapse of the Safavid state in the early 18th century.

---

[157] Ocak., p. 181. Also see Itzkowitz, pp. 68-69: "The Safavids were both a militant state and [from the Ottoman perspective] an heretical Shi`ite sect. Religious propaganda emanating from Persia, and directed toward the nomads and peasants in eastern Anatolia, undermined Ottoman authority among disaffected elements. That propaganda was spread by the shah's missionary agents…." Also see Mitchell, p. 202.
[158] Barkey, p. 175.
[159] This means "redheads" and referred to red headgear, not hair color.
[160] Barkey, p. 175.

In the 16th and 17th centuries the Ottomans were challenged by another brand of rebels: the Celalis.[161] Named after one of the first of such, Şeyh (Shaykh) Celal, who led Turcomans in revolt, Celalis were usually less threatening to the sultan than the aforementioned Sufi movements, not least because they were more akin to bandits, with no overarching ideology—much less a religious one. Often they were disaffected or demobilized soldiers who simply wanted better pay, pensions or higher positions. Some of these uprisings were, nonetheless, quite powerful and bloody; in the early 17th century one group of Celalis in Anatolia numbered some 20,000 men, which took considerable forces of janissaries (shock Ottoman infantry) and sipahis (cavalry) to suppress.[162]

The 17th century saw yet another group throw down the gauntlet to Ottoman rule: the Kadizadelis.[163] In some ways the Kadizadelis presaged the Wahhabis of the next century—and indeed most conservative-fundamentalist-"extremist" [sic] Islamic movements, down to today—in that their founder Kadizade Mehmed Efendi (d. 1635) preached an austere Sunni Islam that had no room for Sufism in general, or in particular with mystical Islam's veneration of shayhkhs' tombs, music, tobacco, wine or even coffee. All of these were deemed *bida`h*, or unacceptable "innovations."[164]

---

[161] Pronounced "Jelalis." On these movements see Barkey, pp. 178-181; and Itzkowitz, pp. 92, 93.

[162] Itzkowitz, p. 93.

[163] As per Madeline C. Zilfi, "The Kadizadelis: Discordant Revivalism in Seventeenth-Century Istanbul," *Journal of Near Eastern Studies*, Vol. 45, No. 4 (Oct. 1986), pp. 251-269; also, Barkey, pp. 181-187.

Kadizade eventually was appointed Friday preacher at the mosque of Sultan Selim I, then later at Aya Sofya Mosque—the most prestigious preaching post, at the huge former church originally ordered built by the Eastern Roman Emperor Justinian in the 6th century AD. Kadizade then "used the grand pulpit of Aya Sofya to promulgate a kind of 'fundamentalist' ethic, a set of doctrinal positions intended to rid Islam of beliefs and practices that had accumulated since the era of the Prophet Muhammad's Medina."[165] As mentioned earlier, "according to the Kadizadelis, deviation flowed from the influence of the Sufi orders…. If the Sufis were not tamed…the entire community would be plunged into unbelief."[166]

---

[164] Such an approach was not new with Kadizade, either. It had been around since at least the 12th century AD, after which "Islam presented persistently two faces: one, Shari`ah-minded, concerned with outward, socially cognizable behavior, accepted as their care by the Sunni `ulama ["clerics"]; the other, mystical-minded, concerned with the inward, personal life of the individual, accepted as their care by the Sufi pirs [shaykhs]." There was a third, albeit less-followed, "stream of piety"—Shi`ism, or "`Alid loyalism with its chiliastic vision." The Ottoman state exhibited both the Shari`ah-minded and the Sufi aspects; the Safavids, for their part, merged Shi`ism with Sufism. See Marshall G.S. Hodgson, *The Venture of Islam: Conscience and History in a World Civilization Volume Two. The Expansion of Islam in the Middle Periods* (Chicago and London: University of Chicago Press, 1974), p. 203. But the openly hostile attitude toward Sufism was really first legitimized by Ahmad Ibn Hanbal (d. 1328), who had "insisted that spiritual progress was not toward knowing God but toward serving Him more perfectly; and that what the devout must learn to love is not God's essence (unknowable) but His command—in effect, the Shari`ah" (Hodgson, p. 470). Ibn Taymiyyah, via his later interpreter and re-popularizer Muhamad b. Abd al-Wahhab (d. 1792), would become a huge influence on not just Wahhabis but Salafis of all stripes within Sunni Islam, down to today. Also see Arvind Sharma, "The Wahhabi and Sufi Approaches to the Qur'an in Relation to the Modern World," *Bulletin of Christian Institutes of Islamic Studies*, V, 3-4 (July-December 1982), pp. 62-65.

[165] Zilfi, p. 253.

[166] *Ibid.*, p. 254

After their founder's death in 1635, these ideas survived, promulgated by Ustuvani Mehmed Efendi (d. 1661) from Damascus, who tried to make Kadizadelism part of the Ottoman state apparatus (alongside, or displacing, Sufism). The final paroxysm of the movement was inspired by Mehmed Bistam (d. 1685) from Van, "Vani" Mehmed.

Sultan Murad IV (d. 1640) at first supported the Kadizadelis, seeing in their severe Sunni orthodoxy a way to help centralize the Empire and silence critics.[167] But others opposed them: the head of one Sufi order in particular, Abdulmecid Sivasi of the Halvetis,[168] was the chief foil of the Kadizadelis. And as we have seen, the Sufis were an integral part of Ottoman society, and even government. In fact, to a considerable extent, for much of the 17th century, the Sufis represented the establishment—the Ottoman "deep state," if you will—while the Kadizadelis were the new, fresh, popular yet rebellious advocates of Islamic piety. Their popularity began to suffer, however, once they began practicing vigilantism—at first attacking Sufi shaykhs and their lodges and thus, by the 1630s, helping convince Sultan Murad IV to shut down not just taverns but coffeehouses—which Murad saw as dens fomenting sedition more than affronts to Islam—and even executing smokers.[169] While Kadizade was the movement's man of action, its primary ideological

---

[167] Barkey, p. 185.

[168] This is their Ottoman Turkish name. In Arabic, they were (and are) known as the Khalwatis. See Trimingham, pp. 74-78, in particular.

[169] Zilfi, p. 257.

architect and inspiration was the `alim Birgili Mehmed (d. 1573), whose writings laid out a Sunni fundamentalist program in which only practices with clear precedents in the Qur'an and/or the Hadiths were to be followed.[170]

The Kadizadelis seem to have pulled Ottoman public and foreign policy further in their direction between the mid- and late-1600s, making it (more) acceptable to attack dhimmis (non-Muslims under Islamic law) as well as Sufis. This was especially the case under Sultan Ibrahim I (1640-48) and Mehmed IV (1648-87)[171]—the former being ill and possibly mentally deranged, the latter coming to the imperial throne at a young age and easily swayed by others for the first decade of his reign. Power vacuums under both gave the Kadizadelis almost carte blanche to carry out activities such as these:

> The great conflagration in Istanbul in the summer of 1660 was followed by a decree banning Jews…and ordering them to sell their property and give their trusts to Muslims. In 1661…Jewish and Christian property was confiscated, and some churches and synagogues were destroyed. In 1662, seven churches were razed [in Istanbul]. Between 1663 and 1667, Jewish palace physicians were converted, and many public conversions were performed (1666-1687). During these years, Sufis were actively persecuted, some executed, and their ceremonies banned….Other assaults on Jews and Christians included…finally, the public stoning of a Muslim adulteress whose Jewish convert partner was beheaded in 1680.[172]

---

[170] *Ibid.*, pp. 260, 261.
[171] *Ibid.*, p. 258.

This cannot help but remind of the throwback ISIS caliphate which straddled Iraq and Syria from 2014 until early 2019, as well as more legitimate states, enforcing strict Islamic law. The latter would include Sunni Saudi Arabia and Pakistan but also the Twelver Shi`i Islamic Republic of Iran. Perhaps, in the near future, the Republic of Turkey may fit into this category—which would no doubt please the Kadizadelis.[173]

Acrimony and open violence between the Kadizadelis and Sufis (especially the Halvetis) reached such a fever pitch, and caused such social and political problems, that Murad IV's grand vizier, Köprülü Mehmed Paşa (in office 1656-61) and a "forceful opponent of preacher zealotry, as well as a strong advocate of calm and order in the capital,"[174] got fed up with the Kadizadelis efforts to turn Istanbul into an idealized 7th century Medina.[175] With armed Kadizadelis marching through the imperial capital, he met with the **Ottoman ulama who "declared the Kadizadelis' claims to orthodoxy false and their actions liable to punishment"[176]**

---

[172] Barkey, p. 184.

[173] There are 15 countries with a majority, or large minority, Muslim population that enforce at least some aspects of *shari`ah* law. See "Sharia Law Countries 2020," *worldpopulationreview.com*; accessed June 15, 2020. The Turkish Republic disposed of Islamic law when it replaced the Ottoman government in the 1920s, but it may be moving back in that direction: "Diyanet, 'Homosexuals,' Erdoğan and a Painful Future," *Observatoire de la Turquie Contemporaine*, April 28, 2020; accessed June 15, 2020.

[174] Barkey, p. 186.

[175] Zilfi, p. 262.

[176] *Ibid.*

[emphasis added]—whereupon the grand vizier had Ustuvani and the movement's other leaders banished to Cyprus. This provided a respite, but only until Köprülü had passed from the scene and his son Fazil Ahmed (d. 1676) replaced him as vizier. Fazil had been caught in the spell of the third influential Kadizadeli preacher, Vani Mehmed—even inviting him to Istanbul, whereupon the new vizier made Vani his own personal shaykh. An empowered Vani Mehmed then reintroduced the severe Kadizadeli condemnations of, and prohibitions against, Sufi music, ritual dancing,[177] wine and tobacco.[178] Vani went even further than had his predecessors Kadizade and Ustuvani, however, in that he attacked the Ottoman practice, rampant in the military and its Sufi members, of allowing "noncombatant boys"[179] to go on campaign with the army. Vani saw in this officially illegal but widely accepted practice, which would have encompassed some of these boys being sexually abused, a moral failing that was contributing to the military defeats the Ottomans began suffering at this time.[180] Vani even prevailed upon

---

[177] Almost all Sufi orders practice *dhikr*, or "remembrance" of Allah, which includes prayers and chanting (usually of Allah's various names) along with rhythmic breathing and body movements, to include clapping, swaying and what might be described as holy "dancing." See Trimingham, "Ritual and Ceremonial," pp. 200-207 especially.

[178] Zilfi, p. 263.

[179] *Ibid.*, p. 264.

[180] This problem still bedevils parts of the modern Islam world. Just three years ago, in Afghanistan, US forces regularly watched its Afghan allies engage in the same practices, *mutatis mutandis*. See Anuj Chopra, "Afghan Soldiers Are Using Boys As Sex Slaves, and the US Is Looking the Other Way," *The Washington Post*, July 18, 2017. This is a problem not just in Afghanistan: "Pakistan: Sexual Abuse of Young Boys Rises," *Aljazeera*, November 18, 2015;" also Raymond

Sultan Mehmed IV to cancel joint prayers by the leading Muslim ulama and the top Christian clerics as the army prepared to attack Christian Austria—showing that he wielded more power than even the Şeyhülislam (Shaykh-al-Islam), the top Islamic official and chief `alim. But when the Ottomans were soundly defeated at Vienna in 1683, the major proponents of that campaign—Vani foremost among them—were declared *persona non grata.* Vani was exiled across the Bosporus to the Asian side, and died (or was murdered) there two years later.[181] "With Vani gone, Kadizadeli puritanism lost its commanding voice" and the movement "sank into the background of Istanbul's religious life."[182]

Ibrahim, "Muslims Sexually Enslaving Children: A Global Phenomenon," *Frontpagemag,* September 3, 2014. For an overview of the relevant Qur'anic and Hadith texts, see Mark Brustman, "Queer Sexuality and Identity in the Qur'an and Hadith,"*people.well.com,* June 14, 2017. For a take that argues that Islam is not necessarily anti-homosexuality, consult Barbara Zollner, "Mithliyyun or Lutiyyun? Neo-Orthodoxy and the Debate on the Unlawfulness of Same-sex Relations in Islam," in Samar Habib, ed., *Islam and Homosexuality.* Volume 1 (Santa Barbara, CA: Praeger, 2010), pp. 193 221. For an eyebrow raising defense of the Ottomans in this regard, see Niki Gamm, "Male Sexual Quirks among the Ottomans," *hurriyetdailynews,* February 28, 2015; in particular: "the members of the Sufi…orders…included many of the most powerful men in the Ottoman government and possibly even the sultan himself. Some of the Sufis even organized what were known as 'sema' during which ceremonies they would sit in a circle and concentrate on the beautiful young boys in the center, concentrating to such an extent on what they perceived as beauty that they might fall into a trance. Since these ceremonies often lasted all night, the people who were opposed to these mystic orders were quick to accuse the participants of engaging in sodomy…. A 17th century reformist movement [the Kadizadelis]…condemned this boy-gazing [sic] as heresy and equated it with sodomy even though the physical act itself had not occurred." All of the aforementioned online sources were accessed June 15, 2020.
[181] Zilfi, p. 265.
[182] *Ibid.*

One other aspect of the Kadizadelis in general, and Vani Efendi in particular, is worth noting, however. Their oppression of Jews in the Ottoman Empire probably helped created the movement headed by the Jew Sabbatai Sevi (d. 1676), who proclaimed himself the Jewish messiah before converting to Islam at the threat of death in 1666.[183] After becoming a Muslim, Sevi, "now Aziz Mehmed, became the companion of Vani Efendi…. Together, they convinced many Jews to follow them into the Islamic fold."[184]

The Kadizadelis' preaching success in the 17th century initially convinced them that they might be able to take Istanbul back to an imagined glorious future resembling Arabia of a millennium before—to re-make the Ottoman state (if not the entire empire) over in their proto-Salafi image. But they ultimately failed because "in general the ulema-statesmen of the highest…ranks continued to represent the empire's Sufi-leavened theological center."[185] The Sufis won this round over the Salafis, if you will. It may have been the case that the Ottoman authorities manipulated the situation by promoting the Kadizadelis at certain times so as to, in the end, strengthen the state-preferred Sufis and to re-center the state on its majority-Muslim identity in a period when the Ottomans were beginning to lose wars to the Europeans and the Russians.[186]

---

[183] See Barkey, pp. 187-191.
[184] *Ibid.*, p. 189.
[185] Zilfi, p. 269.
[186] Barkey, pp. 189-190.

This theory is rather conspiratorial and may well grant the Ottomans much too high a level of strategic brilliance, however.

From the 16th to the 19th centuries, the Ottomans encountered another brand of rebellions: those of the Druze. Then, as now, the Druze were located in the Levant—today's Syria, Lebanon, Israel and Jordan—and considered a heterodox, if not heretical, branch of Islam along with the Nusrayris (now called Alawis). The Druze are an offshoot of Isma'ili Shi`ism, and venerate the Fatimid Caliph al-Hakim bi-Amr Allah (d. 1021 AD) as Allah incarnate.[187] This, to put it mildly, locates the Druze light-years outside the Islamic mainstream—and in fact as far back as the early 14th century the aforementioned Sunni jurist Ibn Taymiyah issued an *istifta'*, or short *fatwa*, on the *Durziyyah* and Nusayris which ruled them "heretics" who "[e]ven if they apparently declare their belief [in Islam] and accept its doctrines[188]…should still be considered heretics by all Muslims."[189] The Mamluks who ruled Egypt and the Levant before the Ottoman conquest were, like their subjugators, Sunni. Therefore, they largely accepted Ibn Taymiyah's scorn for not

---

[187] Whereas the Nusayris/Alawis venerate Ali. See Matti Moosa, *Extremist Shiites: The Ghulat Sects* (Syracuse: Syracuse University Press, 1988), p. xiii. See also Paul E. Walker, *Caliph of Cairo: al-Hakim bi-Amr Allah, 996-1021* (Cairo and New York: The American University in Cairo Press, 2009); and Khuri, *Imams and Emirs*.

[188] This is almost certainly a reference to *taqiyah*, "dissimulation," or *kitman*, "secrecy"—the Twelver Shi`i practice of pretending to be Sunni and hiding one's true religious allegiance in order to escape persecution.

[189] Yaron Friedman, "Ibn Taymiyya's Fatawa against the Nusayri-`Alawi Sect," *Der Islam*, Vol. 87 (2005), pp. 349-363. The specific quote is from p. 355.

only the Druze and Nusayris but also both major sects of Shi`ism
(Twelver and Sevener, or Isma'ili). The Mamluks, in effect, " 're-
invented' [all of them] as non-Muslim, and then treated as heretical
whenever any of their members proved to be a menace to the
dynasty's stability and sovereignty."[190] The Ottomans continued this
approach to the Druze, since they shared with the Mamluks the
same Sunni orthodox view of sects.

Shortly after the Ottomans conquered Greater Syria and
Egypt in the early 16th century, and up until almost the end of the
17th century, the Druze engaged in a series of protracted revolts
against their Turkish overlords[191] rooted in "their refusal to pay
taxes to the Ottoman state and their continued possession of
firearms."[192] There were others who fought the Ottomans as well.
Janbirdi al-Ghazali (d. 1521) had been an Egyptian Mamluk official
and in fact fought for that losing side at the pivotal battle of Marj
Dabiq, Syria, in 1516,[193] defected to the Ottomans and was made
governor of Damascus—only to revolt against Sultan Süleyman's
authority in 1518. Al-Ghazali was defeated and beheaded three years

---

[190] Rula Jurdi Abisaab, "History and Self-Image: The `Amili Ulema in Syria and
Iran (Fourteenth to Sixteenth Centuries)," in H.E. Chelabi, ed., *Distant Relations:
Iran and Lebanon in the Last 500 Years* (London and New York: I.B. Tauris, 2006),
pp. 62-95. The specific quote is from p. 65.

[191] See Abdul-Rahim Abu-Husayn, "The Long Rebellion: the Druzes and the
Ottomans, 1516-1697," *Archivum Ottomanicum*, 19 (2001), pp. 165-191. Also see
"Challenges to Ottoman authority: the Jhulads and the Ma`ns," *The New
Cambridge History of Islam, Volume 2* (Mobile Version). ["Jhulad" is wrong; it
should be "Janbulads."]; accessed June 15, 2020.

[192] Abu-Husayn, p. 171.

[193] "Janbirdi al-Ghazali," *Wikipedia*; accessed June 15, 2020. Also Douwes, *passim.*

later. Lingering pro-Mamluk sentiments may have been a factor in subsequent Druze revolts, as well, such as the one that broke out in 1520 which was waged in support of a Sunni Arab chieftain, one Muhammad b. al-Hanash. [194] A historian in Damascus, Ibn Tulun, suggested that at least some of the rebellious Druze leaders may even have been cooperating with unspecified "Frankish" troops (possibly supported by Venice) who landed forces at Beirut but were driven off.[195] Ottoman responses to these Druze uprisings were mostly military, and brutal: razing villages and mass beheadings were a favorite tactic, as well as soldiers raping Druze women. On a more ideological plane, Druze religious texts "testifying to the community's hostility to Islam" were seized.[196] This perhaps reflected (if it didn't excuse) the situation that, overall, "[t]he Lebanon posed special problems for Ottoman authority…. Though the Lebanese peasants were affiliated with the religious communities,[197] the local political order was not based on religion, but on allegiance to village and valley chiefs who were subordinate to feudal suzerains, in turn subordinate to the governor of Damascus and the Sultan in Istanbul. This hierarchy of authority was at best unstable and subject to fluctuations in the balance of central and local power."[198] The

---

[194] Abu-Husayn, p. 167.

[195] *Ibid.*, pp. 168-169.

[196] *Ibid.*, p. 170.

[197] These included (then as today) Sunni Muslims, Shi`i Muslims both Twelver and Sevener (Isma'ili), sects (especially Druze and Nusayris/Alawis), and Christians.

[198] Ira M. Lapidus, *A History of Islamic Societies* (Cambridge: Cambridge University Press, 1988), p. 363.

Ottomans even engaged in pre-emptive execution—as when the Druze chieftain Yunus Ma`an was enticed into coming to Damascus and killed by the Ottoman governor. This failed to head off revolts[199] in many Druze villages, however. By 1575 "a state of open rebellion had spread to all the Druze districts and beyond."[200] Within a few more years, Shi`is (presumably Twelvers) in some parts of Lebanon had joined in the anti-Ottoman violence,[201] although the Druze were the main perpetrators—or at least were viewed as such by the Ottoman authorities.

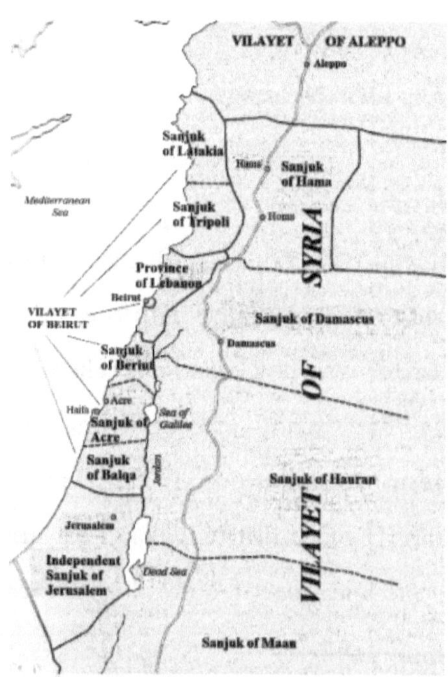

The 19ᵗʰ century Ottoman "Levant." [202]

---

[199] Pun absolutely intended.
[200] Abu-Husayn, p. 172.
[201] *Ibid.*, p. 173.

Finally fed up, the Ottomans in 1585 launched "a massive…punitive expedition" with "troops drawn from all over Syria and Anatolia"[203] which seized thousands of muskets as well as unpaid taxes, killed hundreds of Druze and literally sent heads back to Istanbul.[204] The weapons, as alluded to earlier, very likely came from the Venetians who had previously established close commercial relations, involving trade in cotton and wheat, with the Mamluks of Egypt and had assisted some of the Turkoman tribes fighting the Ottomans back in the 15th century—besides having fought a war directly with the Ottomans themselves in 1463.[205] (The Ottomans suspected as much, which was one reason why they seized Cyprus from the Venetians in 1570). It should come as no surprise, then, that the Venetians would actively work to undermine the Ottomans, who at the time were threatening to conquer even more deeply into Europe and had been stopped from complete control of the Mediterranean, and possible occupation of Rome, only by the massive naval defeat inflicted on them by the combined Christians forces led by Venice and Spain at Lepanto in 1571.[206]

---

202 "Map of Ottoman Levant," subcategory of "Beirut Vilayet," *en.wikipedia.org*, accessed June 13, 2020.

203 Abu-Husayn, p. 174.

204 *Ibid.*, p. 175. Decapitation as punishment for "enemies of Islam" was not devised by ISIS in recent years. See my article "Beheading in the Name of Islam," *Middle East Quarterly* (Spring 2005), pp. 51-57; accessed June 16, 2020.

205 *Ibid.*, pp. 176-177.

206 As per T.C.F. Hopkins, *Confrontation at Lepanto: Christendom v. Islam* (New York: Tom Doherty Associates, 2006).

In the early 1600s, the Druze revolts were renewed under the leadership of Fakhr al-Din Ma`an (d. 1635). This Druze leader at first sided with a Kurdish one fighting against the Ottomans, Janbulad Ali (d. 1620)—whose rebellion is usually classified as part of the aforementioned Celali uprisings in this time frame.[207] After Janbulad Ali's defeat, arrest and exile (and eventual execution), Fakhr al-Din "was able to buy his way back into the sultan's[208] good graces"[209] and get himself appointed *sanjakbey* of Beirut and Sidon. But Fakhr al-Din was also intriguing with the Grand Duke of Tuscany,[210] Ferdinand I (d. 1609). This Christian ruler had also earlier supported Janbulad Ali (as well as the Safavid leader Shah Abbas) over against the Ottomans—out of a combination of Catholic sympathy for their cousin Maronites[211] in the Levant, as well as a desire to obtain commercial entry into the area since Tuscany had not been granted capitulation trade rights in the Ottoman domains to match those of other European powers.[212] Fakhr al-Din was even commended by the Pope (Paul V) for his kind treatment of not just Maronites but Christians in general.[213]

---

[207] "Challenges to Ottoman Authority…."

[208] This would have been Ahmed I (d. 1617).

[209] "Challenges to Ottoman Authority…."

[210] The Grand Duchy of Tuscany was a northern Italian state, nominally part of the Holy Roman Empire but actually independent, for some 300 years, between the mid-16 to the mid-19th centuries. See "Grand Duchy of Tuscany," *Wikipedia*; accessed June 16, 2020.

[211] Maronites are Middle Eastern Catholics, mainly in Lebanon, who came back under papal authority after the Crusades. See Khuri, pp. 153-160.

[212] Abu-Husayn, pp. 181-183.

[213] *Ibid.*, p. 184.

Overall, however, Fakhr al-Din's attempt to "mobilize Roman Catholic military might against the Ottomans"[214] came to naught, as he was captured and put to death in Istanbul by the Empire in 1635.[215] Afterwards, in order to head off any more such Druze challenges to their rule in Lebanon, the Ottomans revamped their administration, which was "intended to bring Druze areas under direct and hopefully more effective imperial control."[216] However, under Ahmad Ma`an (grand-nephew of Fakhr al-Din), many Druze joined Shi`is in the Jubayl district (northeast of Beirut) in revolting against the Sultan's rule throughout the 1680s and indeed until 1697, when Ahmad Ma`an died.[217]

Overall, for this first major period of Druze chafing under the Ottoman yoke, it's clear that the Ottoman center and its representatives in Aleppo and Damascus (Lebanon being part of greater Syrian administration under the Ottomans) had a love-hate relationship with local emirs, especially Druze ones. The latter were crucial to Ottoman rule as governors, but the Sultan and his advisors were (rightly) suspicious of their motives and ultimate loyalties[218]--not least because "Druze rebellion against the Ottomans, certainly until 1633, and probably to the very end [1697], was fueled, to a large extent, by European political, commercial and religious designs

---

[214] *Ibid.*, p. 187.
[215] "Challenges to Ottoman authority…."
[216] Abu-Husayn, p. 190.
[217] *Ibid.*, p. 191. Abu-Husayn also notes that the Ottoman documents refer to these Shi`is as *kizilbaş*!
[218] "Challenges to Ottoman authority…."

upon Syria."[219] This was probably one reason why the Ottomans favored the aggrandizement of the Sunni Shihab tribe over against the Druze, granting the Shihabs a *de facto* "hereditary principality."[220]

Matters changed in Ottoman Syria and Lebanon during the 18th and 19th centuries, thanks to three developments: the increased wealth and power of Maronite Christians and their church; Maronite expansion south into majority Druze areas; and the alliance with the Maronites made by the Shihab tribe and the unexpected conversion of many of them to Christianity.[221] A major complicating factor was the Egyptian occupation of Lebanon and much of Syria in the 1830s by the forces of Egypt, the Empire's nominal vassal. Its ruler Muhammad Ali (d. 1849) leveraged his anger—at the broken promise of Sultan Mahmud II to hand over administration of Syria as a reward for Egypt trying to put down the anti-Ottoman Greek Revolt—into not just occupation of the Levant but a serious attempt to overthrow the Ottoman dynasty, which was prevented only by European intervention.[222] Bashir II, the major Shihabi amir who was a Christian, not a Sunni Muslim, worked with the Egyptian Muslim regime ruling Syria and Lebanon and in fact crushed at least one Druze revolt.[223] This happened when the latter turned pro-Ottoman because the Egyptians were seen as being pro-Maronite.[224]

---

[219] Abu-Husayn, p. 191.
[220] *Ibid.*
[221] M.E. Yapp, *The Making of the Modern Near East, 1792-1923* (London and New York: Longman, 1987), p. 135.
[222] *Ibid.*, pp. 70-71.
[223] *Ibid.*, p. 131.

But after a few years the Maronites themselves turned against the Egyptian occupiers, as well as against Bashir II—and in any event the French and British helped the Ottomans regain Levantine control and push the Egyptians back across Sinai.

Beginning in 1858 Maronites around Mount Lebanon began fighting Druze landowners, and within two years thousands of the former were dead and as many as 100,000 homeless. Perhaps 10,000 Maronites were killed by the Druze in Damascus. "Although efforts have been made to explain the Damascus massacre in terms of factional rivalries and economic changes there was also a substantial element of Muslim [sic][225] popular hostility to the new pretensions of Christians…"[226] Simply put, Sunni and (Twelver) Shi`i Muslims allied with the Druze to settle long-standing scores with Maronite Christians. Many of the local Ottoman troop garrisons, albeit not necessarily the Ottoman government, effectively sided with the Druze and Lebanese Muslims by refusing to stop their depredations—for this time, unlike several centuries earlier, the Druze were seen to some extent as fighting on behalf of the

---

[224] There may have also been long-standing resentment of the Egyptian Muslims for not acknowledging the divinity of the Fatimid caliph al-Hakim—deified by the Druze, recall—and expelling the Druze, even though this had happened many centuries earlier. See Gregory A. Francioch (2008), "Nationalism in Ottoman Greater Syria 1840-1914: The Divisive Legacy of Sectarianism" (unpublished Master's thesis), Naval Postgraduate School, Monterey, California; accessed June 16, 2020.

[225] Although, at as noted earlier, the Druze were not considered Muslim by mainstream Sunni scholars—even then.

[226] Yapp, p. 136.

Ottoman Muslim ummah over against the recalcitrant *dhimmi*s, especially by "the small numbers of imperial troops, who were poorly supplied and often unpaid [and who] neglected their duties and participated with sectarian partisans in looting."[227] Perhaps more importantly, the Ottomans were preoccupied with defending their territorial integrity vis-à-vis European Christian powers, especially Russia, on their northern borders and so were unable to devote the time and manpower necessary to put down Druze violence. "While the Ottomans were not the sole source of the political failures that enabled the violence, they abdicated their responsibility as a modern territorially based state to exercise a monopoly of violence within their borders."[228] This gave the French not just an excuse but a legitimate rationale to intervene, which Napoleon III did by sending 6000 troops and pressuring the Ottomans to create a separate *mutasarriflik*, or provincial subdistrict, of Mount Lebanon for the Maronites. This would be "autonomous under international guarantee with a Christian governor assisted by an elected council on which all communities were represented (4 Maronites, 3 Druzes, 2 Greek Orthodox, and 1 each from Greek Catholic, Sunni and Shi`i communities)."[229] But the Druze had one final, massive anti-Ottoman spasm still in them. In 1909 those in the Hawran, the far-southwestern part of Syria, revolted under the leadership of the al-

---

[227] Francioch, p. 43 [p. 54 in online text].
[228] *Ibid.*, p. 44 [p. 55].
[229] Yapp, p. 137.

Atrash family.[230] The Ottomans tried negotiations but eventually responded with massive military force a year later and, in the summer and early fall of 1910, crushed the uprising. Several thousand Druze were killed. The Ottomans also drafted a huge number of Druze men into the imperial army, and set out to seize weapons from member of that community. The al-Atrash would later foment insurrection against the French, as well. The overall Ottoman failure to prevent such sectarian violence, then, would eventually result in a substantial loss of control of Lebanon and Syria to Europeans and a diminution of authority and prestige of the Sultan's government among all the Levantine Arabs—and indeed, arguably marked the beginning of the end of Istanbul's control of its Arab provinces.

Another recalcitrant Ottoman Arab province, albeit much farther afield from Istanbul, proved a major problem for the Sultan-Caliphs: Yemen. The Ottomans ruled, or at least occupied, that southwestern corner of the Arabian peninsula from 1538 to the mid-1630s, and again from 1849 until the end of World War I.[231] For

---

[230] "Hauran [sic] Druze Rebellion," *Wikipedia*; accessed June 25, 2020.

[231] Relevant sources on Yemen vis-à-vis the Ottoman empire include: Yapp, *The Making of the Modern Near East, 1792-1923*; Vincent Steven Wilhite (2003), "Guerrilla War, Counterinsurgency, and State Formation in Ottoman Yemen" (unpublished doctoral dissertation), The Ohio State University, Columbus, OH; Caesar E. Farah, *The Sultan's Yemen. Nineteenth-Century Challenges to Ottoman Rule* (London and New York: I.B. Tauris, 2002); Jane Hathaway, "The Mawza' Exile at the Juncture of Zaydi and Ottoman Messianism," *AJS Review*, Vol. 29, No. 1 (April 2005), pp. 111-128; Paul Dresch, *A History of Modern Yemen* (Cambridge: Cambridge University Press, 2000), especially pp. 1-27; and "The Zaydis and Ottomans" "and "Ottoman Return," under "History of Yemen," *Wikipedia*. See,

much of the second Christian millennium Yemen—or at least the northern highlands, from Sana`a to Sa`dah—was ruled by Zaydi (Fiver Shi`i) leaders: "hero imams"[232] who could and would wage jihad to protect their faith and their community. The Ottoman occupation of Yemen was intended to head off attacks from the south on Mecca and Medina, and safeguard Red Sea trade with India threatened by the Portuguese and, later, the British; it may also have sprung from a realization of the importance of the newly-developed coffee trade.[233] The Ottomans, however, as Sunnis were anathema to the Shi`i Zaydis,[234] over and above their role as disliked non-Arab, Turkish invaders.

Various and sundry Zaydi states existed in the region between the 10th and 17th centuries.[235] After the initial Ottoman conquest, by imperial forces from Egypt, the petty Zaydi states were replaced by a more substantial and unified Qasimi Imamate, created by al-Mansur al-Qasim (d. 1620). He then spearheaded armed opposition to the Ottomans, while his son al-Mua`yyad Muhammad (d. 1644) oversaw a guerrilla war that finally resulted in Ottoman

---

as well, "Rassids," *Wikipedia.* Both the online sources were accessed June 16, 2020.

[232] As per Khuri, pp. 113, 114. The Ibadis of Oman share much the same belief, although manifestations thereof have been much less of a historical occurrence. The hero imam is quite different from the occulted "martyr imam" of the Twelver Shi`is, as per his excellent book.

[233] Jane Hathaway, "The Ottomans and the Yemeni Coffee Trade," *Oriente Moderno,* Nuova serie, Anno 25 (86), Nr. 1 (2006), pp. 161-171.

[234] Much as the Saudis are today.

[235] As I detail in my unpublished paper "The Shi`a of Yemen and Arabia and their Relationship to Iran," 2012.

withdrawal. Both men led "jihad against the Ottomans focused on the perceived injustice and immorality of the Ottoman state"[236] (to include the presence of Sufis in the Ottoman military and regime—which the fundamentalist Zaydi Shi`is abhorred—and lax enforcement of shari`ah[237]). The most powerful and prestigious Zaydi leader in this era was al-Mutawakkil Isma'il (d. 1676), who filled the power vacuum left by the Ottoman departure with jihads against the Shafi`i Sunnis[238] of the lowlands, deemed virtual infidels (*kuffar*), as had been the Ottomans, for their lack of correct Zaydi Shi`i doctrines.[239] The Ottomans, for their part, had viewed the Yemeni Shi`is much as they did the Safavids and their "fifth columns" within the Empire: as heretical enemies. But by the mid-17th century they had more pressing concerns, mainly in their European provinces.

The Ottoman Empire largely ignored Yemen for some two centuries afterwards. But by the mid-19th century, British inroads into the Red Sea and the continuing Wahhabi-Saudi threat[240] (on which more below) led the Ottomans to attempt another

---

[236] Wilhite, p. 35.

[237] *Ibid.*, p. 74.

[238] There are four major school of Sunni fiqh, or religio-legal jurisprudence, each named after its famous founder: Shafi`i, Hanafi, Maliki and Hanbali. There are also at least two recognized Shi`i "schools" of such: that of the Twelvers (also called Ja`fari) and the Fivers (Zaydis), per 2005's "The Amman Message." In Yemen, most Sunnis are Shafi`is and in fact Imam Shafi`i himself seems to have lived there for some time, according to "A Brief Outline of the Shafi`i School's Transmission," *shafiifiqh.com.* Both online sources accessed June 16, 2020.

[239] Wilhite, pp. 83ff.

[240] Yapp, p. 263.

intervention there—or perhaps more accurately, the *Egyptians* intervened in southwestern Arabia. At this time Egypt was ruled by the still-loyal Ottoman vassal Muhammad Ali.[241]   That *vali*, or "governor," of a vilayet had already pacified the obstreperous Wahhabis in the Hijaz for the Sultan, and Istanbul seemed if anything to trust him and his family more than did, ironically, the British.[242] From the early 19th century Egyptian troops, on behalf of the Ottomans, worked—mostly successfully—at pacifying recalcitrant tribes in Arabia, including Yemen. Of course, within six years Muhammad Ali was aiming far higher than Yemen. His eyes were fixed on Istanbul, as he sent Egyptian forces to invade Syria and Anatolia with the ultimate goal of replacing Sultan Mahmud II (d. 1839). This probably would have worked if the British and French had not stopped it, reasoning that the status quo ante was preferable to this particular problematic resolution of the so-called Eastern Question, "considering that state [the Ottoman Empire] to be a material element in the general balance of power in Europe."[243]

So by 1840, Yemen "was momentarily pacified, but the pacification had abetted British, not Ottoman, aims in that corner of Arabia….[T]he reaffirmation of imperial Ottoman sovereignty was to be achieved only with the conversion of Yemen into an Ottoman

---

[241] As per Farah, chapter 2.

[242] *Ibid.*, pp. 17,18.

[243] "Palmerston to Campbell, 4 Feb. 1833, Public Records Office, FO 78/226," quoted in Yapp, p.71. Henry John Temple, 3rd Viscount Palmerston (d. 1865) as serving as British Prime Minister at the time.

vilayet."[244] In essence, Egyptian intervention had destabilized (via the law of unintended consequences) the tribal power balance in southwestern Arabia to such an extent that the Ottomans gradually came to the conclusion that either they or the British would have to step in—and the Ottoman establishment much preferred itself in that role. The Brits had already taken over Aden, in 1839, primarily as a coal refueling stop for the Egypt-to-India steamer route. But "both Ottoman and British power was confined almost exclusively to the coasts"[245]—a situation which the Ottomans would try to remedy.

During the 1840s, Aden twice suffered attacks, one of which was a jihad led by a man claiming to be the Mahdi—a certain Faqih Sa`id, whose eschatology the Zaydis thwarted by capturing and executing him.[246] In 1849, after entreaties from Sunni ulama and tribal leaders, Sultan Abdulmejid I decided to send in 1500 troops and get control of a degenerating situation, which was in no small measure caused by Zaydi power struggles between rival imams.[247] The Ottoman commander tasked to do so sided with Ali b. al-Mahdi Abdallah "al-Hadi," who, so empowered, "cruelly suppressed al-Mutawakkil ibn Muhammad, confiscated his property and possessions on the grounds of treachery...and had his head cut off

---

[244] *Ibid.*, p. 29.

[245] Yapp, pp. 176, 177.

[246] Dresch, p. 4. It is unclear whether Sa`id was a Zaydi or a Sunni—but considering the former's beliefs, which normally do not include the Awaited Mahdi, he was likely the latter.

[247] Farah, pp, 58, 59.

in prison...."[248] A parade of different imams arose and challenged one another, with the Ottomans sometimes supporting one, then another, until 1872—when the Zaydi tribes agreed to allow Ottoman forces some measure of power in the highlands, not just the lowland coastal areas.[249]

Before that came to pass, however, the Ottomans had their hands full simply "calming tribal rivalries" and "suppressing resistance."[250] Imam Muhammad b. Yahya, the most powerful Zaydi ruler in the highlands, did allow an Ottoman garrison of 1000 men in Sana`a, and the Turks in return permitted him to keep half the tax revenues from the region.[251]  But others rebelled, including thousands of tribesmen from `Asir (northwest of Yemen) and from Yam (around Najran). By 1864 Istanbul was, once again, requesting Egyptian military assistance, and its ruler Isma'il, "remembering only too well how his grandfather, Muhammad Ali, had done the Ottomans' bidding in Arabia against the Wahhabis in the earlier decade of the century only to gain nothing in the end,"[252] was hesitant. But he finally provided a force of 4000 men, which helped the Ottomans successfully face down the rebels. A larger Ottoman force, of at least 6000 troops, put an end to the `Asiri rebellion in 1871 and allowed them effectively to pacify the highlands of Yemen

---

[248] *Ibid.*, p. 60.
[249] *Ibid.*
[250] *Ibid.*
[251] *Ibid.*, p. 61.
[252] *Ibid.*, p. 74.

by the next year.[253] Following that, the Ottoman conquerors made Sana`a the administrative capital of the new Yemen vilayet.[254] (The Suez Canal, which opened in 1869, had made it easier for the Ottomans to transport their forces there by ship, as opposed to overland through the Hijaz.[255]) The Ottomans set up schools, established the first police forces and in general tried to balance force and repression with such conciliatory measures; but the latter failed miserably among the Zaydi tribes of the highlands, especially as not a few Ottoman officials proved venal and corrupt.[256]

Between 1869 and 1872, at least 22,000 Ottoman troops served in Yemen, with 4000 of them dying on campaign there.[257] One major reason was that the Ottoman army was, in effect, fighting in a Napoleonic mode—maneuvering to seize the initiative via rapid campaigning so as to bring superior firepower to bear and crush the enemy—while its opponents, particularly the Zaydis, were engaged in unconventional or asymmetric warfare.[258] The Ottoman state's adoption of European conventional warfare, and its application of such in Yemen (indeed, throughout the Empire) had been made possible by a massive expansion of the Ottoman army, to some 800,000 men, in the second half of the 19th century.[259]

---

[253] *Ibid.*, p. 76.
[254] "Ottoman Return."
[255] Farah, p. 81.
[256] *Ibid.*, p. 97.
[257] *Ibid.*, p. 100.
[258] Wilhite, p. 133.
[259] *Ibid.*, pp, 137, 138.

Nonetheless, Ottoman manpower and successes were still insufficient to head off further rebellion by Yemeni tribal elements, Zaydis and even at least one Jewish messianic pretender, Shukri Kuhayil.[260] But the greatest problems came from the rival Zaydi claimants to their imamate, and the incessant Zaydi highlanders' bitter rivalries with the mostly-Sunni inhabitants of the lowlands, coasts, and Hadramaut[261] (the region along the southern coast between Yemen and Oman). In a novel attempt to counter such sectarian recalcitrance,, the Ottomans began organizing, for the first time, units called "Hamidiye battalions" (after the new Sultan, Abdul Hamid II) which were composed of locals;[262] the concept was likely modeled on irregular Cossack troops deployed by the Russian imperial army.[263] These units, "well-trained and disciplined,"[264] acquitted themselves well and were popular with many Yemenis; "often rebellious tribes would submit merely on the appearance of these troops, because... 'the rebels feared to kill their brother Muslims'"[265] However, this popularity was undercut by the indigenous officials who embezzled so much money that the units ran out of local funding—whereupon the Ottoman administration, unwilling or unable to pay for these units, disbanded them. This

---

[260] Farah., p. 101.

[261] Wilhite, p. 81.

[262] Farah, p. 104.

[263] As per Mesut Uyar and Edward J. Erickson, *A Military History of the Ottomans* (Westport, CT: Praeger, 2009). This specific information is from p. 204.

[264] Farah, p. 105.

[265] Wilhite, pp. 230, 231.

complicated matters by injecting yet more armed groups with grievances into Yemen's already fractious political landscape.

By 1882 the situation on the ground for the Ottomans in Yemen was this: "[t]he progress achieved in pacifying the tribes, promoting education and economic projects, constructing public works and solving administrative problems…[had come] to naught. The inhabitants' main priority was security and protection from extortion, which did not last. The importance of this strategic part of Arabia to the protection of the holy sites…was not lost on Istanbul and attempts were still being made to find solutions. But the treasuries, central and local, could not muster the necessary funds."[266] However, "in all fairness to the Ottomans…in the ten years since their return to the highlands they [had] expended every sincere effort to pacify the land, appease its tribes by forgiving rebellious chiefs even to the extent of appointing them to administrative posts, and introducing reforms to enhance the country's economic welfare"— but these exertions failed mainly because of "the tribes' lawlessness and their chieftain's greed, not to mention the feud over the imamate, more than any misadministration on the part of the Ottomans."[267] In addition, by 1872 the Ottomans "had reached the practical limits of expansion in the region"[268] with the *rub` al-khali* ("Empty Quarter") to the north and east and British protectorates in

---

[266] Farah, p. 106.
[267] *Ibid.*, pp. 106, 107.
[268] Wilhite, pp. 190, 191.

the south.[269]   Thus, the Empire effectively wound down its conquests via conventional war which, in any event, had demonstrated its limited utility against the Zaydis' guerrilla warfare which would ultimately prove the undoing of the Ottoman presence in Yemen.

By 1888-91, much of Yemen was once again in open revolt against Ottoman rule, led by the Zaydis but also including the smaller population of Isma'ili Shi`is.[270] Reasons for discontent included the usual suspects: Ottoman persecution (both real and perceived), taxation and accompanying extortion and violent collection measures, as well as inveterate Zaydi aversion to their Turkish overlords' lax Islamic standards in matters such as wine-bibbing.[271]   Sultan Abdül Hamid II's attempts at placating the locals—via incorporating them into police forces, building new roads, cracking down on corruption[272]—had profited little. By 1891 the Zaydis, now led by Muhammad b. Yahya Hamid al-Din (d. 1904), had exploited these grievances and ejected the Ottomans from the Yemeni highlands.   Hamid al-Din's movement was powered by his declarations of a full-fledged jihad against the occupiers, in which "denunciation of the Ottomans was paralleled by an equally forceful assertion of the Imam's [his] legitimacy."[273]

---

[269] As per Farah, pp.132ff.
[270] *Ibid.*, p. 155.
[271] *Ibid.*, pp. 164, 165.
[272] *Ibid.*, p. 173.
[273] Wilhite, p. 247.

Propaganda to that effect was disseminated by Zaydi ulama, who served as intermediaries below the Imam and as exhorters to jihad; this, in effect, "focused on channeling the competitive energies of the tribal system toward a goal transcending the honor culture of this system"[274] against the "quasi-colonial attitudes of many Ottoman officials...."[275]

This revolt, however, was quashed in rather short order by the Ottomans, as the commander brought in from the Hijaz, Feyzi Paşa, proved highly competent not only in running the rebels out of Sana`a, but reestablishing control of the other major cities.[276] But the 1888-91 jihad set the stage for a longer asymmetric struggle against Ottoman rule which would soon erupt.[277] In no small measure the 19th century violent Yemeni opposition to imperial Turkish administration stemmed from many Yemenis' hatred of Istanbul's *Tanzimat* reforms. These "regulations" or "orders," which were intended to bring many aspects of Ottoman society and administration in line with modern Western practices, had kicked off in 1839, during the reign of Sultan Abdulmejid I. They included replacing the janissaries with a more modernized force; revamping the provinces and their administration, to include official recognition of non-Muslim religious *millets*, or communities; establishment of secular, Western-style schools running parallel to Qur'anic ones; and

---

[274] *Ibid.*, p. 253.
[275] *Ibid.*, p. 262.
[276] *Ibid.*, pp. 292-299.
[277] *Ibid.*, p. 301.

new legal codes that incorporated elements of Western law alongside shari`ah.[278]  The latter two aspects, in particular, were anathema to the Yemenis in general and the fundamentalist Shi`i Zaydis in particular.[279] Since Hamid al-Din "al-Mansur" had been neither captured nor killed in 1891, he continued to stir up jihad against the Ottomans, particularly via *isabat*, "bands" of Zaydi tribesmen, who were paid as "soldiers of the Imam" to fight.[280] "The *isabat* would be dispatched into territory under Ottoman control, accompanied by scholar-propagandists for the Imam…. The *isabat* would circulate through the villages, collecting the *zakat* for the Imam, while the scholar-propagandists…would urge the people to take part in the *jihad*."[281] This more closely resembles modern guerrilla warfare than it does what had been practiced in Yemen previously.[282] By the 1890s the Zaydi tribesmen were formidable opponents of the Ottomans, by virtue both of jihad-infused "tribal quasi-state"[283] organization and modern weaponry—in particular breech-loading rifles, obtained from the French and, later, the Italians.[284]

---

[278] Yapp, pp. 108-114. There was even an attempt at creating a constitutional monarchy in 1876, which was eventually short-circuited by Sultan Abdül Hamid II. See Yapp, pp. 115-120, as well as my essay "Are Islam and Democracy Incompatible? Some Reflections from Ottoman History," *Sects, Lies and the Caliphate*, pp. 259-264.

[279] Farah, p. 178.

[280] Wilhite, p. 311.

[281] *Ibid.*, p. 315.

[282] *Ibid.*, p. 318.

[283] *Ibid.*, p. 325.

[284] *Ibid.*, p. 324. Wilhite also points out that "[t]hese weapons had, in fact, a longer range than the Martini-Henry rifle with which the Ottoman troops were armed…."

By the early 1900s hit-and-run attacks on Ottoman garrisons and forces throughout Yemen were the norm, and while the Ottomans might have wanted to continue the "punitive repression" tactics of Feyzi Paşa which had worked so well for him—treating insurgency mainly militarily; utilizing severe reprisals such as destroying village, crops and livestock; and employing harsh policing to disrupt insurgent networks[285]—they lacked sufficient numbers of troops, as well as the will, to do so. Instead, Huseyin Hilmi Paşa (later to become Ottoman Grand Vizier) was made governor of Yemen and pursued a carrots-over-sticks policy of trying to "win hearts and minds" there,[286] wherein reform programs intended to improve the plight of the population would take precedence over military operations—although the latter were not abandoned entirely. In fact, Hilmi's agenda was something of a "state-building

---

[285] *Ibid.*, pp. 336, 337. The French had crushed the insurgency of `Abd al-Qadir in Algeria, and the Italians that of the militant Sanusi Sufis in Libya, with just such an approach. On the former, see Jamil M. Abun-Nasr, *A History of the Maghrib in the Islamic Period* (Cambridge: Cambridge University Press, 1987), pp. 259ff: "The tribal method of razzia (Ar. *ghazya*)…was henceforth employed by the French army as a basic instrument of war. Muslims encampments and villages were destroyed, the cattle were taken away, harvests were burnt, and trees hewn down. This method of fighting is not foreign to the Maghribi tribal community, but it was made especially brutal by the efficiency and cold-blooded planning with which the French army command employed it." As for the Italians next door, in the 1920s, "[i]n Cyrenaica [eastern Libya], the Italians had to fight an exasperating war for eight years before tribal resistance to them collapsed" (*Ibid.*, p. 398). Ultimately, Italian victory there "involved the destruction of the tribal structure, combating the Sanusiyya, and the establishment of Italian schools for the Libyans" (*Ibid.*, p. 401) and "the Sanusi *zawiyas* were either destroyed of converted into military posts. But the Italians were also careful to uphold the general Islamic customs and institutions" (*Ibid.*, p. 402).
[286] Wilhite, p. 346.

project,"[287] seen as part of Sultan Abdul Hamid's promotion of the general Muslim welfare as an Islamic ruler. It encompassed discerning the wishes of the population, reforming the tax system while clamping down on corruption, and improving infrastructure by building a railroad, upgrading what few roads existed in Yemen, and building primary and "industrial" schools."[288] However, "only the educational program was implemented with any degree of thoroughness"[289] such that some elementary schools, and one "industrial" (trade) one, were established; and ultimately Hilmi Paşa's kinder, gentler methods "had little if any effect on those at whom they were ultimately targeted: that is, the disaffected Zaydis of the northwest and central plateau"—although Hilmi was popular in Sana`a itself.[290]

But even more popular in rural highland Yemen was Yahya Hamid al-Din (d. 1948), who had succeeded his father al-Mansur as chief Zaydi Imam in 1904. The revolt was renewed shortly after Yahya came to power, and this time not a few Sunnis lined up with their Shi`i cousins against the Ottomans. The cross-tribal alliances and cooperation which al-Mansur had cultivated in his lifetime proved instrumental[291] in his son's guerrilla war, not least in that they allowed coordinated attacks on Ottoman forces. San`a fell

---

[287] *Ibid.*, p. 348.
[288] *Ibid.*, p. 352.
[289] *Ibid.*, p. 357.
[290] *Ibid.*, p. 365.
[291] *Ibid.*, p. 379.

from the Ottoman grasp in early 1905.[292] About the same time, the Sa`udis launched attacks in the Nejd,[293] complicating Ottoman planning.  Ottoman forces (mainly Syrian troops) did re-take San`a in August 1905, losing perhaps 30,000 men;[294] and soon after their troops mutinied over a lack of pay.[295] These Ottoman forces in Yemen suffered from debilitating problems: a shortage of funding, troops' distaste for serving there, and bafflingly inconsistent policies from Ottoman officials.[296] Faced with such self-defeating behaviors, Yahya's war of attrition was very likely to succeed—and it eventually did.

In the early years of the 20th century the Ottoman government finally, grudgingly, came to the realization that a total military defeat of the Zaydis and their allies, which by this time including the Isma'ili's and some Shafi`i Sunnis, was impossible, whereupon they dispatched well-known ulama from Mecca to negotiate terms with the Zaydi Imam Yahya.[297] This initial peace mission failed, however, and Yahya would foment yet more rebellion in the coming years before the Ottomans would finally agree to terms and depart at the end of World War I. But Yahya was not the only headache for the occupiers. In 1907 one Muhammad b. Ali al-Idrisi (d. 1923) took over in `Asir, proclaiming himself the Sunni

---

[292] Farah, p. 215
[293] *Ibid.*, p. 223.
[294] Dresch, p. 6.
[295] Farah, pp. 227,228.
[296] *Ibid.*, p. 227.
[297] Wilhite, p. 425.

Mahdi, promulgating Wahhabi Islam[298] and fighting against the Zaydi Imam as well as the Ottomans.[299] Fortunately for the Ottomans, Mahdi Idrisi's differences with the former outweighed his with the latter, preventing them from creating a united anti-Ottoman front. But the *mutamahdi* (false Mahdi) still had perhaps tens of thousands of men at his disposal, and Imam Yahya was said to command at least 60,000. The Ottomans had fewer troops[300] but they were, of course, better-trained conventional forces fighting non-conventional ones—and, at this time, on two fronts (Yahya and al-Idrisi). Also, by 1911 the Italians moved forces into (at least nominally) Ottoman Libya, and the Ottomans finally agreed to a truce more-or-less along the lines proposed a few years earlier.[301] The Ottoman government had come to realize that "the [Zaydi] Imamate…was too deeply rooted in Zaydi society to be eliminated by anything other than the mass slaughter of Zaydis themselves"[302]— a bloodbath too far for even for Istanbul, especially as Sultan Abdül Hamid II saw, and presented, himself as the ruler of all Muslims, to include wayward heretics like the Zaydis. Furthermore, Ahmed Izzet Paşa (d. 1937), who because of political intrigues in Istanbul

---

[298] Al-Idrisi's Mahdism was, thus, something of an earlier version of the Juhayman al-`Utaybi Mahdism of 1979 Saudi Arabia. See Joshua Teitelbaum, *The Rise and Fall of the Hashimite Kingdom of Arabia* (New York: NYU Press, 2001), pp. 60, 61.

[299] Farah, p. 240.

[300] Exact numbers for Ottoman military forces in Yemen across time are all but impossible to pin down, despite recourse to numerous sources.

[301] Dresch, p. 7.

[302] Wilhite, p. 429.

had been put in charge in Yemen in 1911, considered the Idrisid Mahdist rebellion the more pressing problem. Izzet Paşa saw al-Idrisi as a Mahdist pretender (of course), whose movement had much shallower, but potentially broader, roots than did that of the Zaydi Imam, thus making it easier to extirpate in Yemen, at any rate. But at the same time, he viewed such a Sunni uprising as a threat in the rest of Arabia, with the potential to develop into a religio-nationalist one against the Empire.[303]

After months of negotiations, the Ottomans via Izzet Paşa and the Zaydis via Imam Yahya reached an agreement in Da`an[304] in October, 1911. In addition to the aforementioned factors, the Ottomans also needed to relocate troops to the Balkans, where the discontent that was brewing would bubble over into war in 1912. The terms under which the Ottoman Empire agreed to evacuate Yemen's highlands included: the Zaydi Imam's right to appoint Zaydi *qadis* (judges); control of the revenues from *awqaf* religious endowments; taxes to be collected by the Imam's men, with a portion going to the Ottomans; and respect for the borders between the Zaydi-dominated highlands and the Sunni-majority lowlands and coastal areas, where the Ottomans retained a presence, and to the north where the Ottomans retained control in the Hijaz.[305] Unlike

---

[303] *Ibid.*, p. 430. Izzet Paşa's views might have been influenced by the Sudanese Mahdist movement some three decades earlier—on which more below.

[304] This is a village outside of Sana`a.

[305] Dresch, p. 7. See also Farah, "Annex J, Terms of the Truce of Da`an," pp. 297, 298.

al-Idrisi, who remained a thorn in the Ottomans' side—he tried to ally with the Italians against them, and then took up with the Allies in World War I from his perch in `Asir—Yahya "expressed his determination to help preserve the greatness of the Ottoman sultan and to offer all his cooperation to defend the unity of Islam" by "remaining neutral during the First World War, though he moved quickly to consolidate his authority over the entire country after the Turks had evacuated it."[306] He was content to share power in Yemen with the major Islamic power, and have it conduct foreign policy, as long as his community was given its domestic autonomy under imperial rule.[307] Yahya wanted, above all, the right to re-impose shari`ah norms in lieu of the hated "foreign" Tanzimat laws. He thus never really questioned the legitimacy of the Ottoman Sultan-Caliph as the world's Islamic standard bearer, following the example of earlier Zaydi leaders who seem to have cast aspersions on the Ottomans as "bad" Muslims primarily as a means of denigrating their right to rule Yemen's highlands, not in order to call for their replacement—much less calling for "Zaydification" of the Empire.

Another Arabian peninsula challenge to the Ottomans, however, did strike at the Turkish state's very Islamic bona fides: the Wahhabis.[308] The Empire had extended its sway to central Arabia

---

[306] Farah, p. 272.

[307] *Ibid.*, p. 273.

[308] On this topic, see: Teitelbaum; Yapp, pp. 173-177, 260-264; David Commins, "Traditional Anti-Wahhabi Hanbalism in Nineteenth-Century Arabia," in

by 1517, when after Selim I "the Resolute" had conquered co-religionist Mamluk Egypt the sharif of Mecca pledged *ba`yah*, or "loyalty," to the Sultan. Ottoman rule of the Hijaz and *al-Haramayn*, the "two holy sites" of Mecca and Medina, would remain crucial to imperial Islamic credentials for centuries afterwards (as, indeed, it is to the legitimacy of the modern Kingdom of Saudi Arabia). In the 18th century the rulers of the Sa`ud tribe residing in the Najd, the geographical interior of Arabia, adopted the Sunni fundamentalism being preached and written about by Muhammad b. Abd al-Wahhab (d. 1792), which "transformed a small Bedouin principality into a legally-instituted theocracy."[309] What eventually became known as "Wahhabism"[310] amounted to a revival of many of the teachings of

---

Itzchak Weisman and Fruma Zachs, ed., *Ottoman Reform and Muslim Regeneration: Studies in Honour of Butrus al-Manneh* (London: I.B. Tauris, 2005), pp. 81-96; Jacob Goldberg, "The 1914 Saudi-Ottoman Treaty—Myth or Reality," *Journal of Contemporary History*, Vol. 19, No. 2 (April 1984), pp. 289-314; Talip Kŭcŭkcan, "Some Reflections on the Wahhabiya and Saunusiya Movements. A Comparative Approach," *The Islamic Quarterly*, Vol. 37, No. 4 (1993), pp. 237-251; George S Rentz (unpublished doctoral dissertation), "Muhammad ibn Abd al-Wahhab and the Beginnings of Unitarian Empire in Arabia" (University of California-Berkeley, 1948); Shaikh M. Safiullah, "Wahhabism: A Conceptual Relationship between Muhammad Ibn Abd al-Wahhab and Taqiyy al-Din Ahmad Ibn Taymiyya," *Hamdard Islamicus,* X, 1 (Spring 1987), pp. 67-83; M.S. Zaharaddin, "Wahhabism and its Influence Outside Arabia," *Islamic Quarterly*, XXIII (1979), pp. 146-157; *Encyclopedia of Islam* [*EI*], *s.v.* 'Ibn Abd al-Wahhab;" Elizabeth Sirriyeh, "Wahhabis, Unbelievers and the Problems of Exclusivism," *British Society for Middle Eastern Studies Bulletin*, XVI, 2 (1989), pp. 123-132; J.E. Peterson, "The Arabian Peninsula in Modern Times: A Historiographical Survey," *The American History Review*, XCVI, 5 (1991), pp. 1435-1449; "Ottoman-Wahhabi War" and "Unification of Saudi Arabia," *Wikipedia*; both accessed June 16, 2020.

[309] "Ibn Abd al-Wahhab," *EI*.

[310] Adherents of al-Wahhab's teachings reject the label "Wahhabi," and call themselves *ahl al-tawhid*, "people of [divine] unity" (as per Kŭcŭkcan, p.238). I

Ibn Taymiyah, focusing on two cardinal sins which were, in this view, rife among the Ottomans: *shirk*, "polytheism" and *bid`ah*, or "innovation."[311]     Alleged Ottoman religious laxity, and indeed heresy, in both regards included practices such as privileging of Sufism, with its attachment to revering shaykhs and their tombs'; Istanbul's refusal to destroy Twelver Shi`i shrines to their Imams in Iraq; smoking of tobacco; shaving the beard and leaving only a large mustache; and imperial relations with Christian powers in lieu of waging constant jihad against them. Under Abd al-Aziz b. Sa`ud (d. 1803) and Sa`ud II b. Sa`ud (d. 1814) the Wahhabized Sa`udis conquered territory both east and west in the peninsula, raided into Ottoman Iraq and Syria (allegedly killing thousands of Shi`is at Karbala in 1802[312]), occupied Mecca,[313] interdicted Ottoman commercial caravans, and harassed the *hajj* pilgrims. "By their criticism of the [Ottoman] laxities of Muslim observance the Wahhabis constituted a challenge to orthodox[314] Islam, and by their disregard of his claims they presented a challenge to the political legitimacy of the Ottoman sultan….[Therefore] it became the object of the sultan to crush them."[315]   The Wahhabi Sa`udis were

---

personally encountered this in a lecture at the US Army War College several years ago, when two Saudi military officers took umbrage at my using the term "Wahhabism," insisting that their beliefs were simply "true Islam."

[311] Rentz, p. 41.

[312] "Ottoman-Wahhabi War."

[313] "Unification of Saudi Arabia."

[314] A poor choice of words by Yapp, p. 175; much better would have been "establishment" Islam.

[315] *Ibid.*

weaponized Kadizadelis, as it were—but promoted outside takeover of the Ottoman state, instead of simply a domestic makeover.[316] Therefore, the sultanic regime had to respond forcefully, and (as noted above in the section on the Zaydis), Istanbul did so by outsourcing the campaign against the Wahhabi Sa`udis to Muhammad Ali and his Egyptian forces—albeit this when he and his dynasty were still staunchly loyal to the sultan, then Mahmud II. Between 1811 and 1819 Ibrahim Paşa, Muhammad Ali's son, moved against the Sa`udi state via military campaigns and diplomacy with affiliated tribes, to include bribes. Despite sometime inept generalship, Ibrahim used the top-notch European-style military that his father had created[317] to good effect against the Arabian rebels, who had not yet learned the value of asymmetric warfare. The end result was that the so-called "First Sa`udi State," centered on al-Dir`iyyah, was razed by the Ottoman Egyptian forces, and its leader, Abd Allah b. Sa`ud, was sent to Istanbul and publicly beheaded in 1818.

Egyptian forces were totally withdrawn by 1840, leaving a power vacuum in which the second Sa`udi state, headquartered at

---

[316] Note that these Wahhabi and Kadizadeli grievances against the Ottomans were very much akin to those of the Zaydis. But the former both being Sunni meant that they posed a greater headache for the Sunni Ottomans; the Zaydis, on the other hand, could be written off, at least in religious terms, as heretics and, indeed, cranks.

[317] Vladimir Boresovitch Lutsky, "The Military Reforms of Mohammed Ali" in Chapter III, "Egypt under the Rule of Mohammed Ali," *Modern History of the Arab Countries* (1969), *marxists.org*, accessed June 16, 2020.

Riyadh, could arise under the leadership of Turki b. Abd Allah b. Muhammad[318] of the Sa`ud family. This state lasted from 1824 until 1891, and "[t]hough he had succeeded in reestablishing a viable Saudi polity, Turki chose to remain a nominal vassal of the Ottomans rather than challenge them openly, due to what had happened to Abdullah bin Saud."[319] This Sa`udi state was not, however, as pro-Ottoman as its contemporary rivals the Rashidis were—and the latter received Ottoman military assistance sufficient to allow them to win the Rashidi-Saudi conflict at that time and establish the Rashidi Emirate, also known as the Emirate of Ha'il. Claims from pro-Ottoman ulama that the Wahhabi Saudis were dangerous Islamic separatists[320] made it all the way to Sultan Abdül Hamid II,[321] and probably influenced Istanbul's pro-Rashidi tilt. When the Rashidi state's leader, Muhammad b. Rashid, died in 1897 Abd al-Aziz b. Sa`ud (d. 1953) emerged from exile in Kuwait, gathered supporters, and seized Riyadh. He subsequently led more territorial conquests, including driving out Ottoman garrisons, thanks to his powerful Ikhwan: "nomads who had adopted the Wahhabi code…and who were ready and willing to assist in the extension of Wahhabism by war (and also to derive some profit from raids)."[322] Once ensconced in central Arabia, Ibn Sa`ud began

---

[318] "Turki b. Abdallah b. Muhammad," *Wikipedia*; accessed June 16, 2020.
[319] *Ibid.*
[320] *Khawarij*, or "Kharijis"—"those who go out"—was a term that had been applied to schismatics in the early days of Islam, and is still employed to this day in many contexts.
[321] Commins, p. 87.

playing the Ottomans and British off one another: asking the Ottomans to be recognized as their vassal in al-Hasa (the Persian Gulf environs), he simultaneously pursued British financial support against the Turks.[323]

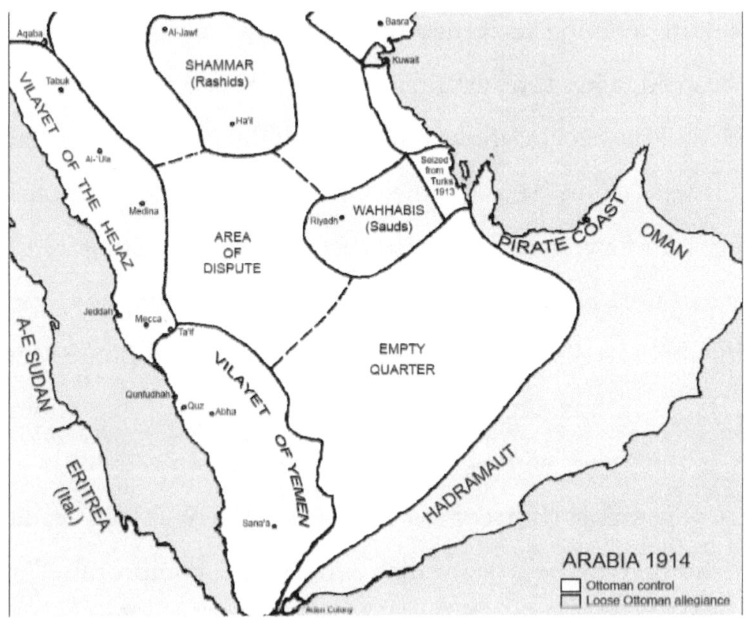

Arabia, c. 1914.[324]

The Brits' demurred, however, and Ibn Sa`ud remained an Ottoman subject, at least diplomatically, when World War I broke out—as

---

[322] Yapp, p. 261.

[323] *Ibid.*

[324] "Source: *Collapse of Empire: Ottoman Turks and the Arabs in the First World War,* itself from *King Husain and the Kingdom of Hejaz* by Randall Baker," *commons.wikimedia.org,* accessed June 12, 2020. Baker's book was published by Oleander Press, Cambridge [UK], 1979.

shown by the Ottoman-Sa`udi Treaty of May 15, 1914, in which Ibn Sa`ud "recognized Ottoman sovereignty over Najd and himself as an Ottoman subject" in return for which the Sultan, Mehmed V, "appointed Ibn-Saud the *Wali* of Najd, and the *Wilayet* was conferred upon the Saudi family on a hereditary basis."[325] Despite this seeming coming to terms, Ibn Sa`ud, in 1915, broke ranks and allied instead with Great Britain.[326] Of course, the British would reward this by backing Sharif Husayn of Mecca, not Ibn Saud, as ruler of Arabia in lieu of the Ottomans[327]—and, famously, by sending T.E. Lawrence to help in that endeavor, starting in 1916.[328] However, the House of Sa`ud eventually triumphed, perhaps primarily because "[d]espite all the funds Britain had poured into the Hijaz, Husayn was unable to keep the loyalty of his tribes. In contrast, Ibn Saud, with a much more modest subsidy, was able to do this very thing with comparative ease; the Wahhabi leader had shown himself to be a statesman who could compromise."[329] In

---

[325] Goldberg, p. 307.

[326] *Ibid.*, p. 294.

[327] Teitelbaum, pp. 99ff.

[328] Some might wonder why I am not analyzing the uprising in Arabia led by T.E. Lawrence. There are two major reasons why I have decided against doing so: 1) the "Arab Revolt," despite its undeniable indigenous anti-Ottoman elements, was in no small measure fomented by an outside, non-Muslim power: Great Britain; and 2) entire forests have been felled producing books about Lawrence, and he has been a favorite—indeed, obsessed-about topic of study in US military circles since the 2003 US invasion of Iraq. See, for example: David Kilcullen, *Counterinsurgency* (Oxford: Oxford University Press, 2010), pp. 24, 25; and Alasdair Soussi, "Lawrence of Arabia, Guiding US Army in Iraq and Afghanistan," *The Christian Science Monitor*, June 19, 2010; accessed June 16, 2020.

[329] Teitelbaum, p. 266.

addition, the aforementioned Muhammad b. Ali al-Idrisi—he of the Mahdist pretensions during the Ottoman wars in Yemen—was still around, fomenting eschatological-tinged plans and, by the early 1920s, coming to terms with Ibn Sa`ud and fighting solely against Sharif Husayn until al-Idrisi died in 1923.[330] "By then, however, Husayn was no longer a factor"[331] in the Arabian peninsula—and neither were the Ottomans.

While al-Idrisi's apocalyptic schemes may have been more apparent than real, those of Muhammad Ahmad in the Sudan were fervently pursued—and realized. The "Sudanese Mahdi," portrayed by the great Sir Laurence Olivier in the 1966 movie *Khartoum*,[332] was the most successful Mahdist claimant ever in the Ottoman Empire, as well as one of the most effective rebels overall. He not only convinced legions of Sudanese that he was Allah's rightly-guided, End Times emissary, but detached and created as a separate polity an enormous area to the south of Ottoman Egypt[333] which survived

---

[330] *Ibid.*, p. 270.

[331] *Ibid.*, p. 271.

[332] Bosley Crowther, "Screen: 'Khartoum' Opens: Olivier Excels in Tale of Blood and Sand," *The New York Times*, July 14, 1966. To see the impressive movie poster, contraposing Olivier's Mahdi and Charlton Heston's General Charles Gordon: "Khartoum (1966)," *IMDB*. Both accessed June 16, 2020.

[333] The secondary literature on Muhammad Ahmad and his *Mahdiyah*, or Mahdist State, in Sudan is voluminous, but most of it has been covered and summarized in chapter three of my Ohio State University doctoral dissertation, "Eschatology as Politics, Eschatology as Theory: Modern Sunni Arab Mahdism in Historical Perspective" (2001), as well as in my book *Holiest Wars: Islamic Mahdis, their Jihads, and Osama bin Laden* (Westport, CT: Praeger, 2001), particularly pp. 45-58. Other valuable sources are John O. Voll, "Wahhabism and Mahdism: Alternative Styles of Islamic Renewals," *Arab Studies Quarterly*, 4, 1 & 2 (1982), pp. 110-126; Major Daryl W. Morrell (2012), "An Institutional Analysis of

until 1898. Muhammad Ahmad, a pious Muslim in his youth in northern Sudan, joined the Sammaniyah Sufi order as a young man and traveled throughout the *Turkiyah*, which was the name given to Sudan under Ottoman Egyptian rule. (Much of this region had been conquered by troops of Muhammad Ali's state in the early 1820s, although periodic Egyptian expeditions incorporating more territories—creating a "secondary empire," in a sense, for the Ottomans[334]—continued for another 50 years.[335]) Muhammad Ahmad, like many Sudanese, chafed under the rule of those he deemed foreigners from the north who were, worst of all, poor Muslims: Ottomans and their "Turkified" Egyptian vassals consorted with infidel Christians (especially the British); onerously taxed their fellow Muslims, above and beyond the zakat; and worst of all, attempted to reduce the slave trade (which was legal under Islamic law).[336] The latter, which the Ottoman Sultan and the Egyptian *Khedivate* agreed to following the Anglo-Ottoman Convention for Suppression of the African Slave Trade of 1880,

General Sir Charles Gordon's Counter-Insurgency Campaign in the Sudan" (unpublished Master's thesis), Canadian Forces College; F.R. Wingate, *Ten Years' Captivity in the Mahdi's Camp 1882-1892* (London: William Clowes and Sons, Ltd., 1892) [Minneapolis: Filiquarian Publishing, 1990]; and Winston S. Churchill, *The River War: An Account of the Reconquest of the Sudan* (1902 edition), Amazon Kindle.

[334] Furnish, "Eschatology as Politics…," p. 100.

[335] See Furnish, "The Egyptian Conquest and Administration of Sudan," in "Eschatology as Politics…," pp. 96-109; also "Egyptian Invasion of Sudan 1820-24," *Wikipedia*, accessed June 16, 2020.

[336] The Mahdist complaints about the Ottomans shared some aspects with those of the Kadizadelis, Zaydis and Wahhabis. But they differed in that the main issue was the Empire's attempt to eradicate the lucrative slave trade.

"was tantamount to throwing down the gauntlet to the frontier society of independent *jallaba*s, or 'petty traders,' as well as many other Sudanese who made a lucrative living from selling the Africans captured further south on the slave market."[337]   Add to these grievances Muhammad Ahmad's subjective experiences of Islam's founder Muhammad and deceased Sufi shaykhs appearing to him and informing him that he was the Mahdi, and the stage was set for an eschatological war.[338]

In 1881 Muhammad Ahmad openly declared himself the Mahdi. The hŭkŭmdar, or governor, in Khartoum sent a delegation to dissuade Muhammad Ahmad—to no avail. A few months later a small force was sent to arrest or kill him, but the Mahdists defeated it.[339]   Immediately after, the Mahdi and his followers went on a "hijrah" to southern Sudan, out of the firm orbit of Ottoman Egyptian control, "not only to buy time and muster his forces but perhaps more importantly to fix in people's minds the legitimacy of his jihad"[340]—consciously emulating not only the Islamic prophet's one, but others performed by previous Islamic movements in western Africa, such as the al-Murabits, al-Muwahhids,[341] and the movement that created the Sokoto caliphate.[342]   They remained in

---

[337] Furnish, "Eschatology as Politics…," p. 105.

[338] *Ibid.*, p. 125.

[339] *Ibid.*, pp. 127-128.

[340] *Ibid.*, p. 129.

[341] These two medieval North African movements will be the focus of a later section in this volume.

[342] Furnish, "Eschatology as Politics…," pp. 128-129.

defensive mode in that part of Sudan (Aba Island, al-Jazirah and Kurdufan) for at least a year, issuing a *da`wah*, "summons" or "call," to Sudanese everywhere to follow Muhammad Ahmad as the Awaited Mahdi. This movement was energized by the approach of the Islamic year 1300 (1882-1883), as the turn of every Islamic century is rife with expectations of a *mujaddid*, or "renewer" of Islam[343]— of which the Mahdi is the ultimate example. Abandoning the hijrah and going on the offensive in summer 1881, Muhammad Ahmad's proclamation of jihad swelled the ranks of believers such that they conquered Kurdufan province in 18 months, and his lieutenant Uthman Diqna was sent to open another front on the Red Sea coast.[344] Ottoman Sultan Abdül Hamid II "was quite concerned about rebel contagion in his Arab domains…. First, the Hijaz…contains the two holy cities of Mecca and Medina…. With forays into the Red Sea coastal region of Sudan, the Mahdi threatened the Hijaz."[345] Thus, the Mahdists presented much the same threats to Ottoman interests in Arabia as had the Zaydis and Wahhabis, as we have seen. However, Muhammad Ahmad was perhaps even more of an ideological threat, for not only did he denigrate Ottoman claims to leadership of the Islamic world—as the Mahdi he arrogated to himself, *ipso facto*, the Caliphate. For that reason loyal and high-ranking ulama, from the beginning of this (from the Ottoman

---

[343] As per "Mudjaddid," *EI*.
[344] Furnish, *Holiest Wars*, p. 53.
[345] *Ibid.*

perspective) mutamahdi's appearance, had been issuing *fatwa*s delegitimizing him.[346] Points raised against Muhammad's Ahmad's eschatological claims in these fatwas included:

- The Mahdi would come from Arabia, not Africa
- The Mahdi would be a "red" Arab, not a "black African."
- Jesus and the Mahdi were to work together. So where was the former?
- Relatedly, the Mahdi and Jesus would combat the Dajjal, the Islamic "antichrist"—but he was also nowhere to be found.
- The Mahdi would kill the Sufyani[347]—an End Times figure arrayed against him—not other Muslims.
- The Mahdi's appearance would be in a chaotic time at the death of the caliph—but the Ottoman Sultan-Caliph was alive and well, and Muhammad Ahmad was undermining him and his rule.
- Instead of filling the earth with equity and justice, Muhammad Ahmad was bringing death and destruction.
- Allegiance would be sworn to the Mahdi in Mecca, not in Sudan.
- Followers of the true Mahdi would come from al-Sham (Syria) and al-Iraq, not from areas where people did not even speak good Arabic.
- No evidence existed that Muhammad Ahmad was of the Prophet's family.

---

[346] *Ibid.*, pp. 78-79.

[347] Wilferd Madelung, "The Sufyani between Tradition and History," *Studia Islamica*, 63 (1986), pp. 5-48.

- Self-validation via dreams and signs was purely subjective, and ran counter to the criterion of *ijma`*, "consensus" of the scholars.

Therefore, Muhammad Ahmad was an eschatological pretender, not the true Mahdi.[348] The latter, for his part, responded with derision as well as, more theologically, *naskh*: he "abrogated" any doubts about his status by disregarding hadiths that seemed not to apply to him.[349] In the final analysis, however, the Sudanese Mahdi based his claim on his irrefutable experiential visions, the fervor of his followers—many of whom came from the rank-and-file of the Sufi orders—and the unpopularity of a Turkish sultan in Sudanic Africa.

The Ottomans might have hoped that their Egyptian client would deal militarily with Muhammad Ahmad's movement, but in September 1882 the British occupied Egypt for two reasons: to ensure continuing payments on the debt for the Suez Canal's construction; and because of the threat posed to the government's stability by the mutiny of Lieutenant Colonel Ahmad Urabi (d. 1911), "Urabi Paşa," who led a populist revolt of Arab officers against their Turkish-speaking Ottoman generals.[350] Once the British took over in Cairo, they initially still deferred (at least on the surface) to the Khedivate in policy matters regarding Sudan. Subsequently, in 1883, Cairo ordered Colonel William Hicks, a British officer in their employ in Khartoum, to confront the Mahdist

---

[348] Furnish, *Holiest Wars*, pp. 79, 80.
[349] *Ibid.*, p. 80.
[350] Yapp, pp. 221-226.

forces. This he did with close to 10,000 men—almost all of whom were killed, along with Hicks, in November 1883 at the Battle of Shaykan/El Obeid. The Egyptian government then turned to General Charles Gordon,[351] the famous British officer who had helped the Qing (or Manchu) dynasty put down the messianic Taiping rebellion some decades earlier. Isma'il, who was even more of Westernizer than his father, liked to hire both British and American (mostly former Confederate) officers to serve in military and government positions. This was the major reason Gordon had served as governor of Equatoria province, then as Governor-General (hŭkŭmdar) of the entire Sudan, in the 1870s. As a zealous Christian and abolitionist, Gordon tried mightily to end the Islamic slave trade in Sudan. Nonetheless, while "Gordon was a dreamer and an eccentric…he was not a fool. His approach to many of the problems he faced was realistic…. He recognized the obvious fact that slavery was the keystone of the economic and social structure of the country, and…that any tampering with it must be done in such a way that the socio-economic structure…did not come tumbling down…. He made no attempt to interfere with domestic slavery…."[352] Still, his efforts to curtail the slave trade ran afoul of many in Sudan (as noted earlier), helping propel Muhammad Ahmad to power. Gordon eventually resigned as administrator of Sudan in 1879.

---

[351] On Gordon see Byron Farwell, *Prisoners of the Mahdi* (New York and London: W.W. Norton and Company, 1989); "Charles George Gordon," *Wikipedia*; accessed June 16, 2020.
[352] Farwell, p. 70.

By 1884 public opinion in Britain, inflamed by the press, prevailed upon the government to send Gordon back to Sudan, initially on a fact-finding mission about the Mahdist movement that would recommend ways of evacuating British and Egyptian forces in Khartoum. But he was also tasked by the Khedive Tawfiq to (re)establish effective Turco-Egyptian rule there[353] and Gordon felt—not unreasonably—that the Mahdi's forces had to be defeated before they threatened to conquer Egypt.[354] So once in Khartoum, February 1884, Gordon took up the defense of the city against the coming Mahdist siege, while also exchanging letters with Muhammad Ahmad in which the former offered the Mahdi a position in the Egyptian administration of Sudan, while the latter recommended Gordon either convert to Islam or remove himself to Cairo.[355] By May 1884 Khartoum was cut off and besieged by the Mahdi's legions; Gordon had perhaps 8000 mostly Egyptian soldiers to protect 25,000 civilians in the city.[356] The Mahdi had as many as 60,000 men.[357] The British government finally agreed to send a relief force of Brits and Canadians, totaling some 6,000 men, which staged to Cairo and departed south from there in October 1884.[358] Held up by harassing attacks, they reached Khartoum on January 28, 1885. But the Mahdi's forces had taken it two days earlier, killing all

---

[353] "Charles George Gordon."
[354] "Nile Expedition," *Wikipedia*, accessed June 16, 2020.
[355] Farwell, pp. 86, 87; "Charles George Gordon."
[356] Farwell, p. 88.
[357] *Ibid.*, p. 90.
[358] *Ibid.*, pp. 92ff; "Nile Expedition."

the combatants including Gordon, whose head was sent to Muhammad Ahmad. The women "were herded into pens, like cattle, until they could be divided among the conquerors, the Mahdi taking first choice...."[359] The relief expedition retreated back to Egypt. Six months later the Mahdi would die, probably of malaria.[360] His state, however, administered by the Mahdi's caliph Abd Allah b. Muhammad (d. 1899), or "Abdullahi," survived for another 13 years, until a British force under General Kitchener brought it back under Cairo's control.

---

[359] Farwell, p. 97.
[360] Furnish, "Eschatology as Politics...," p. 133.

***The Mahdist State, late 19th century.*[361]**

The Mahdiyah, or Mahdist polity proper, only lasted as long as Muhammad Ahmad lived. Its successor state was the "Khalifah," headed by Abdullahi. Between January and June 1885, the Sudanese Mahdi "repudiated the Ottoman caliphate and sultanate; dissolved all Sufi orders so that loyalty to one's shaykh would not undermine loyalty to the Mahdi; and called for the abolition of the four *madhahib*[362]… on the basis that they had not existed in the original Islamic community. Islamic law, as defined by his own esoteric explication and ascetic proclivities, was strictly enforced…. Women were banned from the marketplace and ordered to be veiled whenever they left their homes, under penalty of lashing. Divorce was mandated for anyone married to a Turk or a spouse who doubted that the ruler of Sudan was the Mahdi of Allah. To supervise the legal system in Sudan he appointed a *qadi al-Islam* who was to base his decisions on only three sources: the Qur'an, the Sunnah [or Hadiths] and the Mahdi's edicts. And in what came to be seen as his most egregious departure from Islamic tradition, acknowledgement of Muhammad Ahmad's Mahdi-hood was made a virtual sixth pillar of the faith…."[363] The Mahdiyah, and the Khalifah after it, collected a great deal of taxes (in currency and in kind, such as weapons,

---

[361] "Extreme Limits of Mahdist-controlled territory (area enclosed by dotted line; 1891)," *en.wikipedia.org*, accessed June 13, 2020.

[362] Schools of *fiqh*, or Islamic jurisprudence, which interpret Islamic law.

[363] Furnish, pp. 139-140.

livestock and slaves) in the form of zakat. Before he died Muhammad Ahmad tried to ally with both the Sokoto Caliphate (in modern Nigeria) and the parts of what is now Libya ruled by the powerful Sanusiyah Sufi order, to no avail.[364] The Khalifah fought a major war with Christian Ethiopia (Abyssinia), and invaded Muslim, but ardently non-Mahdist, Egypt in 1889,[365] only to be soundly defeated by British-commanded Egyptian troops in Upper (southern) Egypt[366] at the Battle of Tushkah/Toski.[367] By the 1890s the competition for influence and territory in Africa between the European powers convinced the British that the Mahdi's successor state had to go. So between 1896 and 1899 Sudanese and Egyptian troops led by British officers, notably General Herbert Kitchener (d. 1916), rolled south into Sudan and defeated the Khalifah's forces in every battle, climaxing with the Battle of Omdurman in 1898.[368] Abdullahi escaped but was killed by British troops in late in 1899, while Osman Digna, perhaps the Mahdists' most capable field commander, remained at large until 1900 when he was captured, imprisoned in Egypt for eight years, freed, then lived on until 1926.[369] "Thus ended the most recent example in world history of Mahdism as a conquering and state-building movement, not merely an

---

[364] *Ibid.*, p. 141.
[365] "Mahdist State," *Wikipedia*; accessed June 16, 2020.
[366] "Wadi Tushka: Egypt," *Geographical Name*; accessed June 16, 2020.
[367] "Battle of Toski," *Wikipedia*; accessed June 16, 2020.
[368] "Anglo-Egyptian Invasion of Sudan," *Wikipedia*; accessed June 16, 2020. Churchill, *The River War, passim.*
[369] "Osman Digna," *Wikipedia*; accessed June 16, 2020.

oppositional, revolutionary one. Muhammad Ahmad's Sudanese Mahdism....[i]s the Mahdist movement par excellence for understanding that important mode of Islamic resistance."[370] As Winston Churchill put it: "There are many Christians who reverence the faith of Islam[371] and yet regard the Mahdi merely as a commonplace religious impostor whom force of circumstances elevated to notoriety. In a certain sense, this may be true. But I know not how a genuine may be distinguished from a spurious Prophet, except by the measure of his success."[372] Muhammad Ahmad was largely successful in his eschatological Sudanese nationalism, in that he broke that part of northeast Africa away from the Ottoman Empire's ambit. But while it took the world's foremost military power—and, ironically, a Christian one at that—to dispose, ultimately, of the polity he created, the Sudanese Mahdi's insurgency was always aimed squarely at the Sultan in Istanbul.

---

[370] Furnish, *Holiest Wars*, p. 57.

[371] Perhaps the best example of this, in this specific context, is Morrell's thesis paper—which not only excoriates the 19th century British army for allegedly being so "imbued with Christian virtue" that it suffered "reduced...ability to successfully adapt [sic] to the conditions in the Sudan" (p. 46), but also blames Muhammad Ahmad's movement entirely on Gordon's anti-slavery vehemence (p. 58). Alas, Morrell never actually gets around to analyzing Gordon's military methodology in Sudan.

[372] Churchill, *The River War*, p. 33.

CHAPTER THREE—STRATEGY AND TACTICS

Success, as per Winston Churchill's observation on the Sudanese Mahdi, is the most obvious gauge by which to measure oppositional movements within an Islamic context[373]—but it is not the only one. As narrated in the previous chapter, there were seven major clusters of insurrections against the Ottoman Empire, from the 12th to the early 20th century: various and sundry Sufi uprisings; Celali mutinies; domestic Kadizadeli unrest; Levantine Druze revolts; Yemeni Zaydi rebellions; Arabian peninsular Wahhabi Saudi insurrections; and Sudanese Mahdist war. Many of these fought the Ottoman law, and the law won—using a definition of victory in which the central state itself emerged intact. But Istanbul's rule did not always make it through unscathed; nor was its success always quickly achieved, and that often at considerable cost to imperial coffers, manpower—and sometimes even Islamic credentials. Thus, the similarities and differences between these movements need to be examined, as well as the mode and effectiveness of Ottoman responses to each, before any lessons can be gleaned for modern counterinsurgency against groups in opposition to extant Islamic states.

In the medieval and early modern period, a number of Sufi shaykhs battled the Ottoman state. Although some of these

---

[373] Or within any context, for that matter.

rebellions contained ethno-linguistic elements (Turcoman, for example), an even more prominent theme was waging jihad against the sultan's allegedly illegitimate regime. Most of these Sufis were from the Sunni branch of Islam; but some were Twelver Shi`i. Certain of these non-state mystics' rebellions (particularly the Shi`i ones) also received outside support, from the rival Safavid state. As such, these Sufi movements *in toto* represented a domestic, foreign-supported fifth-column challenge to Ottoman rule. However, all of them were non-state actors, never making it to state status.[374] Most also were spearheaded by charismatic leaders—Sufi shaykhs who then wielded their *barakah*, or charisma,[375] to command the ready-made battalions which comprised each order. A number of these shaykhs were also Mahdist pretenders, or at least tried to incorporate some degree of eschatological fervor into their uprisings. However, none ever seriously threatened to supplant the house of Osman; nor did any successfully separate Ottoman territories from imperial rule for any length of time.

16th and 17th century Celali opposition was about dirhams[376] more than doctrine. These military men fought against the Ottoman state, but in order to get paid more—or at all. They were neither sectarian, nor even religiously disgruntled in any significant way. The

---

[374] Unlike the late 19th century Sudanese Mahdists, Sufis who did achieve their own polity.

[375] The Arabic term literally means divine "blessing."

[376] The dirham was one of the primary coinage units of the earlier Ottoman Empire, having been taken over from the Greek/Byzantine drachma. "Dirham," *Wikipedia*; accessed July 27, 2020.

Celalis mainly had a socioeconomic, and financial, bone to pick with their rulers in Istanbul. Thus, this was the lone case in which Ottoman COIN did not involve an overtly ideological dimension.

The 17th century Kadizadeli movement was unique, of those examined herein, in that it erupted and was carried out in the Ottoman center (mainly Istanbul, but also Cairo), rather than in one of the imperial provinces or peripheries. In fact, in a very real sense, the Kadizadelis might easily be classified as a Salafist[377] restoration movement within Ottoman Sunni Islam, rather than an actual rebellion. But its adherents' fierce antagonism to the Sufi "deep state," as well their frequent employment of violence, places the Kadizadelis firmly in a rebellious register. While to some degree inflamed by socio-economic factors—Kadizadeli preachers were outsiders vis-à-vis the official clerical establishment—the gravamen of Kadizadeli dissatisfaction was the allegedly lax adherence to shari`ah norms exhibited by, mainly, state-supported Sufi imams. As such, this movement did not aim at supplanting or overthrowing the sultan, but rather, as the Kadizadelis saw it, at re-pietizing Islam within the Ottoman Empire, starting in the capital and the official state organs to include the military. This involved reducing the power of, if not eliminating, the Sufi orders in the imperial

---

[377] The Arabic word *salaf* means "ancestors, forefathers." As an Islamic movement, it denotes those Sunnis who aspire to practice their religion as did those in Muhammad's time. By definition Salafis are thus conservative, although not all are fundamentalist—although that is certainly a tendency thereof. It is generally assumed that it developed out of Arab Wahhabism, but the Turkish Kadizadelis, who pre-existed Wahhabis, call that into question.

administration. In that regard, Kadizadelism for a time threatened the Sufi religious monopoly on the Ottoman state apparatus, but ultimately was put successfully back into its nascent Salafi bottle.

The Levantine Druze rebellions against Ottoman rule, from the 16th to the early 20th centuries, are unique among those canvassed here in that they flared up among a group which is really beyond the pale of the Islamic religion *per se*. As noted, although the Druzes are an offshoot of Isma'ili Shi`ism, they did not always envision their resistance to the Sunni Ottomans strictly in religious terms; while the Ottoman state, on the other hand, did tend to employ a religious lens, for its part, and often treated them as recalcitrant heretics. The Druze mainly objected to onerous Ottoman taxation and interference in their community's internal affairs; they were thus not so much separatist as libertarian—wishing to be left alone, or at least less taxed, by Istanbul. The Druzes also received outside help, from Catholic Christian powers hoping to undermine the Ottoman Islamic power threatening Europe. The Druzes did not wage jihad *per se*, but that, of course, did not preclude their engaging in frequent violence against their Sunni overlords. By the later 19th century, when the Ottoman state had shrunk considerably in size and its Islamic nature made even more prominent,[378] Druze religious deviationism was largely overlooked

---

[378] By demographic losses of large Christian minorities, as well as by Sultan Abdül Hamid II's intentional focus on Ottoman Sunni identity over against European Christendom.

when that community began attacking Maronite Catholics—unfortunately, for the Ottomans, leading to French intervention. But the Druzes neither attempted to take the fight to the heart of the Empire, nor tried to detach their domains from Ottoman control. They just desired at first fewer Ottoman rules and taxes and, later, fewer Maronites.

The Zaydis of Yemen constituted, simultaneously, a pro-autonomy, proto-nationalist movement against Ottoman occupation and a militant Shi`i reaction to control by a Sunni empire in two different time frames: the mid-16th through mid-17th and, again, in the late 19th through early 20th centuries. These two incarnations of Ottoman rule were mainly a result of both geopolitical and religious factors: Istanbul's concerns about European encroachment in the Red Sea region that might threaten trade, as well as Fiver Shi'i, and later Wahhabi, threats to Mecca and Medina. However, there was also an element of the Ottoman sultans' Sunni unwillingness to tolerate Shi`i obstreperousness, especially in a strategic province—no matter how far-flung. These Shi`is, for their part, waged jihad-as-guerrilla warfare against what they saw as lax, shari`ah-deficient Muslims who had little if no right to rule in southwestern Arabia. The Ottomans were also seen as meddling foreigners whose attempts at nation-building and modernization were unIslamic and, thus, unwelcome. The Zaydi Shi`is, in addition, detested Sufis, and the Ottoman state's official enfranchisement of several orders therefore rankled. There was furthermore an eschatological patina to the Zaydi rebellions, in that their jihadist Imams were seen as clear and present mahdis (albeit not the final apocalyptic Mahdi of Twelver Shi`ism).   To add insult to injury, from Istanbul's perspective, at least some of the Zaydi tribes of Yemen may also have received outside support in the form of French weapons. And while the Zaydis never wished to overthrow any Sultan, they certainly did reject his right to rule in their part of the Dar al-Islam; and that insubordination was intolerable to the Ottomans insofar as it threatened their control of the Hijaz containing the two holy cities of Mecca and Medina, as well as the Empire's egress from the Red to the Arabian Sea, and thus Indian Ocean.

The Wahhabi movement of the 19th and early 20th centuries, especially after it forged an alliance with the Saud tribe, proved a real thorn in the Ottoman Empire's Arab underside. It was in some important ways analogous to the earlier Kadizadeli movement, notably in being Islamic fundamentalist and anti-Sufi. But the Wahhabis also espoused ardent anti-Shi`ism, as well as jihad against the Ottoman state; thus they had no desire to reform governance and Islamic praxis in Istanbul, like the Kadizadelis, but rather to drive the tepid Turkish Muslims, as they saw them, from the original lands of Islam.   Brought to heel after their first uprising, the Wahhabis were more diplomatic in the 20th century, playing the Brits and their nominal Ottoman overlords off against one another. And although the British ultimately turned against them, the Ottoman departure from Arabia following World War I allowed the

Wahhabized Saudis to carve out a state in the Najd that eventually came to encompass most of the Arabian peninsula. So Wahhabism, in the time frame covered, functioned primarily as an Arab Sunni separatist ideology over against Istanbul—and one that ultimately succeeded.[379] The loss of Mecca and Medina—which the Wahhabis did occupy, briefly—did not jeopardize imperial rule *per se*, but it did threaten to dent Ottoman caliphal claims, since possession of the two sacred sites was a major legitimizing element for the Empire as Islam's bulwark, and the sultan-caliphs as Allah's appointed leaders of Dar al-Islam.

The final insurrection against the Ottomans examined herein is also the most overtly eschatological one: Muhammad Ahmad's Sudanese Mahdist movement, which succeeded in detaching that area of northeast Africa from imperial control. While consisting in part of Sudanese Africa ethno-nationalist resentment at Egyptian and Turkish rule, the gravamen of the Mahdi's and his followers' case against the Turkiyah was that regime's unIslamic habits: allying with infidel Christians, over taxation of fellow Muslims, and interference with the lucrative, and legal, Islamic slave trade. Ironically, Sudanese Mahdism was also, in no small measure, a Sufi movement against the Ottomans—thus a more modern analog of the aforesaid, more ancient Sufi uprisings against the Turkish sultan-

---

[379] Although in the modern world—especially since the failed 1979 Mahdist coup in Arabia—Wahhabism has become the preeminent global brand of Salafi Sunnism, thanks to Saudi petrodollars. This is explained by Trofimov, *The Siege of Mecca.*

caliphs. While not Salafist *per se*, like the Kadizadelis and Wahhabis, Muhammad Ahmad and his followers did share both groups' view of the Ottomans as slipshod Muslims; and, like the latter, were only too happy to wage jihad against the forces of Istanbul and those of its puppet, Cairo. The most obvious and telling aspect of this late 19th century Sudanese revolt was, of course, the bold claim by Muhammad Ahmad to be the eschatological Mahdi who would usher in the ideal Islamic state of the End Times, which would include him supplanting the Ottoman sultan-caliph as leader of all the world's (Sunni) Muslims. Thus, the chief rationale and motivation for Sudanese Mahdism was not just proto-nationalist but religious and, indeed, apocalyptic; in this regard it differed from the similar Sufi mutinies of earlier centuries in degree, but not in kind— insofar as Muhammad Ahmad actually seized power in a sizable province of the Empire. The Sudanese Mahdi openly questioned the Ottomans' right to rule, and indeed claimed to supersede their caliphate with his Mahdiyah. But while he never remotely had the military power to pose a serious threat to the Ottoman center, the Mahdi and his successor "Khalifa" caused problems for Cairo's power in upper (southern) Egypt, and gave Istanbul heartburn over Khartoum's potential threat to Mecca and Medina across the narrow Red Sea.

Although not constituting formal challenges to Ottoman rule in the same way as the above-mentioned seven discrete movements, there were also a number of one-off eschatological irruptions in the

Empire's domains between the 16th and early 20th centuries. As noted in chapter two, in the early 16th century Shah Qulu, Nur Ali Khalifa and Shah Wali each claimed to be the Mahdi or its equivalent, Sahib al-Zaman. In the early 17th century two Naqshbandi Sufis also separately claimed the Mahdiyah, and Sayyid Abd Allah in 1665 was at least at least mahdistic. The Empire even saw a prominent example of Jewish, rather than Muslim, apocalypticism in the mid-17th century, as Sabbatai Sevi claimed to the Jewish messiah before converting to Islam. In the first half of the 19th century, Faqih Sa`id in Yemen declared himself the Mahdi—only to be terminated by the Zaydis. In the early 1870s an aspiring Jewish messiah, Shukri Kuhayil, stirred up some of the Yemeni tribes against the Ottomans. But the greatest messianic pretender of the last several centuries in the Ottoman realms, besides Sudan's Muhammad Ahmad, would had to have been Muhammad b. Ali al-Idrisi, who for some 16 years (1907-1923) as the proclaimed Sunni Mahdi fought both the Zaydis and Sharif Husayn's forces centered in Mecca, as well as the Ottomans.[380] Mahdist movements such as these historically have tended to go through three stages of rebellion against established authority: 1) spreading revivalist-pietist propaganda with the aim of delegitimizing target Islamic rulers; 2) creation of a peripheral militant theocracy which tries to grasp

---

[380] Ironically, some Ottoman sultans were referred to as the Mahdi, as well—notably Selim I (mainly in opposition to similar claims made by the Safavid rulers). See Pinar Emiralioğlu, *Geographical Knowledge and Imperial Culture in the Early Modern Ottoman Empire* (Burlington, VT: Ashgate, 2014), p. 17.

power; 3) formation of a territorial polity in opposition to, or in replacement of, the   targeted regime which eventually fades away or is in turn supplanted.[381]   Most Mahdist rebellions against the Ottomans stalled out in the first phase; Ali al-Idrisi might be said to have attained level two; of the examples covered in this work, only Muhammad Ahmad's much larger and more powerful uprising made it to the third stage.[382]

Six of these seven resistance movements to Ottoman rule were religious, at root—and, indeed, all involved Muslims (either Sunni, Shi`i or Sufi) with the arguable exception of the Druzes, whose centuries-old departure from the Islamic mainstream had long rendered them a *de facto* separate religion.   Trimingham, adduced several times earlier in this work, formulated an influential observation about 19th century movements in the Arab and African regions of the Dar al-Islam—one that might well be extended across space and time to all of the anti-Ottoman ones examined above. That famous scholar of Sufism identified three major groupings of Islamic revivalism in the 1800s:

- Wahhabism:[383]   Salvation   through   return   to origins/Islamic Law

---

[381] As per Jan-Olaf Blichfeldt, *Early Mahdism: Politics and Religion in the Formative Period of Islam* (Leiden: E.J. Brill, 1985).

[382] Later in this book, chapter four, I examine an earlier Mahdist movement that emerged from a periphery and actually conquered its Islamic center: Ibn Tumart's Almohads, who excoriated, rebelled against, then ultimately supplanted the Almoravids.

[383] Another major brand of Salafism—South Asian Deobandism, which was influenced by the Arabian kind but developed separately—should be mentioned

- Mahdism: Salvation through the divinely-guided one
- Sufi Revivalism: Salvation through ecstasy, following charismatic shaykh(s).[384]

Of course, there was, and still can be, overlap between the categories. The Zaydis waged jihad to maintain Islamic law, although they were fighting for the Zaydi Shi`i brand. The Kadizadelis were proto-Wahhabi, in the sense of being fundamentalist Salafis, before Abd al-Wahhab was even born. A number of Sufis in the early days of the Ottoman Empire were also Mahdist. And Muhammad Ahmad of Sudan was a Sufi Mahdi who levied Wahhabi-style criticisms against the Ottoman Sultan and his rule.

The Ottoman responses to such challenges included, if they did not entirely revolve around, Islam norms—or, perhaps more precisely, around whose definition of that religion was the correct one. The Empire, as the quintessentially Sunni power bloc, stood for, and on, "state structures, exoteric understanding of the Qur'an,[385] the centrality of religious consensus, the resort to coercive measures in government, the tendency to standardize procedures—all these constitute a 'fabric' fitted together by the logic of power and conquest."[386] Sects of Islam, on the other hand, tended to be located on the peripheries (both geographically and in relation to the power

---

here, as well.

[384] Trimingham, p. 245.

[385] That is, reading and understanding that holiest Islamic text literally, if not necessarily fundamentalistically, as it were. This type of exegesis is contraposed to the esoteric kind, which finds abstruse, indeed secret, meanings therein.

[386] Khuri, *Imams and Emirs*, p. 19.

structure), assign cryptic meanings to the Qur'an which allegedly only they could fathom, and claim superior moral, even spiritual, status[387] over against the official Islam of the establishment. Peripherality, in particularly, could be a key indicator of how rebellious a sect of Islam may become. Indeed, there is almost certainly "an inverse correlation between the status of the state and the rise of sects...."[388] When the state is strong, sectarianism finds little room to maneuver; but when the center lacks power, or even is perceived as weak, non-establishment belief systems can arise—and even flourish.

Not all enemies of the Ottoman caliphs examined in this work would qualify as sects. The Druzes and Zaydis certainly would. Probably the Sudanese Mahdists would qualify, too, since they made belief in their founder's eschatological character, *inter alia*, a key belief. But Sufis are not actually sectarians, however—Kadizadeli and Salafi protestations notwithstanding. Nor, for that matter, would the Kadizadelis or Wahhabis constitute such a religious clique; they are more properly, as noted, categorized as reform movements via return to fundamentals—although the Ottoman state apparatus definitely branded the latter a dangerous sect. In brief, here is how the Ottomans responded to the seven major challenges arising within their Islamic realm:

---

[387] *Ibid.*
[388] *Ibid.*

- Against the Sufi rebellions in the first few centuries of the Empire, the Ottomans seem to have usually resorted to overwhelming military force in tandem with mass executions. This was especially the case with those non-state Shi`i and quasi-Shi`i orders which were aligned, overtly or covertly, with Istanbul's hated Safavid state rival. No doubt the Sunni Ottomans also deployed counter-Shi`i ideology and propaganda, about which we can only surmise as no comprehensive study of such utilizing the old imperial archives has yet been done.

- The Empire segued between kinetic operations and more accommodating co-optation in opposing the Celalis, who were disgruntled soldiers and not religious deviationists. Non-state sanctioned violence could not be tolerated, of course; especially when it rose to the level of attempting to detach any towns or areas from Istanbul's control. But dissension in the military ranks, even former ones, seems to have been treated more circumspectly by Ottoman authorities than, in particular, religious-based revolts.

- On the other hand, Ottoman ripostes to the Kadizadeli movement leaned more on finesse than raw military force, as in this case the opponent was a domestic one with impeccable—if irritating—religious bona fides. And, somewhat ironically, by the 17th century the state brand of Islam was heavily infused with Sufism—making (at least some of) the orders the defenders of the regime rather than its attackers. The Kadizadeli v. Sufi struggle did sometimes descend into violence—especially on the part of the former—but the Ottoman state responded, for the most part, judicially and legislatively rather than militarily: co-opting (by accepting them into the government and military apparatus); then, when that proved unsuccessful, exiling Kadizadeli preachers and prevailing upon state ulama to issue denunciatory fatwas. The Ottoman response was shock and law, if you will.

- The Ottomans dealt with the many armed Druze uprisings as those of non-state Islamic heretics, and ones who sometimes had state sponsors—but in this case Christian Europeans rather than a rival Islamic polity. As such, the relevant sultans responded to this double insult to their rule with something close to scorched earth campaigns: razing villages, mass beheadings, sanctioned rape and targeted killings. But the Ottoman authorities used non-kinetic approaches, as well: they ordered destroyed copies of *Raziel al-Hikmah*, *Epistles of Wisdom*—the Druze holy book—thus demonstrating a counter-ideological element; and after later rebellions they placed Druze population centers under direct Ottoman control, in an attempt to remove the excuse of allegedly-unendurable Maronite rule. Istanbul also took to frequently rotating senior administrative posts in the Syria *vilayet* and specifically the Beirut and Lebanon *sanjaks*[389] so that power bases could not be built up among the Druze chiefs who, despite their obstreperousness, sometimes served as Ottoman government proxies.

- Yemen's refractory Zaydi population was subjected to Ottoman sticks and carrots during the Empire's two separate occupations of that strategic southwestern Arabian area: the former via "police repression" and "counter-guerrilla tactics;" the latter through "programs of social and economic development."[390] More specifically, the Ottoman sticks—clubs, really—in Yemen included: 1) overwhelming firepower 2) brutal punishments as well as 3) explicitly punitive expeditions, to include burning of crops and killing of livestock 4) divide-and-rule tactics against Yemen's tribes. The carrots employed were grounded in 1) granting of

---

[389] Dick Douwes, *The Ottomans in Syria. A History of Justice and Oppression* (London and New York: I.B. Tauris, 2000), p. 212.
[390] Wilhite, p. ii.

"practical autonomy in return for formal loyalty,"[391] and 2) creation of indigenous police forces, as well as the earlier mentioned 3) infrastructure building of roads and schools, in particular. The latter was predicated on the Ottoman hope that "a Yemeni elite educated in the Ottoman fashion would influence the population at large to support the Empire,"[392] as had been the case elsewhere in the Empire's Arab provinces. But although some of Yemen's leadership did eventually come to support Istanbul, it was not because of education but rather due to the Empire's acquiescence in the Zaydi Imams' right to rule parts of Yemen.

- The Wahhabis exhibited, from the Ottoman point of view, the worst of two previous rebellions. These Bedouin reactionaries fused a Kadizadeli-like critique of Turkish Islam to a Zaydi-esque revulsion with outside rule. Furthermore the Wahhabis, like their Yemeni cousins, posed a threat to Ottoman control of Mecca and Medina—whence the Sultans drew no small measure of their Islamic legitimacy—but a Sunni, not a heretical Shi`i, one. As such, the Empire could tolerate this central Arabian movement even less than the southern Arabian one. At first Istanbul delegated dealing with the Wahhabized Saudis to their Egyptian proxy. But when they resurfaced, the Wahhabis were more circumspect, working the diplomatic and geographical margins between the Ottomans the British and, in fact, gaining the status of rulers of the Najd[393] vilayet under Ottoman overlordship during World War I. Eventually the Wahhabi Saudis outmaneuvered all other Arab players in the peninsula and, by the 1920s, created Saudi Arabia—a state that would outlast the Ottoman one.

---

[391] These five were taken from Wilhite, pp. 43-55.

[392] *Ibid.*, p. 228.

[393] Or "Nejd"—the highlands of the central Arab peninsula.

- The final challenge to the Ottoman Sultans examined herein is the most overtly eschatological one: the late 19th century Sudanese Mahdist. This one, too, combined elements of several other anti-Ottoman movements: the apocalyptic zeal of some of the earlier Sufi ones—and Muhammad Ahmad, recall, was a Sufi himself; the questioning of Ottoman Islamic bona fides, similar to the Kadizadelis and Wahhabis; and finally, the borderline xenophobic dislike of distant, different rulers which resembled that of the Yemeni Zaydis but raised the stakes in terms of ethnolinguistic and even racial aversion. The Sudanese Mahdist insurrection was perhaps the most pointedly religious in nature, which perhaps stands to reason as its leader claimed to be the End Times defender and renewer of the entire Islamic world—an arrogant assertion that no doubt infuriated the Ottoman establishment even more than the criticisms levied by the likes of Wahhabis, Zaydis or even Kadizadelis. The self-styled Mahdi ultimately prevailed over surrogate Ottoman forces from its client Egypt, even under British leadership, and detached an enormous northeast African territory from imperial control. In that sense, the Sudanese succeeded, although their ardent apocalyptic movement never actually threatened the Ottoman state itself—as much as their leader would have liked doing so.

Broadly speaking, the Ottomans, like any state dealing with uprisings, operated in several major counter-insurgent registers: military-kinetic, political, socio-economic and ideological-religious. Thus, they did not hesitate to bust some heads—or even remove them; but there were also imperial efforts to win hearts and minds. It is necessary to examine how the Ottoman state brought all these

counter-rebellion approaches to bear on each of their opponents .
But before that can be done, some further definition—or at least
clarification—of terms is in order. Any and all Islamic enemies of
the sultan-caliphs were, by definition, potentially (and probably)
religious; some were, as noted, clearly sectarian. All were also non-
state, and thus engaged in what's now known as irregular, or
unconventional, warfare. *Unconventional warfare* is perhaps best
defined as "activities conducted to enable a resistance movement or
insurgency to coerce, disrupt, or overthrow a government of
occupying power by operating through or with and underground,
auxiliary, or guerrilla force...."[394] *Insurgency* is further defined as "the
organized use of subversion and violence to seize, nullify or
challenge political control of a region. Insurgency can also refer to
the group itself."[395] *Guerrilla force* refers to "a group of irregular,
predominantly indigenous personnel organized along military lines
to conduct military and paramilitary operations...."[396] They "are
neither militias nor mercenary soldiers..., nor are they criminal
gangs...."[397] A more basic characterization of guerrilla warfare
derives from its Spanish context: "small war," which referred to the
hit-and-run attacks which the Spaniards waged against the occupying

---

[394] Taken from "Unconventional Warfare: Pocket Guide," US Army Special
Operations Command, Deputy Chief of Staff G-3, Sensitive Activities Division
G3X, AOOP SA, Fort Bragg, North Carolina 28310, 5 April 2016, p 5;
accessed June 25, 2020.
[395] *Ibid.*
[396] *Ibid.*, p. 6.
[397] *Ibid.*, p. 8.

forces of Napoleonic France. Interestingly, no definition of *conventional warfare* is supplied—the assumption being, perhaps, that one simply knows it when he sees it.

Since this book's opening chapter delineated Islamic terrorism as the main type wracking the modern world, it is necessary to try to distinguish that from guerrilla warfare.[398] The major differences between the two are as follows:

- Guerrillas try to take and control territory; terrorists mainly fight on the psychological, not physical, plane.
- Guerrillas' fighting units, though usually smaller than those of conventional forces, are still sometimes substantial; terrorists attacks in small cells or individually.
- The guerrilla arsenal differs little, if at all, from those of the conventional militaries they battle—although it may lack the larger caliber weapons. Terrorists tend to use, at most, individual weapons such as rifles, as well as homemade bombs and/or IEDs (Improvised Explosive Devices).
- Guerrilla tactics differ little from those of their conventional enemies—whereas terrorists employ quite different ones, such as targeting civilians.

The US State Department defines terrorism as "premeditated, politically motivated violence perpetrated against non-combatant targets by subnational groups or clandestine agents."[399] Another term much in vogue nowadays is "violent extremism." In fact, that is

---

[398] One good source on this topic is Ariel Merari, "Terrorism as a Strategy of Insurgency," in Gérard Chaliand and Arnaud Blin, eds., *The History of Terrorism from Antiquity to ISIS* (Oakland: University of California Press, 2016), pp. 12-51; see especially pp. 24, 25, "Terrorism and Guerrilla War."

[399] "Organization Definitions of Terrorism," *SecBrief*, accessed June 25, 2020. See also Merari, pp. 13-16 in particular.

often preferred to "terrorism." The FBI defines violent extremism as "encouraging, condoning, justifying or supporting the commission of a violent act to achieve political, ideological, religious, social, or economic goals."[400]

The Ottomans, of course, didn't call those engaged in insurrection guerrillas, terrorists or violent extremists; although each of those terms might be accurate, to one degree or another, using them would be committing the historical sin of prochronism.[401] The Ottomans usually deemed them simply rebels.[402] But each of the major groupings of rebellions had its own particular motivations, not always entirely religious—likewise for its goals. A useful chart for differentiating conventional from unconventional warfare, or conflict between states from that with insurgents, is this one by Iris Malone:[403]

---

[400] As per "What Is Violent Extremism?," *fbi.gov*, accessed June 25, 2020.

[401] "[R]epresenting of something as existing before it really did," "prochronism," *wordnik.com*; accessed June 27, 2020

[402] It is quite revealing, however, that the FBI definition of "violent extremism" would describe practically any revolution or war in human history—so what has been the most typical means of effecting change has now been deemed out-of-bounds, radical, beyond the pale.

[403] From her "Regular v. Irregular Wars," *web.Stanford.edu*, 2015, with permission; accessed June 26, 2020.

Comparison of Interstate War with Insurgent Wars

	Regular Wars	Irregular Wars
AKA:	interstate war, conventional war	insurgency, asymmetric conflict, civil war, guerrilla warfare, intrastate war, extrastate war, revolution*
Participants:	State Actor vs State Actor	State Actor vs Non-State Actor
Motivation for War:	Territory, policy change, regime change, status quo	Ideology, religious extremism, ethnic separatism, colonialism, culture, regime change, possibly territory
Goal:	Military, economic, or political change	Political change
War of …	Blitzkrieg	Attrition
Relative Power between Participants:	Symmetric	Asymmetric
Overall Strategy:	**Direct:** orchestrate military offensives to eliminate the enemy	**Indirect:** undermine the incumbent or insurgency's will to fight
Tactics:	Military battles, coercion, fire power, troops, tactics to eliminate the enemy, convince civilians to resist	guerrilla tactics, terror, propaganda, convince civilians to collaborate with insurgency, use local knowledge, fight on own turf
Casualties:	High	Low to Moderate
How is War Changing in the 21st Century?	Drones, WMDs, field medicine, mechanization	Internet, cell phones, "twi-plomacy," new techniques to finance insurgency (oil, minerals)
Outcome:	Stronger power wins	Stronger power *or* weaker power wins conditional on other factors
Examples:	World War I, World War II, Gulf War, War in Iraq (early)	Vietnam War, War in Iraq (late), Tuareg Rebellion in Mali, ISIL

Mutatis mutandis, this taxonomy can help understand the enemies of the Ottomans, as well as, to some extent, the Empire's reactions. Here are some necessary modifications. "Religious extremism" is often in the eye of the (modern) beholder. Today that phrase is coterminous with violent expression of religion—especially Islam.[404] But a Kadizadeli or Wahhabi might have said "extremism in the defense of Islam is no vice." For that matter, the Ottoman state itself was dedicated to upholding Sunni Islamic power and law— albeit not in a way that some sectarians preferred, as this entire work shows. Even as late as 1914 the Ottoman Şeyhülislâm, at the behest

---

[404] The same is true of the aforementioned "violent extremism," so beloved of the FBI.

118

of Sultan Mehmed V, issued a fatwa of jihad against the UK, France and Russia—its enemies in World War I.[405]   That would be condemned as religious extremism today. And a particularly potent brand of "religious extremism" was the eschatological, or apocalyptic kind—exemplified by the Sudanese Mahdi and his fervent followers. Another problematic categorical motivation for irregular war is "colonialism." No doubt the chart's creator means by that term Western—European, or perhaps American—intrusion into, and takeover of, territories in Africa, Asia or perhaps even the Americas. But many of those fighting the Ottomans deemed them guilty of *Turkish* colonialism. Certainly the Zaydis, Wahhabis and Sudanese Mahdists had this view; perhaps, too, did the Druzes. Finally, in terms of counter-rebel tactics employed by the Ottoman Empire: part of the effort to "convince civilians to resist" would have included, in almost every case, a crucial element of religious—Islamic—delegitimization. Hard power alone rarely won the day.

Malone also has created a quite handy "cheat sheet" for analyzing both insurgencies and the states fighting them in terms of causes and tactics.[406] She sees the three main reasons for anti-state uprisings as 1) "grievances and political instability" 2) "greed and poverty" and 3) "competing ethnic/religious groups." Such movements fight the state by 1) gaining the backing of the population 2) escaping and

---

[405] Peters, "Jihad and War Propaganda: the Ottoman Jihad Fatwa of November 11, 1914," *Jihad in Classical and Modern Islam*, pp. 55-57.

[406] "Insurgency and Counterinsurgency: A Cheat Sheet," *web.stanford.edu*, 2016; accessed June 29, 2020.

evading government forces and 3) outlasting and wearing down the state's will to fight by engaging in hit-and-run tactics. For their part, the targeted state has three major avenues of response: 1) search and destroy insurgents 2) clear and hold former insurgent territories and 3) yes, win hearts and minds. Let us now look at each of the Ottoman Empire's collections of nemeses from this perspective.

The early 15th century Sufi uprisings against the nascent Ottoman state, epitomized by Bedreddin, definitely operated in a time of political problems for the Ottomans, who were reconstructing their rule after Tamerlane's ruinous war on them. They also exploited localized disenchantment with Ottoman rule, especially taxation on subsistence-level peasants (both Muslim and Christian). Turcoman nomads also chafed at following rules set up by a sedentary state, while former Islamic holy warriors resented new Ottoman injunctions to lay off Christians—while, at the same time, formerly-Byzantine Orthodox Christians still had not come to terms with Islamic rulers. But the overarching motivation for these mystical Muslim revolts was, of course, Islam of the Sufi variety which was syncretistic enough to allow Christian involvement.[407] So the variegated socioeconomic and political grievances against rising and reconsolidating Ottoman rule were held together under an umbrella of religious fervor—if not exactly extremism. In terms of

---

[407] This is all the more notable when one considers that a rump Eastern Christian/Byzantine state still existed, mainly in Constantinople but also in a few other territories. These would all be extinguished by the Ottomans, of course, in 1453.

how these movements fought the Ottomans: they did seek, quite successfully for a while, civilian support; and Bedreddin's followers did manage to avoid Ottoman clutches for about a year (1416), but eventually were put down violently and their leader publicly executed. Beyond that, we do not know much about the rebellious Sufis' actual tactics.

Similar, but truly extremist, revolts followed in the 16th and 17th centuries. The same Ottoman injustices, real or perceived, were adduced. But Shah Qulu, Shah Wali, Nur Ali Khalifa, and Sayyid Abd Allah kicked their rebellions up a notch by claiming eschatological sanction. And such did not just gain the support of elements of the populace. They were at times backed and assisted by the rival major state power, Safavid Iran—especially when the movement was as least quasi-Shi`i. This made these conflicts both intrastate and interstate. Also, since by the 1500s and 1600s the Ottoman state was firmly established, the uprisings had elements of guerrilla wars bordering on civil ones. There was an element of Turcoman nomad resistance to Ottoman control here, too: taxes and being forced to become sedentary were the main bones of contention. But, overall, it's hard to tell whether the socioeconomic and political motivations drove the religious one—or vice-versa. As best as can be determined, these apocalyptic mutineers at first engaged in hit-and-run raids particularly in the eastern Empire, bordering Iran. Eventually they graduated to attacking Ottoman caravans, even royal ones, as well as entering towns and killing

Ottoman officials.[408] But they would have avoided any conventional battles with the superior Ottoman military, until they were given no choice—at which point the Ottomans would usually win. Often with such movements killing the leader deflated its power—as happened with Bedreddin and Shah Qulu. All told, these Sufi insurgent irruptions only last perhaps 12 years: 1416-20, 1511-17, 1520 and 1565. They are probably best defined as religious and socioeconomic insurgents, although insofar as any of them with Shi`i tendencies served as a *de facto* auxiliary of that Ottoman state rival, the Safavids, the designation of guerrillas is not inaccurate.

The Ottomans then made little, if any effort, to "build community relations" or "implement social/public services"[409] as a means of winning over the Anatolian population vis-à-vis these Sufi uprisings. As noted earlier, the Ottoman state probably worked more in the realm of religious delegitimating of these movements—although we can only speculate about such, lacking data. The Ottomans put much more effort into "search and destroy, followed by "clear and hold," campaigns:[410] imperial forces simply crushed the rebellious mystics, then garrisoned the "liberated" towns and areas. A degree of co-optation took place, however. Some of these recalcitrant orders, such as the Bektaşis, were incorporated into the state apparatus, thus defusing and redirecting their militant zeal.[411]

---

[408] See "Şakhulu Rebellion," *Wikipedia*, accessed June 29, 2020.
[409] "Insurgency and Counterinsurgency: A Cheat Sheet," p. 2.
[410] *Ibid.*
[411] "Shi`sm, which was not tolerated [by the Ottoman state], was forced to seek

So Ottoman COIN in this era and with these enemies was mainly kinetic, albeit including a dollop of appropriating, if not winning, hearts and minds—of the rebels, if not of their followers.

Finally, in this approximate time frame, the Celali Turcoman insurrections did not derive their motivation from religion but were, rather, rooted in socioeconomic grievances. Usually they consisted of Ottoman troops who hadn't been paid, or those who had been involuntarily demobilized, going on violent sprees. There was a major exception to this, however. In 1598-99 Karayazıcı Abdülhalim,[412] a former *sekhan*,[413] who led armed followers to take over several towns in east central Anatolia and established, in effect, a shadow government. Such did not threaten the central Ottoman government in Istanbul, but rather constituted military and political resentment of, in particular, the dominant position of the full-time, professional Janissaries at the expense of the formerly-important auxiliary troops which did, however, segue into separatism. The Ottomans eventually military defeated Abdülhalim's men, with their leader dying of natural causes. His brother Deli Hasan then rebelled in western Anatolia, but was eventually co-opted by the Ottomans

---

asylum within Sufi groups, among whom the Bektashiyya gave its fullest expression." Trimingham, p. 69.

[412] As per Lord Kinross, *The Ottoman Centuries: The Rise and Fall of the Turkish Empire* (New York: Morrow Quill, 1977), pp. 286-87. See also "Celali Rebellions," *Wikipedia*; accessed June 29, 2020.

[413] This was an "irregular musketeer" in the Ottoman army. But Kinross, p. 286, has the term as *sekhan* while it's "Sekban," in *Britannica.com*; accessed June 29, 2020.

who made him governor of Bosnia.[414] Overall, these Celali revolts lasted on-and-off for episodes totaling 57 years: 1519, 1590-1610, 1622-1659.

The Celali insurrections, particularly the most potent, like that of Abdülhalim, were definitely insurgent, bordering on separatist—even if they started out as merely men wanting to be employed, and paid for it. Similarly to how they dealt with the Sufi irruptions, the Ottomans mostly utilized search and destroy missions, followed by clear and hold ones. Likewise, since these Celalis themselves were the problem, *sans* any substantial element of popular support, the Ottoman state had to win them over—not their followers. To that end, they would bring on board rebellious leaders, as they did most prominently with Deli Hasan, granting him a government administrative position. This despite his alleged boast that "I have overthrown in these countries the Ottoman power, and the domination undivided now belongs to me."[415] So, again, we see the Ottoman state employing kinetic operations primarily. Any hearts and minds they won were those of the insurgent leaders—not their followers, nor even the civilian population.

The next major challenge to the Ottomans was a horse of a different color: the Kadizadelis. They were certainly religiously extremist by the standards of the Ottoman state's religious status

---

[414] Kinross, p. 287

[415] *Ibid.* Kinross goes on to note, concerning Deli Hasan, that he and his supporters who followed him to Bosnia "in 1603 were finally annihilated on the banks of the Danube by a force of Hungarians."

quo, which by the 17th century was dominated by several Sufi orders—ironically, considering the rebellious nature of the latter in previous centuries. But the Kadizadeli goals are not so easily fit into Malone's categories. This movement did not so much seek political, as religious, change—or, perhaps more accurately, reform. Kadizade Mehmed Efendi, as well as his epigones and followers, had no desire to alter Ottoman dynastic power, much less to replace it. The aim was to bend the dominant Islamic ideological paradigm from a mystical-oriented, "innovative" one to a more fundamentalist mode, in which only slavish devotion to Islamic holy texts was permitted. Several Ottoman sultans even supported this movement—until its adherents left the mosques and took to the streets of Istanbul attacking Jews, Christians and Sufis, sometimes even meting out vigilante justice. This violence, in tandem with the condemnation of establishment, Sufi-approved sexual practices in military circles, cost the Kadizadelis most of their remaining support and putt their movement perilously close to fitnah status—that of an Islamic insurgency or civil war. The death knell for Kadizadelism was the Ottoman defeat by the Christian coalition at Vienna in 1683, for which that movement's leader, Vani Mehmed, was blamed. He had successfully lobbied against the customary joint Islamic-Christian leaders' prayers for Ottoman success in battle. These Ottoman prigs never really won the support of the Ottoman populace, even in Istanbul; and the violence they employed never rose to the level of guerrilla warfare. The main motivation for this movement was religious, although there may have been some element of socioeconomic envy vis-a-vis the state-supported Sufis. The Ottoman center certainly was not suffering any political instability at the time. The Kadizadelis' main aim was to win hearts and minds in Topkapi palace—a goal which they did achieve for some decades, only to squander by overreaching. But once Kadizadelism had discredited itself, as it were, the Ottoman state prevailed mainly by non-kinetic means. Nonetheless, for 54 years—from 1631 to 1685—this movement vexed the Ottoman state. It was unlike the others examined herein, however, being more one of agitation and religious reform than insurgency. Its adherents did take advantage of Sultanic power vacuums in the mid- and late-17th century, due to rulers' illness/mental instability and youth. And the Kadizadelis did finally segue into sectarian street violence and were met with state force in return. This was only in two cities—albeit rather important ones, Istanbul and Cairo. Still, the Ottoman state had no need to resort to the methodology of search and destroy, and thus not clear and hold. There was a strong focus, however, on winning hearts and minds by delegitimizing the Kadizadelis. Ottoman religious officials issued fatwas declaring Kadizadeli beliefs beyond the pale of Islamic orthodoxy. In the end, the Ottoman state did engage in a kinder, gentler form of search and destroy, exiling prominent Kadizadeli ideologues from the imperial center to the peripheries—probably because certain high-ranking Ottoman officials were sympathetic to that cause.

The Druzes were much closer to a modern insurgency than either the Sufis or the Kadizadelis. As a heterodox religious community, they were often vexed by Sunni Ottoman norms—but mostly by state taxation and attempted limitations on Druze possession of weaponry. At times Druze resistance to imperial control bordered on religio-ethnic separatism. They also periodically resented what they saw as the better socioeconomic status of their Maronite Christian neighbors in the Levant. At other times Druze intransigence, especially when inflamed and assisted by outside powers such as Venice, transmogrified into guerrilla warfare, indeed open rebellion, against the Turks in the late 16ᵗʰ century and, again, several times in the 17ᵗʰ century—the latter including Twelver Shi`is, who allied with the Druzes against the Sunni Ottomans. And, again, western Christian (usually Catholic) powers often aided these uprisings, notably Fakhr al-Din—giving them an interstate aspect. Ottoman responses were both kinetic and non-kinetic: the former including military intervention and bringing captured Druze leaders back to Istanbul for public execution; the later encompassing moves such as revamping Ottoman administration to be less onerous and giving Druze chiefs hereditary positions as governors, as well as collecting, and probably destroying, Druze copies of their main religious text: *Rasa'il al-Hikmah*.[416]   By the 19ᵗʰ century Druze

---

[416] "The full Druze canon…includes the Old Testament, the New Testament, the Quran and philosophical works by Plato…among works from other religions and philosophers." From "Epistles of Wisdom," *Wikipedia*; accessed June 30. Khuri, *Imams and Emirs*, p. 133, elaborates further: "Their [Druze] sources

violence was often directed not so much at the Ottomans as at Maronite Christians, thus falling into the category of competing ethnic/religious group conflict. In these bloodlettings, the Druzes found allies among the Muslims, both Sunni and Shi`i. The Ottomans, preoccupied with the stability and integrity of their northern borders, allowed a power vacuum and, thus, this political instability in their Levantine province—an authority void ultimately filled by a Western European Christian state: France. The Druzes rose in one final anti-Ottoman insurrection on the eve of World War I. The Ottomans crushed the uprising, disarmed many and conscripted thousands of Druzes into the imperial army. Then World War I broke out, after which the Ottomans had bigger problems—such as the survival of the Empire. But the Druzes had been a thorn in the Ottoman Levantine side, all told, for 57 years, from the 16th to the early 20th centuries: 1518, 1520, 1575-85, 1620-35, 1680-97, 1858-60 and 1909. The Druze uprisings often qualified as insurgencies, insofar as they aimed to "challenge political control of a region" by the Ottoman state. But do they qualify as guerrillas? Probably not, since they more closely resembles sectarian militias.

With their Druze opponents, the Ottomans resorted mainly to search and destroy operations, as well as co-optation. They could not win hearts and minds in a religious sense, since the Druze were a

abound in names, ideas and religious traditions that appeared before the rise of Islam…particularly Neoplatonism. After the rise of Islam, the Druzes relied heavily on the writings of the Mu`tazila [Islamist rationalist] writers…as well as well-known masters of Sufism…

heterodox branch of Islam, far departed from Sunni norms. Ottoman forces did destroy copies of the Druzes' holy texts, perhaps hoping to make it harder for them to pass on their religious teachings. On the flip side of this COIN, Istanbul tried to win over some rebellious Druze leaders with government administrative positions—but only after the severe kinetic campaigns, which included razing villages, beheadings and other targeted executions, confiscations of firearms, mass conscription and even, allegedly, rape as a subjugation tool. The Ottomans did also try to cut off the Druzes' outside Christian means of support—as by occupying Cyprus. Ultimately, the Druze situation spiraled out of control, and the Ottomans were replaced as power brokers in the Levant by the French.

The Zaydis of Yemen, along with the Arabian Wahhabis and the Sudanese Mahdists, probably more resemble modern insurgents or guerrillas of the Islamic variety than the previous movements examined. These intractable Shi`is bogged the Ottomans down, twice, in lengthy counter-insurgent wars: from 1538-1635, and again from 1849 to 1911. All told, that's 159 years of Ottoman pacification efforts in the far southwest of the Arabian peninsula. The Zaydis fought the Empire on a number of levels: as Fiver Shi`is who resented Sunni strictures; as Arabs who despised Turkish colonialism; as strict Muslims who found their overlords' practice of the faith to be wanting, exemplified by the Sultans' support for Sufism. Imperial taxation inflamed Zaydi passion, as well. There was also another cultural element: that of quasi-nomadic, bellicose highlanders' scorn for their softer, sedentary—and, in this case, Sunni—cousins. In the first Ottoman occupation, Mansur al-Qasim and, then, his son Mua`ayyad Muhammad led jihads against imperial forces. These, in tandem with the Ottoman need for more forces in the European theater, helped persuade them to withdraw their troops. Almost two centuries later, the Empire belatedly struck back, alarmed by the Mahdist pretensions of Faqih Sa`id, Zaydi infighting and attacks on Sunni lowlanders, and British threats to intervene in the area. At times the Zaydis kept to the highlands and tolerated Ottoman rule along the Red Sea coast and in the lowlands among their co-religionist Sunnis. But rebellion spread out of the mountains, and the Ottomans—once again—requested Egyptian military aid. This helped the Empire restore its rule, temporarily, by 1871. Ottoman attempts to win Zaydi hearts and minds proved insufficient, however. Furthermore, in terms of kinetic operations, the Zaydi tribesmen were masters of making hit-and-run attacks on Ottoman garrisons and caravans, then fleeing back to their mountain strongholds. The Zaydis also had massive support among their co-religionist population.

By the late 1880s the Isma'ilis had joined the Zaydis against the Ottomans, an alliance predicated on the common political grievance of overtaxation combined with mutual Shi`i loathing of Sunni rule. Under Yahya Hamid al-Din, these combined forces' jihad reasserted control of the Yemeni highlands. Yet once again Ottoman forces riposted and retook Sana`a and other major towns. This in turn set the stage for the Ottoman end game in Yemen. The Zaydis ramped up their already substantial support among the populace by "bands" or "gangs" of tribesmen who accompanied Zaydi clerics as the armed muscle, while the latter stirred up yet more jihad. These easily overwhelmed Ottoman attempts to promote the general Islamic welfare and win over the Yemenis. By the first decade of the 20th century, almost constant Zaydi warfare under Yahya Hamid al-Din, coupled with Wahhabi Sa`udi raids further north, al-Idrisi's quasi-eschatological uprising, and the low morale of Ottoman forces, led Istanbul to open negotiations, leading ultimately to the removal of imperial forces by 1911. Thus ended the Ottoman Empire's longest-lasting colonial campaign against other Muslims. The Yemeni Zaydis were insurgents as well as guerrillas, and clearly waged somewhat successful unconventional warfare against the Ottomans: they helped kick out their Sunni Muslim overlords, only to induce a major Western Christian power (Britain) to replace them in southern Yemen..

Ottoman COIN against the Zaydis is perhaps the best-documented of all the Empire's such campaigns treated herein. It was directed, in two chronologically-separated chapters, against an insurgency which was inflamed by many of same grievances as modern irregular warriors: colonialism, ethno-linguistic separatism, religious differences and territorial claims. Ottoman counter-Zaydi efforts, across time, employed all three major COIN modes: search and destroy, clear and hold, and attempts to win hearts and minds—although the last was much more a factor in the second phase thereof. In both periods of occupation and attempted pacification, the Ottoman state used military power as a first resort. But the mode of doing so changed by the 19th century, and the Ottomans added to that a quite extensive agenda of community relations and social/public services—impressive even if it ultimately failed. This latter "nation-building" program included: establishing schools, setting up police forces, recruitment of indigenous militias, appointing rebel leaders to administrative posts, building roads, proposed extension of the Hijaz railway to Yemen, and revamping the legal system.[417] Schools were a sticking point for many there because Istanbul funded Western-influenced ones teaching secular subjects—not simply the Qu'ran. And updating the legal code undermined shari`ah, as the Ottomans had been incorporating elements of Western legal systems starting in 1839 with the Tanzimat reforms. For example, "[u]nder the Penal Code of 1858, which was a translation of the French Penal Code, the traditional *hadd* or defined punishments of Shari`a law were all abolished except for that of the death penalty for apostasy."[418] Needless to say, such changes infuriated the tribal, uber-traditional Zaydis.

---

[417] The US in Afghanistan comes to mind here.

[418] N.J. Coulson, *A History of Islamic Law* (Edinburgh: Edinburgh University Press, 1964), p. 151.

Before embarking upon this heart and minds outreach, the Ottomans waged brutal COIN warfare. By the late 19th and early 20th century Yemeni campaigns, imperial forces under Ahmed Feyzi Paşa embarked on, in effect, a scorched earth policy. In fact, it has been argued that "it was Ahmed Feyzi's counterinsurgency operations, in the 1890s, that radicalized a lot of the population—drove them into the arms of the Zaydi imams, and energized the Shi`a imams' local state-building efforts that then allowed for a much more serious uprising...."[419] Ahmed Feyzi's tactics, as noted earlier, included razing villages, burning crops and killing livestock, as well as intrusive and brutal policing. By 1902 the Ottomans supplemented their sticks with some carrots, by naming Huseyin Hilmi Paşa their man in Yemen—and it was he who presided over the aforementioned infrastructure-building program. However, such benefited mainly San`a, and did little for the highlander Zaydis. So their jihads continued and, prompted by complicating factors such as the Idrisi revolt to the north of Yemen, the Ottomans eventually sued for peace and departed—although the Zaydi leadership gave Istanbul the fig leave of loyalty in foreign affairs.

Throughout the 19th century the Wahhabi Sa`udis of central Arabia tried to establish an independent Islamic state. Unlike the Zaydis, this Wahhabized tribe only occasionally battled Ottoman troops directly; rather, it engaged Egyptian ones, fighting at the

---

[419] See Thomas Kuehn, "Ottoman Hero or Frontier Villain? Ahmed Feyzi Pasha (1839-1915)," *Youtube.com*, April 3, 2013; accessed July 3, 2020.

behest of the Sultan, from 1811 to 1819. The Arab fundamentalists, exemplars of religious extremism (especially vis-à-vis Ottoman Islam), had been attacking imperial territory since 1802, when they ransacked the Imam Husayn shrine in Ottoman Iraq. The Wahhabis not only went after Shi`is, however; they also challenged the Ottoman Sultans' right and legitimacy, accusing them and their subjects of lax Islam and kow-towing to infidels (mainly the Brits). The Wahhabized Sa`udis were interstate, indeed extrastate, Kadizadelis, as it were. Their rebellion also included hatred of Turkish colonialism and, thus, ethnic (Arab) separatism. By 1818 Ottoman Egyptian forces had crushed the movement and sent its leader to Istanbul for public execution. In its next incarnation, the Wahhabized Sa`udi polity did not often take on even the Ottoman proxy, Egypt, in open warfare. Instead, its leadership fought for control of central Arabia with the rival Rashidi Ha'il Emirate, which prevailed by, in part, receiving tacit Ottoman assistance. At the end of the 19th century the Wahhabi Sa`udis went on the offensive against the Rashidis, conquering them by 1907. The only direct Wahhabi Sa`udi attack on Ottoman forces came in 1913, when the garrison at al-Hasa on the central Persian Gulf coast was seized from imperial forces.[420] After that *fait accompli*, the Ottomans recognized the Wahhabi-Sa`udi state's ruler as head of the Najd vilayet. After World War I the Ottomans withdrew, leaving their former rebels to

---

[420] See this map: "Arabia 1905-1923," *i.redd.it/ugnekzlmpmoy.gif*, accessed July 1, 2020.

consolidate the Kingdom of Sa`udi Arabia. Wahhabi Sa`udi grievances were primarily religious, though they did weaponize them in an Arabian context of increasing Ottoman political instability. Much like the Zaydis further south in the peninsula, the Wahhabized tribes deployed their shock force of Ikhwan nomads in hit-and-run attacks which would then often outrun Ottoman pursuit. Sa`udi determination to create their own Wahhabized state then outlasted Istanbul's desire to hold on to Arabia outside of Mecca and Medina—where the Ottomans maintained nominal control via Sharif Husayn until 1916. Overall, the Wahhabi Sa`udi asymmetric agenda against their Turkish overlords (whether directly or, versus the Egyptians, indirectly) only lasted some two decades: 1801-18, 1913-18. But it represents, in tandem with the Sa`udi wars against the Rashidis and, later, British-backed, Meccan-backed Arabs, a masterful example of leveraging popular support, kinetic operations and diplomacy to achieve desired insurgent ends.

The Wahhabi Sa`udi movement was an insurgency that used guerrilla tactics and exhibited characteristics of both intrastate and interstate war, in that its enemies included ones inside the Arab world (Rashidis, Sharif Husayn and his men, Shi`is of southern Iraq) as well as the outside Ottoman colonial power. But unlike that of the Zaydi, this one rose to the level of a civil war in that the Wahhabi ulama openly denounced the religious and political legitimacy of the Ottoman Sultans. Interestingly, despite this movement's actual threat, at a minimum, to the Arabic-speaking provinces of the

Ottoman Empire, Istanbul often delegated the kinetic operations against it to Egypt—unlike what transpired in Yemen. Of course, in the early 19th century campaign, Muhammad Ali's military forces were brutally effective. They sought and destroyed Wahhabized Sa`udis, then cleared and held rebel territory. No real effort at winning over hearts, much less minds, was made—although the Egyptians deftly peeled off some of Abd Allah b. Sa`ud's support with diplomacy, spiced with bribes. Later in that century the movement resurfaced, but carefully avoided invoking Ottoman ire by remaining, at least theoretically, under Istanbul's thumb; they kept their conflicts aimed at the rival Rashidis. In this time frame the Empire did engage in some degree of ideological warfare, however—as with, for example, Shaykh al-Islam Ahmad Zayni Dahlan (d. 1886). His *Fitnah al-Wahhabiyah*, "Sedition of the Wahhabis," excoriates them for their heretical beliefs and activities.[421] But while that many have been popular in Mecca and Medina, it did little to stem the Wahhabi tide in the Arabian interior. On the eve of World War I Abd al-Aziz b. Sa`ud emerged and commanded powerful Ikwan forces, thus gaining Ottoman recognition and status—despite (or perhaps because of) his elimination of at least one Ottoman stronghold. Sa`udi Wahhabi timing was impeccable, too, for World War I proved the death knell of Ottoman power

---

[421] The book is available online in English as *Fitnatul Wahabiyah*, *kanzuliman.org*, June 2019; accessed July 3, 2020. The original Arabic version is at *Fitnah al-Wahhabiyah*, *gulfobserver.org*, n.d., accessed July 3, 2020.

among the Arabs. Overall, to be fair, Istanbul's COIN against the nascent Sa`udi polity was half-hearted at best, however. One wonders why the extensive Ottoman infrastructure-building activities in Yemen to win over the Zaydis were not tried in the territory between Riyadh and the Hijaz. Yet it probably would not have made a difference, considering how fervently the Wahhabis despised Ottoman Islam. Likewise, the question can be asked: why did the Empire never commit its own troops *en masse* to the kinetic operations against this Arab enemy? Two explanations come to mind, one logistical and one strategic. The Ottomans had no easy means of access to the interior of the peninsula, whence the Sa`udis came. On the bigger issue, by the end of the first decade of the 20th century the Ottomans were embroiled in the Young Turk revolution, which saw Sultan Abdül Hamid II eventually deposed; furthermore, its Balkan subjects rose in open rebellion not long after. So Istanbul had its hands full at home and in the north, precluding a more extensive assault on fundamentalist Arab insurgents.

Finally, we come to the apocalyptic war of the Sudanese Mahdi and his followers. Although this was one of the shortest of all the challenges to Ottoman rule examined here—a mere 18 years, altogether—it is perhaps the most relevant and instructive for us today. The Mahdist uprising in northeastern Africa ticked all the insurgent boxes. It exploited political instability in the Ottoman province of Egypt (of which Sudan was a subprovince, conquered decades earlier), caused primarily by the British occupation of that country in 1882. The Sudanese people's main way of alleviating their poverty—the slave trade carried out against non-Muslims further south in Africa—was being discouraged and even interdicted by Ottoman forces, at the behest of abolitionist Britain. The Arabic-speaking Sudanese tribes resented lighter-skinned Egyptians and Turks lording it over them; to make matters worse, the latter spoke an unintelligible language. In addition, not only did the Ottomans and Egyptians practice a shoddy brand of Islam, from the Sudanese perspective—they worked closely with infidel Christians from Britain. So the Mahdi, and his followers, had legitimate socioeconomic grievances; a political power vacuum existed after 1882; and the Sudanese saw themselves as constituting a competing ethnic and religious grouping over against their northern colonizers. Add to this the powerful factor of eschatological religious extremism, and it's easy to see why the heavily-motivated Mahdists triumphed over their enemies. Note that whereas in the Kadizadeli, Zaydi and Wahhabi uprisings, Sufism *per se* was a major irritant, here the Sudanese Mahdi and many of his initial followers were themselves Sufis. But the Sammaniyah order, in particular, did not enjoy the official imprimatur of the Ottoman establishment—and that was Muhammad Ahmad's main mystical membership. Furthermore, Sudanese Sufism was imbued with much more purist ideas and practices than were the Ottoman orders, so much so that its founder has been referred to as a "frontier fundamentalist."[422]

That explains *why* the Mahdi's forces won, initially. But *how* did they? The major methodology was in garnering, and then leveraging, massive popular support for the Mahdi as their leader, and his efforts to expel the extant Muslim colonial power. As we have seen with previous movements, Ottoman taxation was a major irritant to subject populations. That, plus the (admittedly reluctant) Ottoman attempts to proscribe slaving, constituted the socioeconomic planks of Mahdist policy. Muhammad Ahmad added scathing critiques of Turkish Islam, both in terms of its praxis and its heretical alliance with Western infidels. Charles Gordon, remember, was a staunch Christian, as well as a Brit. Muhammad Ahmad was also well aware that the Egyptians were cooperating fully with British occupation. Finally, his claims to be the eschatological Mahdi convinced many, especially after he and his followers went on a *hijrah* to far southern Sudan. This imitation of what the early Islamic community did in in 622 AD, in tandem with the approach of the turn of an Islamic century in 1882-83, convinced the Sudanese masses that Muhammad Ahmad was not just a mujaddid, but the actual awaited Mahdi. Once he had massive civilian support, his forces took on Ottoman Egyptian ones, defeating them in several hit-and-run battles and gaining stores of modern weapons—rifles, machine guns, even artillery—in the process. They then used these weapons in further attacks, in which they increased their arsenal. By

---

[422] John Voll, "The Sudanese Mahdi: Frontier Fundamentalist," *International Journal of Middle East Studies*, Volume 10, Issue 2 (May 1979), pp. 145-66.

summer 1881 the Mahdists controlled Kordofan/Kurdufan (southwestern of Khartoum), from which they captured yet more weaponry. This made the insurrection a separatist movement, if not quite yet a civil war. And the warfare waged changed from simply the former guerrilla tactics to conventional warfare. The Mahdists routed several Ottoman Egyptian-British forces, 1881-1884, then took Khartoum in January 1885, after a five-month siege—despite the best efforts of the Egyptian forces commanded by General Charles Gordon. Muhammad Ahmad thereupon established a theocratic Islamic state, centered around belief in himself as the Mahdi. This marked the transition from separatist rebellion to state-formation. Of course, the Mahdi would go to his eternal reward just six months later, although his frontier fundamentalist state would survive until 1898, when the Brits finally demolished it.

The Sudanese Mahdists made ISIS' jihadists look like insurgent and eschatological pikers. These 19th century apocalyptic warriors fought the Ottomans in just about every mode, and with multiple motivations. Following Muhammad Ahmad, they were empowered by ideology, religious extremism—not just holy, but the holiest, war—ethno-linguistic separatism, anti-colonialism, cultural clashes, and the desire for not just territorial acquisition but regime change (at least in Sudan). Their tactics were quintessentially guerrilla, until they acquired enough arms and manpower to wage conventional warfare and even siege. And they had support of much, if not most, of the population. The main Ottoman COIN response—again, much like that in Arabia against the Wahhabi-Saudi threat—consisted of deputizing the same powerful proxy, Egypt, to conduct kinetic operations. These failed miserably at search and destroy operations, even when assisted by an outside power (Britain), thus making it virtually impossible to conduct any clear and hold ones. The Turkiyah government's attempt to hold on to its major redoubt, Khartoum, also proved futile. On the hearts and minds front, the Ottomans again farmed out their response to surrogates, in the form of Egyptian and loyal Sudanese clerics. *In toto* these amounted to denigrating Muhammad Ahmad's grandiose eschatological claims via relevant Qur'anic and Hadith texts.[423] But the Mahdi knew his people too well, and his subjective claims proved irrefutable by compromised clerics—especially when they were validated by success in battle. The Mahdist state would prove invulnerable to religious delegitimating—but not, some years later, to British firepower.

Now that we have looked at the Ottomans and their internal enemies through a primarily sociopolitical, insurgent conflict prism, let us try another lens. It is quite illuminating to analyze the sultans' foes, and the Islamic empire's responses, through a strictly military history prism. The best paradigm for doing so is that of the eminent military historian Archer Jones:[424]

---

[423] See chapter two, above, for the detailed list.

[424] See two superb works of his: *Elements of Military Strategy: An Historical Approach* (Westport, CT: Praeger, 1996) and his voluminous *The Art of War in the Western World* (Urbana and Chicago: University of Illinois Press, 1987), in particular pp.

Armed forces had two strategic means available for depleting their adversary's military forces: combat and depriving the opponents' armed forces of supplies, weapons, recruits, or other resources…. The former method is easily labeled **combat strategy**, the latter suitably termed **logistic strategy**…. There were also two means of carrying out these two strategies. One used **the raid**, a transitory presence in hostile territory to make a destructive incursion. The other, called **persisting strategy**, had the objective of conquering a significant portion of the territory under the adversary's control…. These are used in lieu of other terms, such as conventional and unconventional warfare…. Thus there are four possible combinations of the strategic means of depletion: combat + persisting, combat + raiding, logistic + persisting, logistic + raiding. The strategy of any military operation is almost certain to fall into one of the four possible combinations…. Guerrilla warfare and other sorts of unconventional   warfare usually took advantage of the dominance of raiding…. **Rather than defining guerrilla warfare as a distinct sort of strategy, it seemed more useful to employ the categories of comprehensive strategy** and, by using other factors, such as the ratio of military force to the area of operations, make it easier to understand how guerrilla forces operated and the conditions under which they had success [emphases added].[425]

Julius Caesar, although he didn't use the terms "combat" and "logistical" for these strategies, clearly knew the difference: the former he called "winning by steel" and the latter "winning by hunger."[426]

679-704.
[425] Jones, *Elements of Military Strategy*, pp. xiv-xv.
[426] *Ibid.*, p. xv.

Guerrillas, or those forces which engage in a raiding strategy—either combat or logistic—against a target power, by definition, have a smaller force to space ratio than the larger armies of their enemy. Thus they depend on making effective use of terrain, operating from at least one base, and, most of all, a sympathetic population. Victory for guerrillas/raiders consists of 1) convincing the enemy to abandon its efforts to bring them to heel and/or eliminate them, 2) decreasing, or forsaking entirely, the amount of territory their enemy holds. The power engaging in counter-guerrilla, or counter-raiders, operations can, broadly speaking, take either the combat or logistical route.[427]   A combat strategy would require capturing or killing the guerrillas/raiders, controlling key nodes of communications and transportation, or undermining their political support—or a combination thereof. Fighting logistically would entail increasing (even more) force to space ratio superiority over raiders, counter-raiding their bases and/or occupying more of the territory in which they operate, and finally removing their bases and undermining their political support.[428]   "Both attack and defense against guerrillas typically have had a political component" because "guerrillas are particularly dependent on popular support."[429] Also since, as explained as some length earlier in this work, the political

---

[427] The full range of options, according to Jones, for a state attempting to counter insurgents/rebels/guerrillas can be found in his "Schematic 12.7: Summary of Alternatives for Combatting a Raiding Strategy or Guerrilla Warfare," *The Art of War*, p. 689.

[428] *Ibid.*, pp. 679ff.

[429] *Ibid.*, p. 688.

and the religious are practically identical in pre-modern Islamic societies, this means that almost every example of Ottoman military operations against the groups examined herein would have had a religious component (the Celalis being the lone exception).

Although Jones deals almost exclusively with Western military history, he does briefly mention the Ottoman Turkish conquest of formerly-Byzantine Anatolia, which includes a political-military option, scorched earth, which the Ottomans rarely took but to which they did resort in the 15th century. "The Turks subdued the Anatolian province of the Byzantine Empire by raids that created such dread that they cowed the population in much of this large area in a matter of only five years. Terror supplied the political ingredient, but the Turks killed so many people and destroyed so much property that one may fairly say they coupled with their political program a military-logistic strategy aimed at human as well as physical resources."[430]

Before applying this paradigm of combat raiding, combat persisting, logistic raiding, and logistic persisting to how the Ottomans dealt with their rebellious enemies, we need to know something about the Ottoman military in each time frame. From the 15th through the late 18th centuries, its main combat branches were basically four: elite infantry or Janissaries; armored cavalry or sipahis; artillerymen; and combat engineers.[431] Like European armies of the

---

[430] *Ibid.*, p. 690.
[431] See John F. Guilmartin, Jr., "Ideology and Conflict: the Wars of the Ottoman

same era, that of early modern land warfare, the main firearm was, eventually, the musket. By the time of the French Revolution, Ottoman land forces were divided as follows: 1) frontier garrisons stationed in citadels 2) provincial troops 3) soldiers hired for duration of a campaign only 4) sipahis and 5) Janissaries.[432] Sultan Selim III (r. 1789-1807) tried to create a new corps, the *Nizam-i Jedid*, but opposition was so fierce that he was deposed. Mahmud II (r. 1808-39) had better luck. Not only had he stocked the upper reaches of the Ottoman administration before moving, Mahmud "went out of his way to forestall accusations of infidel innovations. The instructors were to be Muslims, members of the ulema were to be attached to each company to conduct daily prayers and to act as religious commissars, and the ordinance was accompanied by a *fetva*...to the effect that the reform was in accordance with the *Shari`a*."[433] The hidebound Janissaries revolted nonetheless. But by then they were so unpopular, and Mahmud's preparations so complete, that troops loyal to him killed thousands of Janissaries and eradicated them as a threat. "The way was clear for the establishment of a new, European-style Ottoman army with all the momentous consequences of that innovation."[434]

Empire, 1453-1606," *The Journal of Interdisciplinary History*, Volume 18, Number 4: *The Origin and Prevention of Major Wars* (Spring, 1988), pp. 721-747. Specific info cited here is from pp. 730-731.

[432] Yapp, *The Making of the Modern Near East 1792-1923*, pp. 100-101.

[433] *Ibid.*, p. 104.

[434] *Ibid.*

Of course, the Europeans by that time had gone through the Napoleonic revolution in military affairs. Mass, national armies able to maneuver adroitly on the battlefield and force battle on an opponent, via strategic turning movements and mastery of interior lines, had become the norm, thanks to General Bonaparte. In effect, combat persisting strategy had gained the upper hand over the logistical persisting kind—at least when conventional armies fought one another.[435] The Ottomans in the late 18th century, even before the European quantum leap in power due to Napoleonic tactics and strategy, had begun suffering military defeats, and for the first time, losses of Muslim territory, to the Russians.[436] The ease with which Napoleon's relatively small force defeated Ottoman troops in Egypt in 1798 made the need for Istanbul to update its military all the more obvious—and pressing. Hence the attempted reforms of Selim III, and the successful ones of Mahmud II.

Bu this did not happen overnight. Ottoman troops fared poorly against those of Muhammad Ali's Egyptian ones in the 1830s. It would take a further revamping under Sultan Abdulmejid I (r. 1839-1861) to bring Ottoman forces closer to par with European ones. His Tanzimat reforms, mentioned previously in terms of their

---

[435] As per Jones, *The Art of War*, pp. 320-386, as well as Larry H. Addington, *The Patterns of War Since the Eighteenth Century, Second Edition* (Bloomington and Indianapolis: Indiana University Press, 1994), pp. 1-7, 29-42.

[436] Epitomized by the humiliating 1774 Treaty of Küçük Kaynarca, in which the Ottomans lost Crimea to the Russian Empire. See Bernard Lewis, *What Went Wrong? Western Impact and Middle Eastern Response* (Oxford: Oxford University Press, 2002), pp. 21-23.

legal and educational aspects, began with the military. The army was increased, via conscription, to about 300,000 men, which size was about the same as European armies of the time.[437] The Ottomans, by the late 19th century, had procured rifles in lieu of muskets for their soldiers, as well—to include American Winchesters,[438] British Peabody-Martinis[439] and, eventually, German Mausers.[440] In terms of how these revamped forces were utilized: "*nizami* corps were more frequently used to preserve and extend the reach of central government than to wage warfare against European adversaries...."[441] Or, to put it another way, "the army became the agency for the subjection of unruly groups, for the pushing back of the bedouin by the re-establishment of a fortified eastern defence line and for the socialization of large parts of the population, especially through service in other parts of the empire."[442]

Of course, the Ottoman army was also "the agency for the subjection of unruly groups" centuries earlier. It was certainly used as such against both unmanageable Sufis and Celalis. The available

---

[437] Yapp, *The Making of the Modern Near East*, p. 109.

[438] See "M1866 Turkish Contract Winchester (.44 Henry Rimfire)," *militaryrifles.com/turkey*; accessed July 7, 2020.

[439] As per "M1874 Turkish Peabody-Martini," *militaryrifles.com/turkey*, accessed July 7, 2020.

[440] See "The Ottoman Empire Page 13—Weapons of the Ottoman Army," *nzhistory.govt.nz/war/ottoman-empire/weapons-of-the-ottoman-empire*; accessed July 7, 2020.

[441] Amira K. Bennison, "The 'New Order' and Islamic Order: the Introduction of the *Nizami* Army in the Western Maghrib and its Legitimation, 1830-73," *International Journal of Middle East Studies*, Volume 36, Number 4 (November 2004), pp. 591-612. Specific quote is from p. 591.

[442] Yapp, *The Making of the Modern Near East*, p. 134.

data suggest that the congeries of armed Sufi movements in early Ottoman history pursued mainly a combat raiding strategy which relied on the sympathy of the population of the consolidating Empire (especially in peripheral areas)—or at least on the unpopularity of the Ottoman sultans among newly-conquered peoples, as well as among heterodox Islamic groups. By the 16th and 17th centuries, these insurgents would have probably added a logistical raiding dimension as, for example, when the kizilbaş were empowered by outside help from the Safavid Empire. However, in neither time frame, nor via either approach, were these movements able to convince the Ottoman state to give up its opposition, much less to abandon any territory. So the Ottomans won. Working backwards from that, we can surmise that they operated from secure base areas with a combat strategy. This most likely commenced with a relatively low force to space ratio of government forces, which would have allowed the raiders (guerrillas) to survive by retreating until they could concentrate against weakness. Eventually, and especially after provoked by the overt assistance which their rival Safavids were providing, the Ottomans would have increased the forces in theater, making the force to space ratio support a persisting as well as a combat strategy. This would have included, in particular, interdicting rebel religious groups' lines of communication and resupply with Iran to the east. Increased Ottoman force to space ratio would have also permitted counter-raids to smoke out and defeat or kill the enemy. Backing for the Ottoman state likely would have increased after its ringing victory over the Safavids at Chaldiran, which would have made the Sultan the strong horse—even if he was, from the insurgent Sufi and Shi`i perspective, the wrong brand of Islam. This strategy enabled Ottoman victory over these Sufi and quasi-Shi`i raiders, across time and, to some degree, space.

The Celalis were rather different from these previous mystical marauders. In a very real sense, they can be classified not as guerrillas or raiders at all, but rather "`rambunctious clients' of the center."[443] They accepted the Ottoman state's authority—they simply wanted a bigger piece of the action. Placing them in the guerrilla/raider category is also precluded to some degree by the fact that the Celalis often operated as criminal gangs, or simply bandits. These gangs consisted of not just of "demobilized mercenaries" but also disenfranchised tax collectors, demoralized laborers and farmers, and jobless clerics—many of whom got their hands on the newly plentiful firearms flooding into the Empire[444] and decided to, in effect, raise some hell in order to win concessions from Istanbul. Celalis did at times take over certain towns and redirect the tax revenues to their own use; the culmination of this approach was the Celali leader Abdülhalim's temporary "secession "of a part of east central Anatolia. This might fall into the category of a logistical

---

[443] Caglar Keyder, Review of *Bandits and Bureaucrats: the Ottoman Route to State Centralization*, by Karen Barkey, *American Journal of Sociology*, Volume 101, Number 1 (July 1995), pp. 249-251. Specific quote is from p. 250.
[444] *Ibid.*, p. 250.

persisting strategy, under which government resources were redirected. But there was little effort, or even desire, to make this situation permanent. Still, some Celalis did take up arms against the state, particularly under Abdülhalim and his brother Deli Hasan. Thus while perhaps not technically guerrillas/raiders, the Ottomans responded as if they were, with a two-pronged strategy: a combat persisting aspect, which invaded the Celali base areas and besieged them, coupled with a logistical persisting one of re-redirecting tax revenues to Istanbul while also working for political reconciliation by co-opting bandit leadership into imperial administration. This approach ultimately succeeded.

The Kadizadelis were definitely a threat to the Ottoman Empire—just not a serious military one. This movement is really *sui generis* compared to all the other ones examined herein.[445] If the Celalis were rambunctious clients, the Kadizadelis might be termed "unruly moralizers." As explained earlier, these Ottoman fundamentalists hoped to change the Islamic nature of the Empire, and "were marked by a willingness to use force against their opponents when deemed necessary."[446] But they mostly ran, in a sense, temporarily successful influence operations in Topkapı Palace,

---

[445] Yes, the Kadizadeli movement greatly resembles—if not presages—the Wahhabi one. But the latter mounted armed rebellion against the Sultan(s) as well as derided his Islamic credentials; the former did neither of those.

[446] As per James Muhammad Dawud Currie, "Kadizadeli Ottoman Scholarship, Muhammad Ibn `Abd al-Wahhab, and the Rise of the Saudi State," *Journal of Islamic Studies*, Volume 26, Issue 3 (September 2015), pp. 265-288. Specific quote is from p. 265.

especially during the reign of Sultan Murad IV (r. 1623-1640). This was during the lifetime of the group's founder, Kadizade Mehmed. Later, in the time of Mehmed IV (r. 1648-1687), the Kadizadelis were led by an Arab scholar, Muhammad b. Ahmad al-Ustuwani, or Ustuvani in Turkish. He been appointed preacher to the Palace troops, as well as the personal tutor of the young Sultan, and under him the Kadizadelis "set about implementing a plan for complete reform.[447] Their vision was to…eliminate all religious innovations that had appeared since the beginning of Islam and to destroy Sufi lodges, forcing their opponents to renew their faith or face death. Kadizadelis gathered in the vicinity of the Fatih Mosque with weapons, ready for action and calling the people to rally to arms. Grand Vizier Köprülü Mehmed convened a meeting of scholars who judged the incitements of the Kadizadelis punishable by death."[448] The Vizier had them rounded up, but not executed. Instead, he exiled them to Cyprus, whence Ustuvani eventually made his way back to Damascus and lived the final five years of his life.[449] More violence, against Christians and Jews, broke out in the 1660s.[450] The final influential Kadizadeli was Sayyid Vani Mehmed Efendi. His friendship with Grand Vizier Köprülü Fazıl Ahmed allowed him access to Sultan Mehmed IV, as well as secured for him the position of head preacher to the Ottoman army for the 1683 attack on

---

[447] This was in 1656 as per Currie, p. 271.
[448] *Ibid.*
[449] *Ibid.*
[450] Barkey, *Empire of Difference*, p. 184.

Vienna—which poor results have already been noted. Vani was exiled to Bursa and died a few years later as, for the most part, did the Kadizadeli movement in Istanbul.

This movement did not rise to the level of that of guerrillas/raiders. One might say the Kadizadelis practiced "vigilante terrorism"[451] when they did not think the Ottoman establishment was sufficiently supportive of their Islamic retrenchment agenda. So in this case the combat/logistic and raiding/persisting paradigm does not apply. What does pertain is the political-religious component, both from the Kadizadeli and the Ottoman state side. The retrenchers despised (Sufi, especially Bektaşi) religious innovations, and at the top of their hate list was the mystics' turning the graves of their deceased holy men into shrines. Kadizade Mehmed preached vehemently against such practices. His successor Ustuvani "was willing to use state-endorsed violence to enforce that position."[452] And his heir, Vani, "managed to persuade the Sultan to forbid Sufi dancing rituals"[453] in addition to visiting shrines and, as noted in chapter two, the practice of some in the Ottoman military to sexually exploit young boys.

So when out of power, the Kadizadelis agitated and acted as a 17th century, Islamic version of Antifa. When they had access to, and

---

[451] As per Gérard Chaliand and Arnaud Blin, "Introduction," *The History of Terrorism From Antiquity to ISIS*, Chaliand and Blin, eds. (Oakland: University of California Press, 2016). P. 17.

[452] Currie, p. 271.

[453] *Ibid.*, p. 273.

influence upon, Ottoman leadership they prevailed upon the government to enforce their preferred policies.

Ottoman kinetic responses to the Kadizadelis when they were an out group took the form of police action: arrest, imprisonment and exile—and only sometimes death. The Ottoman reactive agenda of *toleration*, *assimilation*, *persecution* and *expulsion* was thus applied to the Kadizadelis more than to any other movement examined herein—the main reason being that its epicenter and stage of activity was almost exclusively the imperial capital. There was one major exception. In 1711 one al-Rumi[454] sparked a Kadizadelisque uprising in Cairo, demanding an end to Sufi meetings and shrine visitation, converting their meeting houses to Qur'anic schools, and in general "enjoining the right and forbidding the wrong"[455]— according to his fundamentalist Islamic perspective, that is. Perhaps as many as 1,000 Ottoman soldiers supported him. The Ottomans had to send more troops[456] to crush this serious, if short-lived and localized, rebellion.[457]

Other than this one-off example of a combat raiding strategy, the Ottomans responded to Kadizadelis mainly with religio-political refutation. The main example of this comes from Damascus, which was in many ways the second city of the Empire

---

[454] No relation to the famous 13th century mystic Jalal al-Din Muhammad Rumi (d. 1273).

[455] Currie, p. 278.

[456] Whether from other parts of Egypt or from further abroad is not clear.

[457] Currie, p. 279.

and, most relevantly here, had been the home of Ustuvani both before and after his (in)famous interlude in Istanbul. A Damascene Naqshbandi shaykh and scholar, Abd al-Ghani al-Nabulusi (d. 1731), wrote several works aimed at countering Kadizadeli beliefs and practices in which he defended "music, Sufi whirling, and smoking tobacco, as well as...the doctrine of *wahdat al-wujud*."[458] He also staunchly defended visiting graves of holy Muslims, pointing out that they can do miracles even after death for those who seek their help. Al-Nabulusi was thus engaging in anti-Kadizadeli information operations, even if the Ottoman leadership had not formally requested it. "The Ottomans, by this late state, had largely adopted the opinions of those opposed to the Kadizadeli movement, such as al-Nabulusi, and were spreading such opinions all over the Muslim world via their influence over the hajj pilgrimage. This would lead to a prolonged conflict between the post-Kadizadeli Ottomans and the Saudis...."[459]

As we shall see, the Wahhabis have much in common with the Kadizadelis. But first we must examine the Druze, and then the Zaydi, uprisings. The Druze ones were on the other end of the spectrum from Kadizadeli agitation. The Druzes mainly resented Ottoman (over)taxation and perceived preference for Maronite Christians, as well as interference in their internal, sectarian affairs.

---

[458] *Ibid.*, p. 276. Wahdat al-wujud means "unity of being" and has been a key concept of Sufism going back to Ibn `Arabi (d. 1240).
[459] Currie, p. 284.

The fact that their rulers were Sunni Muslims was a complicating, but not causative, factor in the revolts. Druzes can be classified as guerrillas, since they were comprised of irregular, indigenous personnel engaged in paramilitary operations. Thus, as raiders fighting the larger Ottoman army, they made good use of the Levantine terrain, had multiple secure bases, and enjoyed the support of a sympathetic population—which at times grew to include not just their own sect but, at times, Shi`is. Druze goals of convincing the Ottomans to leave them alone met with sporadic success, but they never convinced their overlords to depart their lands. The Druze depredations against Maronite Christians, which triggered long-term French intervention, did that.

Ottoman responses were primarily kinetic. The Empire utilized both combat and logistical strategies, in both raiding and persisting modes. Most likely Ottoman forces deployed against the Druzes would have come from Damascus, as that was not only the major city of the Arab provinces, but by the late 19th century the location of one of the three major Ottoman army corps in Arab lands, along with Mesopotamia and Arabia-Yemen.[460] We can assume the Ottomans operated from secure base areas in Syria, except perhaps in the early 16th century following the Empire's conquest of the rival Mamluk Sultanate in Egypt—a period in which the Turks would have been consolidating their power over former

---

[460] See "Ottoman Army (1861-1922)," *Wikipedia*, accessed July 9, 2020.

Mamluk domains, both in terms of territory and recruitment of warlords to the new dispensation, as with the aforementioned Janbirdi al-Ghazali and Muhammad b. al-Hanash. Remember, too, that outside Christian powers—Venice and Tuscany in the 16th and 17th centuries, France in the 19th—stirred the Druze pot against the Ottomans, to include providing weapons. In the earlier phases of Druze resistance, with the Ottomans' base areas being vulnerable (at least to warlords who been appointed governors repudiating their allegiance to the Ottoman Sultan), imperial forces seem to have utilized primarily a persisting strategy against the Druze raiders. And since the Ottomans, then, had a relatively low force to space ratio in the Levant, the logistic side of their COIN aimed at gradual conquest of rebellious villages, while the combat side, lacking sufficient forces to impose Ottoman will, simply encouraged Druze raids and sometimes defeat of state forces. The Ottomans changed the calculus in 1585 when they greatly increased their force to space ratio, thereby enabling their pursuit to overcome Druze retreats and defeat them, after which the successful state combat strategy allowed the Ottomans to confiscate muskets and demand and receive in arrears taxes. For good measure they beheaded many Druzes—a politically intimidating impact, indeed. In terms of logistic persisting approach, Istanbul also took steps to cut off foreign support, as by seizing the staging area of Cyprus. This contained the Druzes in the 16th century. In the 17th, the Ottomans, even staging from (more) secure base areas and with a higher force to space ratio, preferred political co-optation to kinetic operations—as by appointing Fakhr al-Din governor of Beirut and Sidon. But after he intrigued with European Catholics, the Empire captured and executed him. This might be termed a micro-, or targeted-combat strategy. Istanbul followed this up, not with another massive military incursion, but administrative reform, putting Druze areas under direct imperial control. This logistic persisting strategy allowed some degree of political (re)conciliation, which held until the early 19th century.

The stability was broken in the 1830s by Maronite aggrandizement and Egyptian invasion. Both of these re-inflamed Druze resentment, as they allied with Twelver Shi`is and even some Sunnis to attack the Christians starting in 1858 in Lebanon. Some Ottoman units refused orders to put down the Druzes, more for socioeconomic than religious or political reasons: Istanbul was notoriously poor at paying provincial soldiers on time, and joining the Druze in looting wealthy Maronite estates was appealing. Some Druze and Shi`i forces attacked Ottoman garrisons that did not support them. The Ottomans, even if they had not been preoccupied with wars and rumors of wars in their Balkan domains, lacked the force to space ratio necessary to put down thousands of raiding/guerrilla Druzes and Shi`is not just in Lebanon but even in Damascus. So, as noted, the French intervened to stop the Druze slaughter of Maronite Christians. They also prevailed upon the Ottomans to create the autonomous subdistrict of Mount Lebanon.

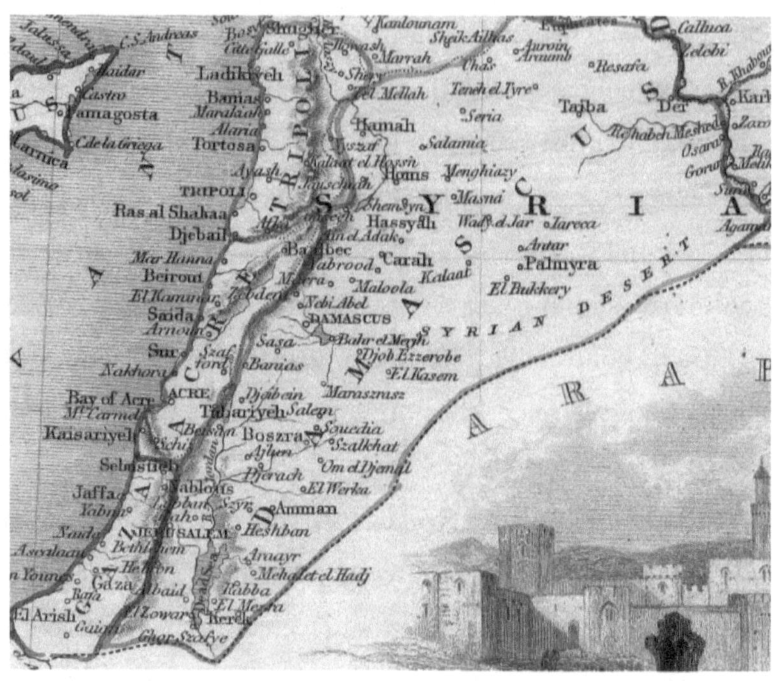

Ottoman Syria, c. 1851 [461]

In the final Druze uprising of 1909-1910, the Empire avoided the mistakes of 50 years earlier. The Ottomans went through the motions of negotiation, then straight to a combat raiding strategy, taking the fight into the heart of the rebellion in *Suveydiye* or, in Arabic, *al-Suwayda*. Fortunately for the Empire, the Ottoman 74th Infantry Regiment was already stationed there, part of the 25th Infantry Division from nearby Dera.[462] But Istanbul sent

---

[461] "1851 map showing the southern Eyalets of Ottoman Syria—Damascus, Tripoli, Acre and Gaza," *Wikipedia*; accessed August 5, 2020.

[462] Both of these units fell under the Ottoman VIII Corps in Damascus. See "VIII Corps (Ottoman Empire)," *Wikipedia*; accessed July 9, 2020.

another 35 battalions anyway.[463] With a predominant force to space ratio,[464] imperial forces killed thousands of Druzes and conscripted at least that many more. They also, once again, appropriated Druze small arms, this time as many as 10,000. Then World War I broke out, after which the Druzes would be a guerrilla headache for the French, instead.

The most protracted and bloody Ottoman counterinsurgency was fought against the Zaydis of Yemen, albeit in two different time frames. As observed earlier, the Zaydis most closely fit the modern definition of guerrillas or, in a military history "Jonesian" sense, raiders. But somewhat different factors were at play during the two distinct phases of Ottoman occupation. The mid-16th century back-and-forth[465] in southwest Arabia was like, and yet unlike, that of the 19th and early 20th centuries.[466] In both periods, the Zaydis and their allies employed both combat and logistic strategies against the government forces (although more the

---

[463] See "Hauran Druze Rebellion," *Wikipedia*; accessed July 9, 2020.

[464] The exact size of an Ottoman battalion is hard to pin down. But, reflecting European structure and organizations, it would have consisted of at least 300, and as many as 800, men. So the Ottoman expeditionary force would have numbered at least 10,500, and possibly as many as 28,000, troops.

[465] I rely here heavily upon the following two sources: J. Richard Blackburn, "The Collapse of Ottoman Authority in Yemen, 968/1560-976/1568," *Die Welt des Islams*, New Series, Volume 19, Issue 1/4 (1979), pp. 119-176; and Clive K. Smith, "Kawkaban, the Key to Sinan Pasha's Campaign in the Yemen (March 1569-March 1571)," *Proceedings for the Seminar of Arabian Studies, Volume 32, Papers for the 35th Meeting of the Seminar for Arabian Studies held in Edinburgh, 19-21 July 2001* (2002), pp. 287-294.

[466] The key source here is John Baldry, "Al-Yaman and the Turkish Occupation 1849-1914," *Arabica*, T23, Fasc. 2 (June 1976), pp. 156-196.

former than the latter in the 16th century); exploited the terrain, with which they were much more familiar; operated from secure bases, particularly in the Yemeni highlands; and for the most part, relied on the support of a sympathetic population. Also, in both the 16th/17th and 19th/early 20th centuries, the raiding guerrillas successfully decreased the amount of territory the Ottomans held, and ultimately convinced them to not just abandon their counter-insurgent operations—but to depart Yemen entirely. On the Ottoman side, in their two occupation periods imperial forces at time operated from both secure and vulnerable bases, depending on the situation. Likewise, the Empire employed both combat and logistic/persisting and raiding strategies, with varying degrees of success depending, in large measure, on the competence of its commanders and administrators in theater at the time. Since considerable historical data is available for insurgency and counterinsurgency in Yemen, it's possible to look at specific campaigns and take a more granular perspective on these matters in southwestern Arabia.

The Ottomans inherited the rule of Yemen, `Asir and the entire Hijaz from the Mamluks of Egypt when the former conquered the latter in 1517. But they didn't exert effective control for some decades. In 1552 the Zaydi Imam al-Din Yahya was made sancakbey of Yemen in return for recognizing Sultan Süleyman as his overlord. Under the competent rule of Özdemir Paşa, "towns were garrisoned with Ottoman gendarmes, pacts were made with tribal leaders, good relations were fostered with non-Zaydi communities, such as the Sunnis and Isma'ilis, the main routes of communication were rendered secure, and fortresses were built or restored...."[467] Yemen became a revenue-producing eyalet, especially via the spice trade.[468] But then the Empire's leading men there then chose poorly in terms of policies, starting with Mahmud Paşa's tenure as governor in 1561. He debased the silver currency, which reduced the value of the Ottoman troops' pay and causing many of them to extort and rob the Yemeni population, and some to desert.[469] Mahmud managed to get himself kicked upstairs, to the governorship of Egypt, and was replaced by Ridvan Paşa. The latter not only raised taxes but imposed them on previously exempt groups such as the Isma'ilis—destroying their loyalty to the Ottomans and driving them into a tacit alliance with the Zaydis.[470] Istanbul also decided, about the same time, to divide the country into two administrative districts, which allowed the new Zaydi Imam, al-Mutahhar (d. 1572)—who had resumed the jihad against the Ottomans in 1556—also to play the two off against one another.

Imam al-Mutahhar employed all four modes of guerrilla warfare against imperial forces and concentrations. His forces took Sa`dah, in the northern highlands, first. Then he "positioned armies to cover Amran and San`a, the only two significant bases of Ottoman armed strength in the northern highlands."[471] When

---

[467] Blackburn, p. 121.
[468] *Ibid.*, pp. 136-37.
[469] *Ibid.*, pp. 125-26.
[470] *Ibid.*, pp. 133-34.

imperial forces moved to retake Sa`dah, the Zaydis routed them. His combat raiding strategy having succeeded, the Imam turned to a persisting one such that the Zaydis more or less came to control all of the north and west of the country. Ridvan Paşa then had no choice but to negotiate with al-Mutahhar, accepting Zaydi power in those areas. The Imam wisely left San`a in Ottoman hands, as he did not want to risk antagonizing the Ottomans into sending reinforcements from Egypt.[472] That would have increased imperial force to space ratio and probably greatly lowered Zaydi prospects. By leaving it alone, the Imam could also plausibly claim that he was still loyal to the Sultan. But when Süleyman died in 1566, and Ridvan was recalled the following year, the Zaydi leader considered his deal with the Ottomans a dead letter, and set out to take over all of Yemen—not seemingly a hard task, as the Empire's held only the capital and a few smaller garrisons at that point.[473]

The Ottomans initially took the power and charisma of the Zaydi Imams far too lightly, seeing the sect in general and its leader in particular simply as heretical Muslims and ragtag tribes. The Egyptians would make much the same mistake in the 1960s, when they sent 70,000 troops to shore up the pro-Soviet Republic of Yemen forces against the Imamic royalist forces. "A major miscalculation in Egypt's decision to intervene was its

---

[471] *Ibid.*, p. 141.
[472] *Ibid.*, pp. 146-47.
[473] *Ibid.*, pp. 150-52.

underestimation of the Imam's strength in the fiercely loyal Zaydi tribes of the mountainous north."[474] The Zaydi Imam in any age is a larger-than-life figure to his people, and "government [is] a matter of the personal achievement of the imam as hero."[475] There are, however, in Fiver Shi`ism two distinct types of Imams: the *sabiq* (predecessor) and the *muhtasib* (accountable). "The first wage wars, levy taxes, defend the community by the sword and therefore hold Friday prayers; the second administer religious law and refrain from holding Friday prayers."[476] It's not hard to imagine which type of Imam showed up more often during Ottoman occupation. Al-Mutahhar was most certainly of the first persuasion.

---

[474] A.I. Dawisha, "Intervention in the Yemen: An Analysis of Egyptian Perceptions and Policies," *Middle East Journal*, Volume 29, Number 1 (Winter, 1975), pp. 47-63. Specific quote is from p. 49. Ironically, considering the current situation in southwestern Arabia, in which the Zaydi Huthis (Houthis) are fighting the Kingdom of Saudi Arabia with Iranian support, in the 1960s the Saudis supported the Zaydis over against the Egyptian- and Soviet-backed San`a government.

[475] Khuri, *Imams and Emirs*, p. 113.

[476] *Ibid.*, p. 122.

"Yemen, Excluding ʾAsir." [477]

Much as he had done in his first campaign, the Imam divided his considerable forces (numbering 10-15,000) into two cohorts, in order to deal with any Ottoman troops disembarking at al-Hudaydah on the coast and marching to relieve their garrison at San`a. When an Ottoman force of 1700 then did exactly as he

---

[477] From Baldry, p. 157.

expected, Zaydi cavalry routed it. This shows that at this time the rebels, in fact, enjoyed a superior force to space ratio over the occupiers. This victory, in turn, won the Imam more support from the tribes, now in the south as well—thereby increasing his margin of superiority in forces. The Zaydis then took the Ottoman garrisons at Ibb and Jublah (or Jiblah)—although putting to the sword the surrendering imperial soldiers, even after offering them terms. The loss of these towns further threatened Ottoman lines of communication and also encouraged yet more tribes to rise in revolt.[478] So al-Mutahhar had begun pursuing not simply a combat raiding strategy, but a combat and logistic persisting one, with multiple objectives of political intimidation of his enemies coupled with winning even more popular support; interdicting Ottoman lines of communication and maneuver; and reducing the amount of territory under imperial control. The Imam ramped up his program of political intimidation when in 1567 his forces routed an Ottoman force retreating to Ta`izz , captured the Ottoman governor, Murad Paşa—and beheaded him. His men sent the head to the Imam, who then flourished it before the walls of besieged San`a, helping persuade the Ottomans there to surrender in August 1567.[479]

The new Ottoman beylerbeyi, Urus Hasan Paşa, just made matters worse—which should come as no surprise. Disembarking with fresh troops, he set up shop in Zabid and immediately imposed

---

[478] This aforementioned data largely comes from Blackburn, pp. 152-56.
[479] *Ibid.*, pp. 159-60.

new taxes on sympathetic Sunnis; he also had the nasty habit of executing wealthy Yemenis on trumped-up charges in order to seize their assets. Militarily Hasan was also clueless. He refused to send any relief to the garrison at Ta`izz, which was then forced to surrender. The Zaydis then also took `Adan (Aden).[480] "By this time, probably later in 975/early 1568, al-Mutahhar had gained control of both the highlands and the northern *tihamah*,[481] either directly by…his own occupying forces or through…alliances with local leaders."[482] The Zaydi jihad against the Ottomans had to this point exhibited every aspect of guerrilla/raider warfare: skillful use of the terrain, staging from multiple bases, exploiting and drawing energy from the sympathetic population. This holy war had also greatly decreased Ottoman-controlled territory. But it had not eliminated it. Nor, most importantly, had the Zaydis yet convinced the Empire to abandon its claims in Yemen.

By the following spring al-Mutahhar, operating from his superior tactical and strategic situation, was planning on doing just that by expelling the Ottomans entirely from southwest Arabia. But Istanbul had other ideas. Having received, finally, accurate intelligence reports and assessment of the situation on the ground in Yemen—the false and duplicitous ones sent by the late Mahmud Paşa having finally been recognized for what they were, and cleared

---

[480] *Ibid.*, pp. 161-64.

[481] This is the Red Sea coastal area. *In toto* it includes not just Yemen but extends along the entire western length of Arabia.

[482] Blackburn, p. 166.

out of the imperial inbasket—the Empire sent Osman Paşa with another large expeditionary force from Egypt. He was also granted the rank of beyberreyli of San`a. His forces reached Zabid, and al-Mutahhar ordered the local Zaydi commander, Ibn al-Shawi, to interdict Ottoman lines of communication and resupply but not to attack the town. He ignored these instructions, however—and saw his forces cut to pieces by Ottoman artillery.[483] Osman had a short tenure in Yemen, pulled out and pushed aside by the more powerful, and even more competent, governor of Egypt: Sinan Paşa.[484] Sinan led thousands of newly-arrived Ottoman troops in Yemen, starting in late 1568, and "over the next year and a half Ottoman Yemen was largely reorganized"[485]—and reconquered.

Probably the most important aspect of Sinan Paşa's campaign of reconquest in Yemen was his successful siege of the Zaydi fortress at Kawkaban, northwest of San`a. His initial "blitzkrieg"[486] defeated the Zaydis in several battles but then stalled out. He then decided to try and take Kawkaban, both because of its strategic location and in the hopes that its commander Muhammad b. Shams al-Din, whose father had been an Ottoman sanjackbey, might resume loyalty to the Empire. Sinan also saw his prospects as

---

[483] Blackburn, p. 169.

[484] See "Koca Sinan Pasha," *Wikipedia*; accessed July 15, 2020. A highly-competent Ottoman official, from Albania, he not only served in Egypt and Yemen but led imperial forces against the Safavids and would eventually serve as Grand Vizier a total of five times.

[485] Blackburn, p. 171.

[486] Smith, p. 287.

good since many Isma'ilis had resumed their Ottoman allegiance.[487] Kawkaban, however, was a mountainside fortress and considered impregnable. Throughout the Ottoman siege, Zaydi tribesmen would raid their lines in hit-and-run attacks, "which infuriated the Turks whose training and superiority in weapons demanded space for pitched battle."[488] The Ottoman forces besieging Kawkaban had not just muskets, but also *darbuzan* (culverins, or hand-held cannons) as well as larger cannons. But they only had about 2,000 troops. Imam al-Mutahhar had perhaps 9,000 he could deploy to harass them, although less than half had muskets, the rest equipped with spears.[489] Eventually the siege proved too much for the garrison—especially when its commander accepted Sinan Paşa's offer of the same position his father had held. The Imam also came to terms with the Ottomans some time later. He agreed to stop the jihad in return for being granted his former autonomy over northern Yemen. So Sinan "had not defeated Mutahhar in the terms in which had been sent...he had simply renewed his earlier authority; and he had certainly failed to send [Mutahhar's] decapitated head to Istanbul...,"[490] as the Sultan probably expected. Nonetheless, Sinan made it appear a huge victory to Selim II, eager for any good news after the massive Ottoman naval defeat at Lepanto in 1571. And Istanbul's new man

---

[487] *Ibid.*, pp. 287-89.
[488] *Ibid.*, p. 289.
[489] *Ibid.*, pp. 291-92.
[490] *Ibid.*, p. 293.

in Yemen had certainly saved Ottoman rule there from almost certain downfall.

For much of this time period the Ottomans were fighting counterinsurgency from vulnerable base areas. Only San`a and the port town of al-Hudaydah stayed secure from Zaydi conquest; the others were, at one time or another, taken by the rebels. When staging from fortified towns and areas which could repel guerrilla attacks, as during their first decades in Yemen and, again, after 1571, the Ottomans' low force to space ratio precluded an effective combat strategy and so they employed, rather, a logistic persisting ones: reliance on the garrisons; political deals with indigenous leaders to include the highest ranking, the Imam; and, most of all, a light taxation hand. When inept and inflammatory Ottoman administrators sparked the Zaydis and their allies to turn to a combat raiding strategy, imperial forces responded first with a combat raiding strategy of their own, as by sending fresh forces from al-Hudaydah into rebel-controlled territory around San`a. But the Ottomans found that their low force to space ratio gave the Zaydis the advantage, as when the latter defeated the San`a relief convoy and went on to take more towns. With a greater number of troops under both Paşas Osman and Sinan, however, the force to space ratio swung back in imperial favor and allowed them to engage in a combat strategy with both raiding and persisting elements. This included, for example, taking the Kawkaban fortress and the concomitant political impact of its commander switching sides, on the combat side. But it also included a logistic persisting aspect, via depriving the Zaydi forces of such bases and the political conciliation one of granting the Imam his former status. So in this mid-16th century phase of their first occupation, Ottoman counterinsurgency triumphed—if barely—over Zaydi guerrilla warfare/raiding.

Perhaps the most crucial facet of Ottoman success was that certain, shrewder Ottoman governors "had been at pains to exploit the religious factionalism that obtained there. Thus, the backing of groups traditionally opposed to the Zaydis, such as the Isma'ilis and Shafi`i [Sunni] orthodox Muslims…was actively sought, usually in return for tax exemptions or concessions"—thus "[i]t is almost inconceivable that al-Mutahhar could have mustered sufficient political strength to reduce the Ottomans to the extent he did, had he not received at least the tacit approval of those elements hitherto allied with his enemies."[491] Building on that policy pillar, Ottoman power in Yemen would last another six decades. It was finally undone, in this incarnation, by the resumption of the Zaydi jihad under Imam al-Mansur al-Qasim (d. 1620) and his son, al-Mu`ayyad Muhammad (d. 1644).[492] The latter adroitly used combat and logistic persisting strategies to defeat Ottoman forces and also to conquer Ottoman-controlled towns and territory, not just in the highlands but in the tihama. Ultimately, the 17th century Zaydi-led rebellion

---

[491] Blackburn, p. 173.

[492] See "al-Mu`ayyad Muhammad," *Wikipedia*, accessed July 16, 2020.

not only convinced the Empire to abandon its efforts to defeat them—it prevailed upon Istanbul to forsake Yemen entirely for two centuries. The Ottomans lacked the necessary force to space ratio to win at this point, because they were involved in titanic state wars with the rival Safavid Empire of Persia,[493] and thus could not spare sufficient forces for this far-flung provincial campaign.

Although the Ottomans were thereafter absent from Yemen for 200 years, "at no time did they abdicate their sovereign rights over the land….This was all the more compelling after the English began to intrude on the southern region…. This intrusion set the tone also for their return physically to the land to alleviate the fears of the custodians of the sacred shrines of Islam, who had suspected the foreign powers' motives even since the Portuguese invaded the Red Sea…."[494] So in 1849 Ottoman forces once again disembarked at al-Hudaydah, with the Imam al-Mutawakkil Muhammad initially agreeing to the Turks controlling the coastlines and San`a as long as he still held the highlands. But many of his men deserted him, violence broke out between them and Ottoman troops, and the Turkish commander Tevfik Paşa helped depose al-Mutawakkil in favor of the former Imam, al-Mansur Ali II.[495] `Asiri tribesmen also periodically attacked the Ottomans, who nonetheless maintained

---

[493] See "Ottoman-Safavid War (1603-1618)" and "Ottoman Safavid War (1623-1639)," both at *Wikipedia* and both accessed July 16, 2020.

[494] Farah, *The Sultan's Yemen*, p. 1. Also Baldry, p. 162.

[495] Baldry, p. 165; "Al-Mutawakkil Muhammad" and "Imams of Yemen," both *Wikipedia*; accessed July 16, 2020.

their garrison at al-Hudaydah, but control of not much else in Yemen, for several decades. Finally in 1870 Istanbul sent thousands more soldiers, giving them sufficient force to space ratio to undertake a successful combat raiding strategy into `Asir and to then plan a campaign in the Zaydi-dominated highlands the next year. The Ottomans felt secure enough to designate Yemen a vilayet, subdivided into four sancaks.[496] This marked the Ottoman turn to a combat and logistic persisting strategy, focusing on invading and occupying guerrilla base areas. Unlike in its first period of occupation, at this time the Ottomans' persisting approach involved a heavy dose of political conciliation: building roads and schools, recruiting indigenous army and police battalions,[497] appointing former rebels to administrative posts, eliminating corruption, reforming the legal code and even sending sons of Yemeni leaders to school in Istanbul.[498] However, as noted in chapter two, the Tanzimat-oriented derived schools and legal reforms--with their derivations, respectively, from Western science and Western-style legal concepts—alienated many Yemenis, who saw them as betrayals of Islam.

---

[496] For the preceding, see Baldry, pp. 165-168.

[497] "Using tribal levies, the Ottoman Turks created four battalions of gendarme and three cavalry regiments." Lt. Cdr. Youssef Aboul-Enein, "The Egyptian-Yemen War (1962-67): Egyptian Perspectives on Guerrilla Warfare," *The U.S. Army Professional Writing Collection* (January-February 2004), pp. 1-8.

[498] On the last, see Eugene L. Rogan, "Aşiret Mektebi: Abdülhamid II's School for Tribes (1892-1907)," *Journal of Middle East Studies*, Volume 28 (1996), pp. 83-107.

So the late 19th century Ottoman logistic persisting and ideological strategy backfired. The Zaydis rose, yet again, in rebellion, led by Yayha Hamid al-Din (d. 1904), this time joined by the Isma'ilis. Very much as they had done two centuries earlier, the anti-Ottoman guerrillas operated from secure bases in the northern highlands and relied on support from much of the population. So by 1891 the Ottomans were ejected from the highlands. They regrouped, under Feyzi Paşa, 1891-98, whom Istanbul put in command with even more troops at his disposal—perhaps as many as 43,000.[499] Brutal but effective, he used a combat raiding strategy that included, really for the first time for the Ottomans in southwestern Arabia, defense with a logistic strategy that included scorched earth policies. Feyzi also employed defense with a combat strategy, which succeeded at time because he could muster superior forces in space in the north and west of the country. San`a changed hands several times in this period. But as the 20th century opened, the revolts spread to the south and to the coastal plain. The Ottomans sent another 18,000 men in 1905,[500] bringing their in-theater total to well over 60,000. But they lost perhaps half of them to battle and disease. Thus the new governor, Hilmi Paşa, tried—once again—to win Yemeni hearts and minds by doubling down on reforms and infrastructure-building. This time Istanbul even agreed to pardoning rebels, freeing prisoners and forgiving tax debt.[501]

---

[499] Baldry, p. 175.
[500] *Ibid.*, p. 176.

Imam Yahya, who became the Zaydi leader in 1904, was having none of it. According to him, "the disturbances in Yemen were the result of misrule by Turkish officials: he demanded the abrogation of Turkish civil law and its substitution by the laws of Islam. He added that he was not against the Sultan but rather against the Turkish officials, owing to their abuse of power and the oppression of the poor."[502] By 1911 the Zaydis were coordinating attacks with the followers of Muhammad b. Ali al-Idrisi of `Asir, he of the Mahdist aspirations. This gave their combined forces the power to engage in not just combat raiding, but combat persisting, strategies against the Ottomans. The Empire did not give up however; it sent 20,000 more troops and began using its Red Sea naval forces to interdict arms being supplied, now, by the Italians.[503] This greatly increased force to space calculus gave the Ottomans the ability to employ an effective combat persisting strategy—thus forcing Imam Yahya to the negotiating table. The end result was the Treaty of Da`an, under which the Ottomans finally agreed to stop fighting the Zaydis in return for the Imam's pledge of loyalty to the Sultanate. He also received a yearly stipend from Istanbul, and the Ottomans were allowed to retain a token force in Yemen.[504] But for all intents and purposes, Ottoman attempts to dictate events in that country ceased. The Ottomans, during this second attempted takeover of Yemen,

---

[501] *Ibid.*, p. 179.
[502] *Ibid.*, p. 180.
[503] *Ibid.*, pp. 185-87.
[504] Yapp, *The Making of the Modern Near East, 1792-1923*, pp. 263, 264.

had episodically succeeded with a combat raiding and, less often, a combat persisting strategy. But in the long(er) run, their attempts at logistic raiding and persisting approaches failed, because their enemies simply enjoyed far too much support among the population—and Zaydi will to convince them to abandon their efforts and leave proved greater than the Ottoman determination to avoid either.

Running in some measure concurrently with its 19th century campaigns in Yemen, the Ottoman Empire was forced to deal with an Islamic rebellion in central Arabia: the Sa`udi Wahhabis.[505] The Ottomans responded to this movement differently than to the Zaydi one further south in the peninsula. Whereas in Yemen the Empire was involved first-hand in the two primary counterinsurgent registers—kinetic and ideological—in the Najd Istanbul, for the most part, delegated the former to its Egyptian proxy and only battled the Wahhabis directly in the latter frame. To briefly recap, the Wahhabi brand of fundamentalist Islam developed in the 18th century, was adopted by the Sa`udi leaders and tribe shortly thereafter, and by the early 19th century the powerful fusion of

---

[505] In addition to sources cited previously, the analysis here utilizes: Elizabeth Sirriyeh, "Wahhabis, Unbelievers and the Problems of Exclusivism," *Bulletin (British Society for Middle Eastern Studies)*, Volume 16, Number 2 (1989), pp. 123-132; M.J. Crawford, "Civil War, Foreign Intervention, and the Question of Political Legitimacy: A Nineteenth-Century Saudi Qadi's Dilemma," *International Journal of Middle East Studies*, Volume 14, Number 3 (August 1982), pp. 227-248; "Nejd Expedition,""Emirate of Nejd," and "Emirate of Diriyah," all from *Wikipedia*, all accessed July 16, 2020.

Sa`udi power and Wahhabi fervor was causing problems for the Ottomans. The Sa`udis so empowered began creating a territorial state, attacked Karbala and its Shi`is as well as Ottoman trade routes, robbed pilgrims going to Mecca and even took over that city at one point. "The Wahhabi/Saudi alliance expanded its power to the shores of the Persian Gulf and to the Hijaz and mounted raids into the Ottoman provinces of Iraq and Syria. The Wahhabis also interrupted the pilgrim caravan from Damascus."[506] So the Wahhabized Sa`udis utilized both combat and logistic strategies, in both raiding and persisting modes. Damaging Karbala's Twelver Shi`i shrines would have entailed attacking its Ottoman garrison, thus amounting to a combat and arguably logistic raid. Holding up religious travelers was logistic raiding. Conquering territory across the Arabian peninsula qualified as the quintessential combat and logistic persisting approach.

Lacking any real power base in the peninsula, and with Sultan Mahmud II threatened by potentially-rebellious Janissaries in the imperial center,[507] the Ottomans initially delegated dealing with the Wahhabized Sa`udis to Egypt, which under Muhammad Ali had been upgrading its military.[508] In 1811-13 Egyptian forces moved into the Hijaz, expelling the Wahhabis.[509] Four years later, the

---

[506] Yapp, *The Making of the Modern Near East*, pp. 174-75.

[507] The hangover from the failed attempts of Sultan III to create a "new order" army, which resulted in his deposition, as well as that of his successor, Mustafa IV. See Yapp, *The Making of the Modern Near East*, p. 102.

[508] See Ali A. Soliman and M. Mabrouk Kotb, "Egypt's Finances and Foreign Campaigns, 1810-1840," unpublished paper, n.d.; accessed July 17, 2020.

Egyptians undertook a more extensive anti-Wahhabi campaign. Its main thrust was the December 1817-September 1818 operation commanded by Muhammad Ali's son Ibrahim Paşa. In less than year he took 30,000 men into the heat of the Sa`udi territory, capturing half-a-dozen defended towns and finally besieging and taking the capital, al-Dir`iyah.[510] Many Wahhabi and Sa`udi leaders were sent as prisoners back to Istanbul, including the leading figure, Amir (Emir) Abd Allah b. Sa`ud—who was decapitated in the imperial capital, his detached head said to have tossed into the Bosporus. Egyptian forces remained in Najd for six more years, evacuated, then returned in 1837—finally leaving for good in 1840.[511]   In 1839 Egyptian forces pursued the Sa`udis to the shores of the Persian Gulf.[512] The main expedition, the 1817-18 one, was a classical example of combat raiding —if 30,000 men can be said to constitute a "raid"—which was followed up with a logistic raiding and persisting one: Ottoman Egyptian forces invaded guerrilla base areas with a force to space ratio sufficient for investing their fortresses, to include the rebels' primary political center, thus depriving the Wahhabi Sa`udis of supplies, bases of operation and, most importantly, political cachet. Depriving the Sa`udi leaders of their heads also undercut their authority.

---

[509] Yapp, *The Making of the Modern Near East*, p. 152.
[510] See "Nejd Expedition," and "Emirate of Diriyah."
[511] Yapp, *The Making of the Modern Near East*, p. 175.
[512] *Ibid.*, pp. 152-53.

But the Sa`udi leadership did not abandon its plans to carve out a state in Arabia, although in the next state-formation attempt the Wahhabized leadership was more modest in its territorial ambitions.[513]   Not willing to risk more Egyptian, or even direct Ottoman, intervention, the Wahhabi Sa`udis carefully avoided military actions that would force a heavy imperial kinetic hand. But it was still the case that "by their criticism of the laxities of [imperial] Muslim observance the Wahhabis constituted a challenge to orthodox Islam, and by their disregard of his claims they presented a challenge to the political legitimacy of the Ottoman sultan."[514] This second Sa`udi Wahhabi state is known as the Emirate of Najd/Nejd, and existed from 1824 till 1891. It was created in 1824 under the leadership of Turki b. Abd Allah b. Muhammad, one of Muhammad b. Sa`ud's grandsons, who led the (re)capture of Riyadh.[515] After Turki was killed by a political rival, his son Faysal b. Turk al-Sa`ud became the amir.   This is when Egyptian forces re-intervened, defeating the movement and dragging Faysal back to Cairo as a prisoner. The Egyptians then played amir-maker, putting Khalid b. Sa`ud, one of Muhammad b. Sa`ud's great-grandsons—who had lived for some years in exile in Egypt—in power in Riyadh, with a praetorian guard of Egyptian soldiers. In 1840 Muhammad Ali withdrew his soldiers, since he was then enmeshed in the fallout

---

[513] "Emirate of Nejd."
[514] Yapp, *The Making of the Modern Near East*, p. 175.
[515] "Emirate of Nejd."

from his failed attempt to overthrow the Ottoman Sultan. Faysal, meanwhile, had been released from imprisonment and made his way back to central Arabia and, with the assistance of the Rashidis, returned to power in Riyadh. He died in 1865, setting off a Wahhabi Sa`udi civil war between his sons: Abd Allah, Sa`ud b. Faysal b. Turki, and Muhammad.[516]

Besides fighting one another, the Wahhabi Sa`udis had to deal with the realm of Ibn Rashid, in the Jabal Shammar region. "This chieftaincy fielded an armed force that included tribal warriors, mercenaries and slaves, and it expanded beyond the immediate area of Ha'il to incorporate Jawf in the north and Qasim and Riyadh in the Najd. In 1891 the Rashidis captured Riydadh and forced the Saudis into exile; during the First World War they supported the Ottomans, and the Rashidi state came to an end in 1921 when Ibn Saud captured Ha'il."[517]

---

[516] For details, sometimes mind-numbing, see Crawford, *passim.*
[517] Joshua Teitelbaum, *The Rise and Fall of the Hashimite Kingdom of Arabia* (New York: New York University Press, 2001). That specific quote is from pp. 74, 75.

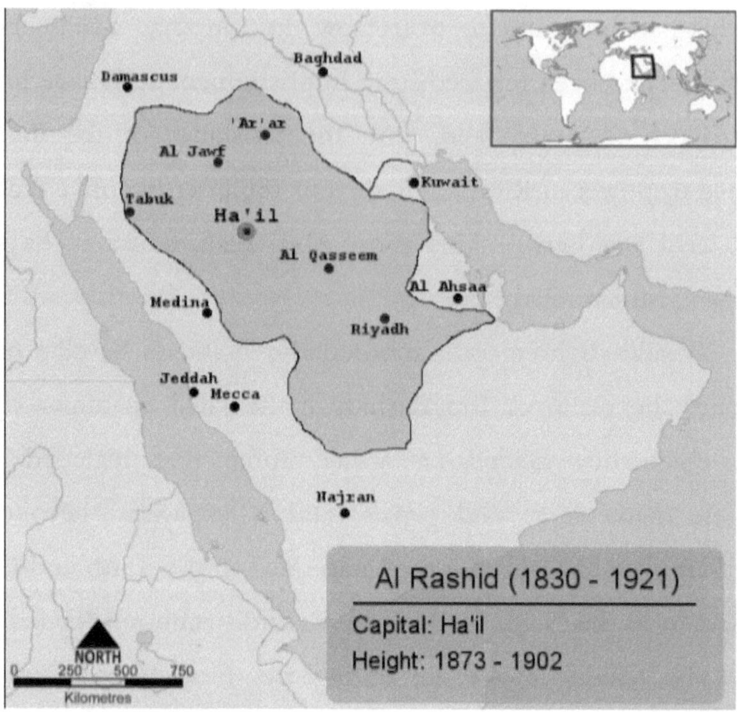

"Emirate of Jabal Shammar." [518]

The Rashidis were pro-Ottoman not just in World War I, but had been during the 19th century as well. So they served as imperial proxies in much the same way that the Egyptians had, albeit less powerfully. The Rashidis would push the Sa`udis out of their domains and into al-Ahsa/al-Hasa by 1891. Ironically, the only substantial Ottoman garrison outside the Hijaz (Mecca and Medina) was to be found here, after 1871. It numbered at various times

---

[518] Public Domain, from the *Wikipedia* page of the same name; accessed July 18, 2020.

between 600 and 1200 men.[519] At one point Abd Allah approached the Ottomans, asking for their help in the civil war against his brothers, particularly Sa`ud.[520] "Although `Abd Allah was regarded as more 'Wahhabi' than his brother, whom they would have been just as happy to help should he have been the one needing restoration, `Abd Allah was appointed *qa'im-maqam*[521] of Najd by imperial firman. In the spring and summer of 1288/1871, a Turkish expeditionary force under the command of Nafidh Pasha landed in al-Qatif....[522] They conquered al-Ahsa without encountering any substantial resistance.... `Abd Allah, who had been defeated by Saud....now arrived at al-Ahsa at the behest of the Ottomans."[523] A number of Wahhabi ulama, notably Shaykh `Abd al-Latif, the preeminent Wahhabi `alim, condemned `Abd Allah for seeking help from "unbelievers" with whom he had forged an "unholy alliance." The Shaykh "incited Saud to jihad, urged other `ulama' to encourage the inhabitants of their areas to wage Holy War, and threatened residents of al-Ahsa with jihad under Sa`ud. He made a specific point of declaring that when the enemy attacked the very territories of Islam jihad became a personal, as opposed to collective, duty."[524]

---

[519] The Ottomans referred to this eastern, Gulf coastal province, confusingly, as the "Najd Sancak," perhaps out of outmoded imperial intelligence—or wishful thinking. This is per the *Wikipedia* entry of that name; accessed July 18, 2020.

[520] Crawford, p.236.

[521] In Ottoman Turkish, correctly, *kaymakam*: "head official of a district" (per *New Redhouse Turkish-English Dictionary*, s.v. "kaymakam," p. 625).

[522] A major port on the Persian Gulf, south of Kuwait and north of Qatar.

[523] Crawford, p. 237.

[524] *Ibid.*, p. 238. Note that the enemy against whom `Abd al-Latif is declaring jihad

The Ottomans were singularly unimpressed, and while they either would, or could, not move further into central Arabia they did consolidate their grasp on al-Ahsa. And Sa`ud lacked the support or the resources to wage persistent insurgent warfare on the Empire's forces there. Drought and high prices also made any trading boycott on the Ottoman-held eastern coast quite unfeasible. Political conditions, too, favored the Empire at this point. "The conduct of Saud's supporters…in eastern Arabia had not endeared Saudi rule to local residents, and indeed, "the anarchical conditions of the Civil War supplied the Ottoman invaders with a propaganda weapon which they did not hesitate to use. Their campaign for support seems to have elicited a generally favourable response from settled elements…attracted by the Ottoman promise of just and stable government…. The fact that some `ulama' of eastern Arabia favoured the Ottomans must have reinforced…anxiety that the people of Najd might also be seduced from their allegiance to Saudi rule and the tenets of Wahhabism."[525]

In 1873 Sa`ud was forced out of Riyadh and moved to attack al-Ahsa, only to be rebuffed by a joint force of Ottoman troops and those loyal to Abd Allah. In the fall of that year, the Ottoman Empire then stepped up its level of involvement in Arabia: no less than the vali of Baghdad, and former Grand Vizier, Ahmed Şefik

---

is the staunchly Sunni Ottoman Empire. ISIS did not invent this approach of declaring other Muslims "infidels" against whom jihad should be directed.
[525] *Ibid.*, p. 239.

Midhat Paşa, arrived in region, heeding requests from eastern Arab notables. He proclaimed that the Ottomans were taking over direct control of Najd and al-Ahsa. Abd Allah and Muhammad b. Faysal fled back to Riyadh.[526] These two now resumed jockeying with Sa'ud for leadership of the rump Wahhabi Sa'udi domains. Then a new factor emerged a year later. Abd al-Rahman, youngest son of the late Imam Faysal (and father of Abd Al-Aziz, who would establish the Kingdom of Sa'udi Arabia), returned from Baghdad and led a failed uprising against the Ottomans. He then fled to Sa'ud in Riyadh, whereupon the latter died.[527] By 1876 the surviving brothers, including Abd al-Rahman, joined together to defeat Sa'ud's sons. But this second Sa'udi state, weakened by all the in-fighting, fell to the Ottoman-assisted Rashidi one, with the Wahhabi Sa'udis seeking refuge in Kuwait—whence they would return yet a third time.

The creation of the next Wahhabi Sa'udi state, which would transform into the Kingdom of Sa'udi Arabia, began in 1901 when Abd al-Aziz b. Abd al-Rahman al-Sa'ud—later simply Ibn Sa'ud— left Kuwait, supplied with horses and weapons from the amir there, to attack Riyadh.[528] He succeeded, and used that conquest as leverage for the ensuring battles with the Rashidis. Despite direct Ottoman military assistance, perhaps by as many as eight battalions

---

[526] *Ibid.*, pp. 239, 240.
[527] *Ibid.*, p. 240.
[528] See "Unification of Saudi Arabia," *Wikipedia;* accessed July 18, 2020.

of imperial soldiers,[529] the Sa`udi forces triumphed in all six major battles over the next five years.  In 1913 Ibn Sa`ud's men took the Ottoman garrison at al-Hofuf, in al-Ahsa. Thereafter he settled into a less bellicose policy vis-à-vis his titular overlords, which balanced Ottoman and British designs on the peninsula to his benefit—sauce for the goose, as the Empire had in no small measure been "maintaining control by playing off against each other the various claimants to power in Arabia."[530] In March 1914 the Ottomans and British agreed to a de facto partition of Arabia, wherein the northern two-thirds of the peninsula would be under Ottoman jurisdiction, the southern one-third under British.[531] Wahhabi Sa`udi-claimed territories, notably al-Hasa/al-Ahsa and Najd, were still theoretically Ottoman. "But this division, while it provided for an amicable settlement between the two principal powers, did not in itself affect the local powers of Arabia. Their relations with their suzerains were to be adjusted in dealings with them; all the agreement provided was that they could no longer play off one major power against another."[532] So the Sa`udi-Rashidi struggle for supremacy could go on. And, of course, eight months later the Ottomans would be embroiled in

---

[529] According to "Saudi-Rashidi War (1903-1907)," *Wikipedia*, accessed July 18, 2020.

[530] Yapp, *The Making of the Modern Near East*, p. 263.

[531] This was the so-called "Violet Line (1914), *Wikipedia*. The actual map can be seen here, "Pervez's Map Thread," *alternatehistory.com*. Both sources were accessed July 18, 2020.

[532] Yapp, *The Making of the Modern Near East*, p. 264.

World War I, and facing an entirely different problem in Arabia: the British-backed revolt of Sharif Husayn of Mecca.

Wahhabi Sa`udi strategies, and Ottoman counter-strategies, during the era of the first Sa`udi state have been examined already. Before moving on to an in-depth look at the ideological battle between the Arab fundamentalists and their Turkish rulers, we need to analyze the insurgency and counterinsurgency methodologies utilized during the second and third Wahhabi Sa`udi attempts to seize power. The second Wahhabi Sa`udi movement, 1824-91, was really more an aspiring guerrilla movement than an operative one. Recall that before they left for good in 1840, Egyptian forces were actually who put one Sa`udi leader in power—and left troops to safeguard his rule. Also, later Abd Allah requested, and received, direct Ottoman support. So it is questionable how "guerrilla" a movement can be when some of its leaders are being installed or propped up by the ostensible target regime. The few times that Wahhabi Sa`udi forces attacked imperial ones, they lost: Sa`ud in 1873, Abd al-Rahman shortly thereafter. Likewise, the state-aspiring rebels lacked the men, weaponry and military cohesion to successfully fight the Rashidis. So by the last decade of the 19th century the Wahhabized Sa`udi forces had had no success in their attempts at a combat raiding strategy against either the Ottomans or their proxies—much less any possible persisting strategy, whether combat or logistic. Both the Ottomans and the Rashidis could wage counterinsurgency from secure bases and, in regards to the former in particular after Ottoman reinforcement in 1873, with the ability to bring superior forces to bear in any possible battle space. Thus when either the imperial power or its surrogate engaged in combat raiding as defense, they were able to pursue and defeat Wahhabi Sa`udi forces. However, the Ottomans, secure in their eastern Arabian stronghold, relied more on a logistic raiding strategy while the Rashidis employed combat raiding and combat persisting intrusions into Wahhabi Sa`udi territory. The upshot was that the second Sa`udi state formation attempt failed, with the remnants of the movement seeking refuge in non-Ottoman-controlled Persian Gulf areas.

By the onset of the 20th century, just a few years later, the Wahhabi Sa`udis returned. Ibn Sa`ud's initial six-year campaign defeated the Rashidis and won for his people the territories of Najd and al-Qassim. The year before the start of World War I, he attacked the Ottomans directly and drove them from al-Hofuf. This added to the movement's control al-Hasa. These military actions, particularly the latter, can be defined as combat persisting strategy (taking territory) combined with a logistic persisting one (taking away the enemy's resources, forts, etc.). But they are also very close to constituting conventional warfare with territorial acquisition, as the Sa`udi state by this time had come to stay. The Ottomans, for their part, having lost their sole remaining relevant stronghold, abandoned their military efforts to bring the insurgents Wahhabis Sa`udis to heel. The Rashidis would survive until 1921, after which their state would be swept away, and their territories incorporated into the new Kingdom of Sa`udi Arabia. It turned out that the "ideological cohesion" provided by the Wahhabi brand of Sunni Islam proved more powerful than that afforded by the "Shammar-based Rashidi chieftaincy."[533] Overall, by the time of the third Sa`udi state, the situation really had passed out of the realm of intra-state insurgency and counterinsurgency and into that of inter-state warfare.

The ideological warfare in this conflict, on both the Wahhabi and Ottoman side, was intense. The Empire and its leadership did not take kindly to Wahhabi slurs against the state's Islamic credentials. Particularly in the first conflict, the Ottomans often dealt more viciously with Wahhabi clerics than with Sa`udi political leaders. As noted earlier, a number of Wahhabi Sa`udi leaders were sent back to Istanbul in chains by the victorious army of Ibrahim Pisa. Besides the beheading of Abd Allah b. Sa`ud, some were dispatched by firing squads and others dismembered by artillery. The Ottomans devised a special execution for Sulayman b. Abd Allah, a grandson of the founder Muhammad b. Abd al-Wahhab, who had served as chief qadi of al-Dir`iyyah and an arch-foe of the Turks. So Ottoman officials, knowing full well the Wahhabi hatred of music, ordered a musician to play the *tanbur* in his presence, before killing him by firing squad. "Temporal leaders might be placated, and some compromise reached with them, but with the [Wahhabi] spiritual

---

[533] Teitelbaum, p. 124.

leadership there could be no compromise."[534] The Ottoman Sultan and his administration clearly, and understandably, detested the Wahhabi attacks on them as *kafir*s.[535] These religious attacks were much more offensive to the sultans than previous ones from the Kadizadelis or Zaydis; the former never questioned the Ottoman state's Islamic bona fides, they simply critiqued its praxis; the latter came closer to the Wahhabis, but their Imams were willing to acknowledge the sultans' right to rule anywhere but Yemen—and, often, they would acknowledge his limited power even there. Kadizadelism had been merely an internal problem, Zaydism an external, indeed marginal (both geographically and ideologically) one. Wahhabism combined the worst of both those worlds. So it required both kinetic and conceptual refutation.

Considerable anti-Wahhabi polemics in the Empire came from the Hanbalis[536]—one of the four major Sunni schools of jurisprudence, and the most conservative one, whence Wahhabism sprang.[537] The Ottomans' primary, official school was the Hanafi one, although since their domain was so large it encompassed scholars of all four. (Shaykh Ahmad Zayni Dahlan, on whom more below, was a Shafi`i who lived in Mecca, for example.) The Hanbalis,

---

[534] Sirriyeh, p. 124.

[535] *Ibid.*

[536] David Commins, "Traditional Anti-Wahhabi Hanbalism in Nineteenth-Century Arabia," in Itzchak Weisman and Fruma Zachs, eds., *Ottoman Reform and Muslim Regeneration: Studies in Honour of Butrus Abu-Manneh*" (London: I.B. Tauris, 2005), pp. 81-96.

[537] See "Islamic Schools and Branches," *Wikipedia*; accessed July 20, 2020.

concentrated in Arabia, perhaps felt responsible, to some extent, for Ibn `Abd al-Wahhab and thus took the Empire's side over against him. They were also much more accepting of Sufism than the Wahhabis. One of their major attacks on the Wahhabis was to question their education and scholarship in understanding traditional Islamic teachings.[538] A related criticism was that Wahhabis practiced dangerous, free-lancing *ijtihad*, or "independent reasoning," unmoored from any of the four schools.[539]

Probably the major extant example of debunking Wahhabism from the Ottoman side came from the aforementioned Shaykh al-Islam in the Hijaz, Ahmad Zayni Dahlan.[540] His *Fitnah al-Wahhabiyah*[541] excoriates the founder of Wahhabism for condemning visiting the tombs of the prophet Muhammad and "righteous Muslims," as well as calling upon them for aid. Shaykh Dahlan also ridiculed Ibn Abd al-Wahhab for claiming to have restored true Islam after centuries of adhering to *shirk*, or "idolatry." He also indicted Abd al-Wahhab for wrongly applying Qur'anic passages meant for non-Muslims, such as sura al-Ahqaf:5 and al-Zumar:3, to Muslims whose practices he disliked. "How can Ibn `Abdul-Wahhab and those who follow him find it permissible to equate the believers, who believed in tawhid,[542] to those blasphemers, who

---

[538] Commins, pp. 88, 89.

[539] *Ibid.*, p. 91.

[540] See "Ahmad Zayni Dahlan," *Wikipedia*; accessed July 18, 2020.

[541] As noted earlier, the English text is available at *kanzuliman.org*; accessed July 19, 2020.

[542] "Unity of Allah" (as opposed to, most notably, Christian belief in the Trinity).

believed in the Godhood of idols?"[543] The Shaykh, further, adduces a number of hadiths which, according to him, authorize Muslims to ask prophets and "righteous Muslims" for succor. He says that at one point in his career Abd al-Wahhab was contradicted in person by a number of scholars in Mecca, after which the Sharif ordered the arrest of many Wahhabis, although some fled to al-Dar`iyyah. "This made the Wahhabis more devilishly haughty, and they started attacking the tribes which were loyal to the prince of Makkah."[544] Dahlan goes on at length about the Wahhabis' barbaric attacks on Muslims, their pillaging of pilgrim caravans, and their occupations of Mecca and Medina. "During this time, the Wahhabis destroyed the domes built on the graves of the righteous Muslims."[545] Well-informed of historical events for a religious scholar, Shaykh Dahlan notes that the Ottomans were preoccupied with fighting the Christians and ordered Muhammad Ali of Egypt to deal with the Wahhabis. He notes that the first Egyptian forces sent in were defeated, but that Muhammad Ali sent another expedition which was more successful, in no small part because of its 18 cannons, and the Egyptians shrewdly deciding to bribe a number of Bedouin to abandon the Wahhabis and join them. This army retook Medina, Jiddah and finally Mecca. Another Egyptian force later routed the Wahhabis and the Saudis in their so-called capital. Dahlan also

---

[543] Dahlan, pp. 8, 9.
[544] *Ibid.*, p. 16.
[545] *Ibid.*, p. 19.

recounts that many Wahhabis were sent back as captives to the Sultan.[546] "The tribulations inflicted by the Wahhabis were a calamity for the Muslims. The Wahhabis shed a great deal of blood and robbed a great deal of money; their harm was prevalent and their evil spread."[547] Wahhabi banning of tobacco in towns they controlled is also criticized. The Shaykh notes, almost as an aside, that it was easy to identify Wahhabis because they shaved their heads, an innovation which at least one hadith warned against. For this eminent, pro-Ottoman religious leader in Mecca, the Wahhabis were both a heretical sect and a violent insurgency, no doubt the same view held by imperial leadership. His position allowed him to contest Wahhabism in the former register, which was necessary but hardly sufficient to counter that movement. Imperial kinetic operations, whether by proxy or directly, were also needed—as we have seen.

The Ottoman Empire's final insurgent challenge examined herein was the hardest for it to counter: Muhammad Ahmad's eschatological Mahdist movement of late 19th century Sudan. The Sudanese Mahdi's beliefs and motivations having already been canvassed, this section will focus on the military aspects of his movement, as well as the Ottoman-Egyptian and British-Egyptian counters.[548]   In several major battles between August 1881 and

---

[546] Shaykh Dahlan is confused about the leadership of this early 19th century Egyptian campaign—he several times says it was commanded by Muhammad Ali himself, when in fact it was his son, Ibrahim, as its head.
[547] Dahlan, p. 27.

January 1885, Mahdist forces defeated each expeditionary force sent against them, and in the final one took the city of Khartoum and killed its commander, British Major-General Charles Gordon.

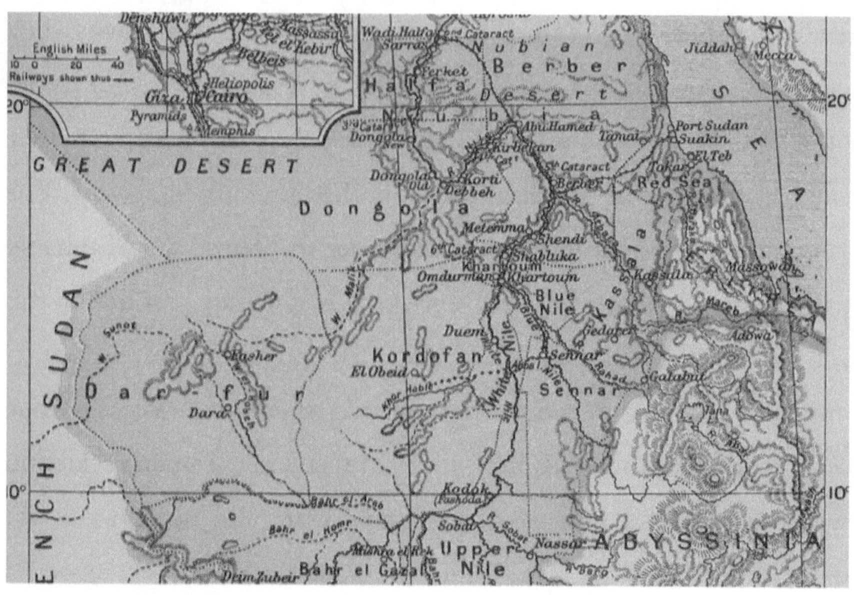

"Anglo-Egyptian Sudan" (relevant part of map).[549]

In 1881 the Ottoman governor of Sudan, Rauf Paşa, having gotten wind of Muhammad Ahmad's extravagant claims, sent his assistant Abu Sa`ud, along with loyal local ulama, to interview the self-styled

---

[548] On this dimension, consult F.R. Wingate, *Ten Years' Captivity in the Mahdi's Camp 1882-1892* (London: Sampson Low, Marston & Company, Limited 1892; reprint by Filiquarian Publishing LLC, 2015); Omer Ertur, *Bones in the Nile: The Omdurman Chronicles* (Omer Ertur, 2010); and for an overview, "Mahdist War," *Wikipedia*, accessed July 20, 2020.

[549] From "Anglo-Egyptian Sudan," *Wikipedia* (public domain); accessed July 27, 2020.

Mahdi.[550] They found him convinced of his eschatological mission, and failed to disabuse him of that belief. So the governor sent Abu Sa`ud back in August with two companies of Egyptian troops to capture Muhammad Ahmad at Aba Island. Despite being armed with modern weapons, they were routed by the Mahdists using only "sticks, stones and spears."[551] This miraculous victory, even over such a small force, of course only increased belief in Muhammad Ahmad's apocalyptic appointment. But "[t]he Mahdi had no intention of waiting on his island for the next attacks. He immediately announced that he must, like the Prophet Mohammed before him, perform a hegira [sic], or flight."[552] He and his followers decamped to southern Kordofan, where many flocked to join him. The second force which the Mahdists defeated was that of the *müdir* of Fashoda, Rashid Ayman, who went against higher orders and attacked the Mahdist camp with a force of some 1400—which was ambushed and mostly annihilated in December 1881.[553] Realizing the Mahdi's forces now constituted a serious threat to Sudan, regardless of his eschatological authenticity, a third attempt to reduce Muhammad Ahmad was made. The acting governor-general in Khartoum—a German, Carl Christian Giegler Paşa, former chief of the telegraph system—pulled together a force of perhaps 5,000

---

[550] Useful details on these military endeavors can be found in Byron Farwell, *Prisoners of the Mahdi* (New York and London: W.W. Norton & Company, 1989).
[551] *Ibid.*, p. 13.
[552] *Ibid.*
[553] *Ibid.*, pp. 14, 15.

commanded by Yusuf al-Shallali Paşa and Abd Allah Dafallah. They moved into southern Kordofan in spring 1882 and by June had camped near Jabal Qadir. But their *zaribah* (camp protected by thorn bushes) was penetrated during the night by Mahdists, who overwhelmed and defeated the government forces—taking thousands of rifles and much ammunition as a result.[554] In May 1882 Abd al-Qadir Hilmi Paşa had replaced his German predecessor as *hükümdar* and by the end of July had raised a force of 12,000 men, some of whom he sent to buttress the garrisons at Khartoum and al-Ubayyid/"El Obeid."[555] But "Abdel Kadir Pasha [sic] was a resourceful man who knew of other weapons besides soldiers. He opened a correspondence with the Mahdi, promising him forgiveness if he would give up his divine pretensions. He commissioned two men to murder the Mahdi. He sent the Mahdi a present of poisoned dates.[556] He requested Cairo to send him some 'dynamite envelopes'. None of Abdel Kadir Pasha's schemes worked."[557]

In early September 1882 the Mahdi led and army of some 30,000 to attack al-Ubayyid. Said Paşa, the müdir, defended the town

---

[554] *Ibid.*, p. 16.

[555] The Arabic is الأبيض, *al-'Abyad.* Various sources use different transliterated versions of this in English.

[556] This didn't work on Dr. Henry Jones, Junior—aka "Indiana"—either. "Bad Dates," *youtube.com*; accessed July 20, 2020.

[557] *Ibid.*, p. 17. The CIA's many alleged, cartoonish attempts to kill Fidel Castro come to mind here: "10 Ways the CIA Tried to Kill Castro," *mentalfloss.com*, February 16, 2012; accessed August 5, 2020.

with 4,000 troops—armed, however, with American Remington rifles, which killed perhaps a third of Muhammad Ahmad's men before the Mahdi abandoned frontal assaults.[558] Abd al-Qadir Paşa tried to reinforce the town, but the forces he sent were decimated by raids and thirst, with perhaps half reaching, instead, the only other surviving government garrison at Bara. Both it and al-Ubayyid fell by January 1883 to siege. Said Paşa was tortured then hacked to death.

That same month Colonel William Hicks, a British officer with experience in India, was put in command of Egyptian forces in Sudan, with the rank of Major General—although his nominal superior, in an effort to assuage Muslim sensibilities, was Sulayman Niyazi Paşa.[559] A month later "this rabble of an army was shipped off up the Nile to Sudan….As there were mass desertions before the men were shipped off, many were put in chains and not released until they reached their destination."[560] Hicks got there on March 4 and began drilling his men. While poorly trained, their arsenal was impressive: "modern Remingtons…rockets, Krupp howitzers,[561] brass mountain guns[562] and even some Nordenfeldt machine guns.[563]"

---

[558] Farwell, p. 21.

[559] *Ibid.*, pp. 27, 28.

[560] *Ibid.*, p. 29.

[561] Probably a 75 mm field artillery piece. See "Krupp gun," *Wikipedia*; accessed July 20, 2020.

[562] Another 75 mm field gun. See "QF 2.95 inch mountain gun," *Wikipedia*; accessed July 20, 2020.

[563] "Maxim's recoil-action machine gun was not introduced to the military world until the following year and the Nordenfeldts, like the Gatlings, were operated by a crank. But they were very efficient weapons, capable, as long as the operator's arm lasted, of firing 1,000 rounds a minute." Farwell, p. 30 is the

General Hicks also commanded a force of Ottoman *bashi-bazouk* irregular cavalry, as well as perhaps 100 Arab cuirassiers. This entire force of some 5000 moved south in April 1883. The power of his artillery allowed Hicks' men to drive off several Mahdist attacks later that month during this sortie in strength.

They returned to Khartoum and Hicks telegraphed his superiors that he would no longer tolerate being under even the ostensible command of Niyazi Paşa—whereupon the Ottoman Egyptian official was kicked upstairs to the governate of the Red Sea provinces of Egypt. In early September 1883 the muster of his forces showed Hicks in command of about 7,000 infantry, perhaps 1,000 cavalry, 14 or so artillery pieces and half-a-dozen Nordenfeldt guns.[564] Once again, they marched south. By October 11 they had made it only halfway to al-Ubayyid "but still not a single tribe had come to support them, no garrisons had been established in their rear and it had been eight days since any word had been sent back to Khartoum."[565] By October 26 Hicks' force was still 40 miles from its destination, and "[w]hile the Dervishes were obviously following every move of the Egyptian army, Hicks Pasha had no information at all as to the movements, size or disposition of the enemy."[566] So he was totally taken by surprise when on November 4, 1883, some

---

source for the text quote and this footnote one. See also "Nordenfelt Gun," *Wikipedia*; accessed July 20, 2020.

[564] Farwell, p. 37.

[565] *Ibid.*, p. 40.

[566] *Ibid.*, p. 42.

40,000 Mahdists attacked from the woods of Shaykan, about 15 miles from al-Ubayyid, in a massive ambush. In two days almost all of Hicks' 8000-man force was killed or captured—the latter shortly thereafter executed. General Hicks himself went down fighting with his sword. His head was sent to the Mahdi.[567] Muhammad Ahmad's men took all the rifles, machine guns and artillery, further bolstering their arsenal. "With the destruction of Hicks Pasha's army, there were few Sudanese who were not convinced by the Mahdi's military victories, if not by his religious dogma, that he was the true Mahdi of Islam. Among Egyptian officials…for whom belief in the Mahdi was impossible, terror spread in ever-widening circles: to the capital of the Sudan in Khartoum and to the remote provinces of Darfur, Bahr el Ghazal and Equatoria…. There was consternation in Cairo, where the danger to Sudan of a Sudan ruled by a militant and hostile religious fanatics was all too apparent."[568]

The Turco-Egyptian government still held the important Red Sea port of Suakin (Sawakin). In December 1883 Cairo sent a police force under a cashiered former British officer, Valentine Baker Paşa, who had received commissions in both the Ottoman and Egyptian armies. He took his 3,500-man force down the coast to El Teb. Here the poorly-trained Egyptians refused to fight or outright surrendered. Most were slaughtered by Mahdists under the command of Osman Dignah (Uthman Diqnah), Muhammad

---

[567] *Ibid.*, pp. 45, 46.
[568] *Ibid.*, pp. 47, 48.

Ahmad's loyal lieutenant in northeastern Sudan.[569] But then London sent 3,000 regular British troops who landed at Trinkitat, south of Suakin in February 1884. Marching inland, Diqnah attacked with 6,000 Mahdists—but this time the disciplined British troops routed them. The following month they again defeated his forces, once more with heavy Mahdist losses. Most of these British troops were then withdrawn, but some stayed to strengthen Suakin garrison. These minor victories over the Mahdi's forces had not altered the grim strategic situation, however. "There was no longer an organized army in the Sudan, and only about 24,000 troops in scattered garrisons. Besides, with British troops in occupation,[570] Egypt was not even sure it was free to act.… The forces of the Mahdi were sweeping the Sudan, and Egypt had neither the men nor the money to reconquer it, or even to continue to hold the ground it still held. Britain had the men and the money but was unwilling to expend them to obtain an unwanted addition to the Empire."[571] The Ottoman Empire's position was somewhere in-between that of Egypt and Britain: Istanbul probably had the men, but neither the money nor the patience, to deal with this frontier fundamentalist messiah—as irksome as they no doubt found his grandiose claims and his undeniable military successes.

---

[569] *Ibid.*, pp. 53, 54.

[570] Recall that the British had occupied Egypt in 1882, ostensibly to help them and the Ottomans maintain stability there.

[571] Farwell, p. 56.

Khartoum still held out against the Mahdi's minions, and the British government resolved to save those within its walls. Who better to manage a strategic withdrawal than Major-General Charles Gordon, who had served previously as governor of Equatoria province and *hükümdar* of the entire Sudan? Gordon was "half military genius and half religious fanatic."[572] He was also "a dreamer and an eccentric, but he was not a fool."[573] London wanted to find "some way to withdraw the Egyptian garrisons now in the Sudan, as well as all the Egyptian officials with their families, and those Sudanese who had exhibited their loyal support...."[574] Scholars differ as to whether Gordon was sent simply to gather intelligence on the situation and to develop recommendations for such a withdrawal, or also to take action to make such happen.[575] In any event, the British public held wild expectations that he would exact revenge for Hicks Paşa and somehow single-handedly master the Mahdi.[576]

Gordon arrived in Cairo January 24, 1884. His view of his mission was decidedly one of more than simply assessing the

---

[572] Ertur, p. 59.

[573] Farwell, p. 70.

[574] *Ibid.*, p. 80.

[575] "From the outset of Gordon's mission doubts existed about whether it was an advisory or an executive role, about what Gordon could accomplish once appointed governor-general of the Sudan and about what would happen if his life became endangered." So says Edward M. Spiers. *The Victorian Soldier in Africa* (Manchester, UK: Manchester University Press, 2004), in chapter six, "The Gordon Relief Expedition," p. 112.

[576] Farwell, p. 81.

situation on the ground. Gordon had devised a plan to restore the rule of local notables who had controlled parts of Sudan prior to the Egyptian conquest in the 1820s. But doing this was, frankly, impossible for most of Sudan. The former dominant families had been stripped of their power and their places taken by supporters of the Mahdi, some in Darfur being the sole exception.[577] Gordon reached Khartoum three weeks later, sans any military escort. He issued an edict that taxes would be suspended for two years, past due taxes written off, and that he would make no attempts to interfere with the slave trade (as he had done in his previous posts). He also offered the Mahdi the position of Sultan of Kordofan—a demotion which, needless to say, Muhammad Ahmad turned down.[578] Gordon did call in as many troops as possible from adjacent areas, which brought the Khartoum garrison strength to perhaps 8,000 men. There would be no more reinforcements, as the Mahdists totally surrounded the city by May 26, 1884.[579]

The British dithered, but finally that summer Gladstone's government approved the dispatch of a relief expedition under General Garnet Wolseley, who had long experience in India, the Crimea, and as the commander of British forces which had occupied Egypt two years earlier. The force was to consist of 9,000 men.[580] It did not set out south until early October. But in August the Mahdi

---

[577] *Ibid.*, pp. 82, 83.
[578] *Ibid.*, p. 87.
[579] *Ibid.*, pp. 87, 88.
[580] Spiers, p. 112.

had set out for Khartoum with 60,000 men. Once there, the Mahdists used captured artillery to bombard the city.[581] Gordon and the city's garrison held out throughout the autumn, but as 1885 loomed Wolseley's force was being help up by harassing Mahdist attacks. Wolseley's men did inflict a major defeat on the enemy at the Battle of Abu Klea (or Abu Tulayh) in mid-January, however.[582] But in Khartoum "hundreds lay dead and dying in the streets from starvation, and there were none to bury them."[583] On January 26 the Mahdists broke into the city via a strip of unwalled muddy land that the falling White Nile had exposed. Gordon died on the steps of the palace, fighting with his pistol and sword. His body was then decapitated and his head sent to the Mahdi.[584] Most of the men in the city were killed, but the women "were herded into pens like cattle, until they could be divided among the conquerors, the Mahdi taking first choice, then the khalifas and emirs in order of rank."[585] The advance guard of the relief expedition arrived two days later, and Wolseley had no hope of retaking the city. The Mahdi would rule all of Sudan until his death, at the age of 40, on June 22, 1885—from malaria or typhoid. British and Turco-Egyptian administration would retain only two peripheral garrisons: Suakin, on the Red Sea coast; and Wadi Halfa, on the border with Egypt. The aggressive and

----

[581] Farwell, pp 90, 91.
[582] "Battle of Abu Klea," *Wikipedia*, accessed July 22, 2020.
[583] Farwell, p. 96.
[584] "Siege of Khartoum," *Wikipedia*, accessed July 22, 2020.
[585] Farwell, p. 97.

Islamic fundamentalist Mahdiyah, after Muhammad Ahmad's death, would be ruled by his appointed successor—the able, if ruthless, Khalifah Muhammad b. Abd Allah—until the British returned with massive force in 1898 and destroyed both him and his no-longer-eschatological state.

The author and General Gordon, London, April 2018.

Muhammad Ahmad's movement had begun as a marginal, Sudanese Islamic one proclaiming him as the End Times Mahdi, but it proved immensely powerful because this figure is predicted in

Islamic traditions, and claims in this vein have often produced jihads—some of which have taken power.[586] The Sudanese Mahdi, along with the founder of the earlier Almohad movement, Ibn Tumart,[587] exemplifies the three-stage creation of a Mahdist state: 1) devising and disseminating Islamic propaganda designed to delegitimize an extant state; 2) forming a renegade military theocracy and attempting to seize power (whether through overthrowing the target establishment or separating territory); and 3) taking the reins of state power or carving off a new polity—which in either case will eventually wane in religious fervor.[588] Muhammad Ahmad's insurgency against the "Turkiyah," the Ottoman administration in Egypt and Sudan—and its British enablers—is unique among the major movements studied herein in that it was the only one which combined apocalyptic expectations and enthusiasm with extensive, ongoing guerrilla operations. All the eschatological hype in the world avails little without accompanying kinetic operations, as Muhammad Ahmad knew full well. So between August 1881 and January 1885 his forces won seven major[589] battles,

---

[586] Even in the modern world, a substantial minority (as much as 42%, according to one reputable poll on topic) of Muslims expects the Mahdi to come while they are still alive. One might well surmise that the belief level in him in Islamic Africa 140 years ago would have been even higher. See my article "Mahdism (and Sectarianism and Superstition) Rises in the Islamic World," *hnn.us*, August 13, 2012; accessed July 25, 2020.

[587] Who will be covered in the next chapter of this book, for reasons that will be explained.

[588] As noted earlier, this paradigm is adapted from Blichfeldt.

[589] Whether in terms of numbers involved and/or significance.

and lost only two—neither of which slowed down their insurgency. They did this primarily by bringing the sympathetic population to bear on the Mahdi's enemies—whether directly, via tens of thousands of ready jihadists; or indirectly, by leveraging the support of hundreds of thousands, perhaps millions, of like-minded Sudanese people. But the Mahdists also superbly utilized the terrain and, indeed, entire geography of their country; and they did so operating from multiple secure bases. In three-and-one-half years, they not only convinced the Istanbul-Cairo-London axis of unbelief to give up the fight—at least for 13 years—but also expelled the Ottoman-Egyptian-British forces from Sudan.

Abu Saud's rather desultory attempt to bring Muhammad Ahmad to heel, using a small military force, was the first attempt at a counter-insurgent combat raiding strategy. Although we don't know how many Mahdists were involved, it's almost certain that they outnumbered, probably substantially, the Egyptian soldiers. So although the regime was staging from a secure base area, its force to space ratio was laughably low—which is why, in tandem with group cohesion and ideological fervor, Muhammad Ahmad's men were able to rout rifle-armed troops using only pre-gunpowder weapons. Following this, the Mahdi led his newly-armed warriors, along with thousands of others, on a hijrah of at least 250 miles, from Aba Island southwest to Kurdufan.[590] Besides its obvious (and

---

[590] It's 256 miles, as the Mahdist marches, from Khartoum to El Obeid. Of course Muhammad Ahmad and his masses set up somewhere outside the latter town—

aforementioned) religious motivation, this strategic withdrawal utilized the terrain to relocate the movement beyond the reach of any government raiding or persisting combat strategy—or so its leader no doubt hoped. But Rashid Ayman, the governor of Fashoda,[591] probably hoping to score points with his superiors in Khartoum, took a substantial force on a combat counter-raid into Kordofan—only to get it wiped out. Once again, an insufficient force to space ratio allowed the Mahdists, with far fewer modern weapons, to concentrate against weakness and win. The third government anti-Mahdist foray involved even more troops. This time, with Khartoum's imprimatur, about 5000 soldiers penetrated Mahdist territory in south Kordofan and set up a camp the security of which, alas, proved slipshod and penetrable. This government foray represented the first serious attempt at a persisting combat strategy: it invaded guerrilla domains, heading for the latter's primary base, with the aim of either wiping them out or, barring that, at least politically intimidating the Mahdi into changing his eschatological tune. But neither came to pass, as even a legion of men proved inadequate to do either. At this point (summer 1882) the Sudanese governor-general realized the gravity of the situation and, knowing that he had to maintain secure bases from which to stage, reinforced the garrisons in both Khartoum and al-Ubayyid. But by early fall the

where, we don't know for certain. So this is a rough metric. See "Distance from Khartoum to El Obeid," *distancecalculator.net*, accessed July 25, 2020.

[591] Now Kodok, and located in the separate country of South Sudan. See "Kodok," *Wikipedia*, accessed July 25, 2020.

Mahdist guerrillas nonetheless attacked al-Ubayyid, with at least 30,000, some seven times the force of the garrison there. The Mahdi lost one-third of them in frontal assaults against a force with superior weaponry—whereupon he switched to siege. Any attempt to relieve or reinforce the town was itself attacked, and al-Ubayyid fell after four months. In this instance, al-Ubayyid proved a vulnerable base area: it represented an attempt to employ combat persisting strategy (albeit not by taking Mahdist territory, but by holding onto it); but Muhammad Ahmad's forces had a greater force to space ratio and the government "invasion" was overcome by a massive Mahdist raid/siege.

The next three encounters between Mahdist and government forces would find the apocalyptic jihadists facing off, to one degree of another, with British forces—or at least British-led ones. And the world's preeminent 19th century military power fared little better against the "dervishes" than had the Ottoman Egyptian soldiers. Hicks' extremely well-armed 8,000-man force moved from Khartoum into Mahdist-held Kordofan, in south central Sudan, but was ambushed at Shaykan near al-Ubayyid. A Mahdist force five times larger was hiding in the forest there and it surrounded British-led Egyptian one. In two days the government troops were wiped out, the Mahdi's men taking Hicks' machine guns and artillery, as well as the rifles. Once again, the state attempted a combat persisting strategy by taking the fight to the insurgents' base area with the hopes of (re)taking al-Ubayyid and thus transitioning to a logistic persisting approach by occupying Mahdist territory. But though they started from a secure base area (Khartoum), the Turkiyah troops were eventually operating from vulnerability, especially by failing to establish garrisons along their line of movement. They were also operating blind, sans intelligence as to the massive combat raiding party that would soon engage them. Yet again, as well, the government force to space ratio was woefully insufficient—and so the hunted turned the tables on them and became the hunter. The hoped-for political impact—diminution of Muhammad Ahmad's authority and power—also went the other way, as the Mahdi now gained more supporters and a competent commander in the Red Sea littoral.

That deputy, Osman Dignah, would then defeat the next offensive by government forces: Valentine Baker's, whose 3500 ill-equipped and ill-trained Egyptian troops staged from Suakin in late 1883/early 1884 and were promptly slaughtered by Mahdists. This operation seems to have been intended as a logistic raiding one, as its main objective was to lure out the enemy to fight rather than (re)taking territory. If so, it failed miserably—although not so much this time because of a low force to space ratio, but because of the extremely poor training of the forces deployed. Shortly after regular British troops disembarked at Trinkitat, and although outnumbered two to one, in two separate battles they devastated attacking Mahdist forces. This showed that a combat raiding strategy with competent troops (and commanders) could succeed. Had the British, or the

Ottomans, been willing to deploy sufficiently large numbers of their regular army to Sudan and take on a full-scale combat raiding strategy, then expand it into a logistic persisting one, the Mahdi and his movement likely would have been defeated. But political factors, mainly at home, precluded that option—until the end of the century.

The decisive battle that won the day for the Mahdist insurgency was the successful siege of Khartoum in late 1884 and early 1885. It was imperative that the Ottoman Egyptian administration, and its British ally, hold onto Sudan's strategically-located largest city and capital if there were to be any hope of defeating Muhammad Ahmad's forces. Seemingly secure, and with a substantial relief force under Wolseley trying to relieve the city, Cairo and London were hoping to engage in defense with a combat strategy—if his forces could reach Khartoum in time. Then they might be able to transition to a combat persisting strategy by adding at least some of the 8,000 men in garrison there in order to block Mahdist lines of communication and take the fight to them. But it was not to be. Muhammad Ahmad's 60,000 men surrounded, starved out and eventually sacked the city before reinforcements could arrive. The abortive relief force did deal the Mahdists a major loss while attempting to reach Khartoum. But with no secure bases within reach in country,[592] the British expeditionary force had to withdraw, leaving Muhammad Ahmad in control of almost all of

---

[592] Other than the aforementioned Wadi Halfa on the border with Egypt and Suakin in the far northeast on the Red Sea—neither close to Khartoum.

Sudan. The Mahdist insurgency had won, successfully enacting all three phases of eschatological rebellion in an Islamic context.

Perhaps the most crucial aspect of Muhammad Ahmad's victory was the first stage—when he waged information or ideological warfare to convince a critical mass of the Sudanese people that he was the Awaited Mahdi and that the extant Turkiyah regime was Islamically illegitimate. This topic has already been addressed to a large extent, so at this juncture only a few additional points will be made. As noted, Ottoman-friendly clerics in Sudan attempted to refute Muhammad Ahmad's grandiosely apocalyptic claims. But so too did one across the Red Sea, in the Hijaz: Ahmad Zayni Dahlan, whom as we have seen was a prominent critic of the Arabian Wahhabis. Observing (as best he could) events in Sudan prior to his death in 1886, Shaykh Dahlan rendered opinions on the man Muhammad Ahmad and his movement at the end of a book entitled *al-Futuhat al-Islamiyah*, or *Islamic Victories*.[593] Surprisingly, he was decidedly more sympathetic to the man claiming to be the Mahdi than he was to any of the Wahhabi leaders. The Shaykh "held the tentative hope that he [Muhammad Ahmad] could be on a God-inspired mission, sent to restore the position of Islam and to fortify Muslims both spiritually and politically."[594] In the end, however, Dahlan opined that while Muhammad Ahmad might be "a" mahdi,

---

[593] See Heather J. Sharkey, "Ahmad Zayni Dahlan's Al-Futuhat al-Islamiyya: A Contemporary View of the Sudanese Mahdi," *Sudanic Africa*, Volume 5 (1994), pp. 67-75.
[594] *Ibid.*, p. 69.

he could not be "the" End Times Mahdi—mainly because the Islamic world already had a legitimate caliph and leader of the Muslims: Ottoman Sultan Abdül Hamid II. Even if he proved to be not even "a" mahdi (more or less coterminous with a mujaddid), the Sudanese rebel might assist the Ottoman Empire by helping eject the infidel British from that region.[595]

Other Islamic clerics were not so sympathetic.[596] First those in Khartoum, then ones in Cairo, wrote fatwas denigrating Muhammad Ahmad's claims. These he based initially on visions of the prophet Muhammad, the four rightly-guided caliphs of early Islamic history, and various and sundry Sufi leaders,[597] in tandem with critiques of the Ottoman Egyptian government for its failure to live by or enforce Islamic norms, and its cozying up to the infidel (Christian) British. By 1882 Muhammad Ahmad was also trumpeting his military victories as proof of his mission. By summer 1882 Sudanese clerics were writing edicts against him: Muhammad al-Amin al-Darir, shaykh al-Islam of eastern Sudan; Ahmad Isma'il al-Azhari; Shakir al-Ghazi, mufti of the Khartoum Appeals Court. Other Sudanese Islamic scholars signed onto these, as well. As noted earlier, these mainly honed in on two areas: how Muhammad Ahmad did not meet the criteria for al-Mahdi al-Muntazar as detailed

---

[595] *Ibid.*, p. 71.
[596] See Fergus Nicoll, "Fatwa and Propaganda: Contemporary Muslims Responses to the Sudanese *Mahdiyya*," *Islamic Africa*, Volume 7, Number 2 (2016), pp. 239-265.
[597] Nicoll, p. 240.

in various hadiths; and that his assertions and jihad undermined the legitimate Sultan in Istanbul—and thus also Ottoman representatives in Cairo and Khartoum.[598] These missives failing in their aim, the following year the propaganda war was kicked upstairs to Cairo clerics who, with the prestigious presence of al-Azhar buttressing their authority, might be expected to carry more Islamic weight than their Sudanese colleagues. The Grand Mufti of Egypt himself, Muhammad al-Abbasi al-Mahdi, wrote an anti-Sudanese Mahdi fatwa. Its core tenet was that "even a personal communication from the Prophet himself did not abrogate the specific provision of *shari`a* law that the *khalifa* must be installed through an oath of allegiance (*bay`a*) approved by 'people of influence or by designation on the part of his predecessor" and that "the pre-existing *bay`a* to the Sultan rendered any subsequent oath to Muhammad Ahmad null and void...."[599] As for the Sultan himself, Abdül Hamid II dismissed Muhammad Ahmad as a mere "rebel" with "vermin" for supporters, and saw him as merely a tool of the British.[600] He was wrong on several of those counts. In the final analysis, Sudanese and Ottoman Egyptian Islamic scholars clung to their loyalty to the Sultan, since he remained a pious Muslim (at least in their eyes) and held the line against fitnah. The Mahdi's supporters, however, argued that the Ottoman Sultan "had forfeited his right to the allegiance of right-

---

598 *Ibid.*, pp. 247-49.
599 *Ibid.*, p. 251.
600 *Ibid.*, pp. 252-53.

thinking Muslims because of his neglect of the *shari`a*, the misrule perpetrated by him and his proxies, and by their collective subservience to non-believers, i.e., the European powers."[601] Muhammad Ahmad's allegations of Mahdihood were necessary, but not sufficient, to propel him to power in Sudan; they had to wedded to a successful counterinsurgent jihad—which they were.

To finally bring to a close this lengthy discussion of insurgents fighting the Ottoman Empire, and the state's responses, let us hazard a COIN scorecard. The Ottomans clearly defeated the 15th and 16th century Sufi movements. Ditto for the Celalis, as much by buying them off as with kinetic operations. The Kadizadelis, too, were beaten—although, as noted several times, they were not so much an insurgency as a domestic attempt at a religious takeover. The Ottoman record against the next four movements was more mixed. In numerous altercations with the Druzes, over a number of centuries, the Ottomans often prevailed on the battlefield temporarily, but would be unable to enforce Druze loyalty to the state once the Empire reduced its force to space ratio. And ultimately the Ottomans found themselves displaced in Druze territories by the French. Similarly to the Druze situation, the Ottomans fought the Zaydis of Yemen in two widely-separated time frames—and in neither did they successfully bring the south Arabian insurgents to heel, despite investing more time, treasure and lives in

---

[601] *Ibid.*, p. 265.

those COIN operations than in any other examined herein. The Ottomans had a number of significant wins over the Wahhabis, again in disparate time periods—or at least their Egyptian proxies did. But ultimately the Wahhabized Saudis detached most of Arabia from Istanbul's ambit, and put it under their control, where it remains to this day. Finally, Muhammad Ahmad's Mahdists did expel the Ottomans, as well as their Egyptian proxies and their British allies, from Sudan and created their own state there. So Ottoman Egyptian COIN in that part of Africa proved ineffective— even when bolstered by British power. Note, however, that while the Ottomans had a mixed record of success vis-à-vis Islamic insurgencies, even the ones that the Empire could not tame did not threaten the state itself. In the following chapter we will take a look at a counter-example: an Islamic state that not only lost territory to a co-religionist challenge—it lost its very existence. Then, in the final chapter, I will apply lessons learned from the Ottomans' long experience in countering insurgencies to some modern contexts.

CHAPTER FOUR—COUNTER-EXAMPLE:

ALMORAVIDS V. ALMOHADS

The Ottoman Empire always managed to hold their internal enemies at bay, whether Sufis, Celalis, Kadizadelis, Druzes, Zaydis, Wahhabis or Mahdists (Sudanese or otherwise). That is, the *dar* wars which these groups provoked[602] could harm the state in a number of ways: killing its soldiers, draining its coffers, denting its political and religious legitimacy, even reducing the scope of its domains. But the Empire always struck back powerfully enough that none of these seven insurgencies ever seriously threatened the rulership of the house of Osman—much less the state's existence itself. By contrast, there was an earlier major Islamic polity which was destroyed by an internal movement that grew from an insurgency to a revolution and ultimately took over the reins of power. The Almoravids (al-Murabitun) created a North African empire in the eleventh century AD, but were challenged then supplanted the following century by the Almohads (al-Muwahhidun).[603] Where the Ottomans succeeded, the Almoravids failed. Why?

---

[602] All except the Kadiazadelis which, as I have pointed out several times, constituted a different sort of threat.

[603] The most salient sources on these two polities, and the conflict between them, are: Jamil M. Abun-Nasr, *A History of the Maghrib in the Islamic Period* (Cambridge: Cambridge University Press, 1987), particularly chapter 3: "The Maghrib under Berber Dynasties," pp. 76-103; Ronald A. Messier, "Re-Thinking the Almoravids, Re-Thinking Ibn Khaldun," in Julia Clancy-Smith, ed., *North Africa, Islam and the Mediterranean World: From the Almoravids to the Algerian War* (London:

The Almoravid state began when a pious Islamic scholar, Abdullah b. Yasin (d. 1059), trekked from Qayrawan (Kairouan, in modern Tunisia) to western north Africa to help the Sanhaja people practice a more orthodox brand of Islam. The chief of the Banu Gudala tribe, Yahya b. Ibrahim, had requested such help on his way back from the *hajj*. "From the moment of his arrival...Ibn Yasin led a rigorous campaign against the practices which he considered incompatible with the *shari`a* and proceeded to create an organized Islamic community."[604] He also set up a state treasury, imposed Islamic taxes and mandated following Islamic law for distributing booty seized in raids. Ibn Ibrahim gave his religious enforcer free rein to implement this agenda, which angered some of the other tribal leaders. As a result, Ibn Yasin took his followers on a "retreat," called a *ribat*, where many flocked to join him and "whom

Frank Cass, 2001), pp. 59-80; Allen J. Fromherz, *The Almohads. The Rise of an Islamic Empire* (London & New York: I.B. Tauris, 2010); Mercedes García-Arenal, *Messianism and Puritanical Reform: Mahdis of the Muslim West* (Leiden & Boston: Brill, 2006), especially chapter six, "The Almohad Revolution and the Mahdi Ibn Tumart," pp. 157-192; H.T. Norris, "Ibn Tumart and the Almoravids: 'The Evil Deeds of the Mujassimūn from Kākudam,' Selected Passages from Iban Tūmart's A`azz mā yutlab," *Journal of Qur'anic Studies*, Volume 13, Number 2 (2011), pp. 155-164; H.T. Norris, "New Evidence on the Life of `Abdullah B. Yasin and the Origins of the Almoravid Movement," *The Journal of African History*, Volume 12, Number 2 (1971), pp. 255-268; W. Montgomery Watt, "The Decline of the Almohads: Reflections on the Viability of Religious Movements," *History of Religions*, Volume 4, Number 1 (Summer 1964), pp. 23-29; Pascal Buresi, "Preparing the Almohad Caliphate: the Almoravids," *Al-`Usur al-Wusta: The Journal of Middle East Medievalists*, Volume 26 (2018), pp. 151-68; "Almoravid Dynasty" and "Almohad Caliphate," both *Wikipedia*, both accessed July 28, 2020. See also "Abdallah Ibn Yasin," "Ibn Tumart" and "Abd al-Mu'min," all *Wikipedia*, all accessed July 30, 2020.
[604] Abun-Nasr, p. 80.

he subjected to strict religious discipline and moulded into a militant reforming movement."[605]   Ribats were more than simply retreat centers—they were, in effect, small frontier forts; each one was a primarily a "jihad war outpost."[606] Those staging from such locales came to be known as *al-Murabitun*, "those of the ribat"—which, in Western languages, became "Almoravids."

Ibn Yasin led his followers out of their ribat(s) in 1042 and allied with the new head of the Lamtuna tribe, Yahya b. Umar (Ibn Ibrahim having died). Years of warfare against enemies in western north Africa ensued, in which Ibn Yasin's organizational skills were matched perhaps only by his brutality.[607] In 1059, however, Ibn Yasin was killed in battle with the heretical Barghwata.[608] The leadership of the movement then passed to Yusuf b. Tashfin who "determined the course of Almoravid history through his military successes in the Maghrib and Spain."[609] They expanded eastward during the 1070s, and in 1086 invaded the Iberian peninsula,

---

[605] *Ibid.*

[606] See Hodgson, *The Venture of Islam* 2, p. 269; also "Ribat," *Wikipedia*; accessed July 30, 2020.

[607] He had no qualms about having even pious Muslims in conquered towns, such as Awdaghast, slaughtered. And his cruel treatment of dogs went beyond even normal Islamic distaste for canines. See Norris, "New Evidence," pp. 266, 267.

[608] This was a tribal alliance on the Atlantic coast of what is now Morocco which practiced a strange, syncretistic brand of "Islam," which adhered as much to the teachings of their 8th century predecessor Salih b. Tarif as to mainstream Islam. Ibn Tarif has claimed to be not only the Mahdi, but to be the recipient of new revelations from Allah, constituting a new "Qur'an." Needless to say, the Almoravids hated them and their ideas. See "Barghawata" and "Salih Ibn Tarif," both Wikipedia, both accessed July 30, 2020.

[609] Abun-Nasr, p. 81.

although "the Muslim princes who had encouraged the Almoravid intervention soon regretted it."[610] Some of these Muslim rulers even allied with Christian powers from the northern peninsula, but by 1110 all of Islamic "Spain"—the southern half of Iberia—was ruled by the Almoravids.

The Almoravid state was "not a mere predatory amirate,"[611] however. Ibn Tashfin tried quite hard to rule in accordance with Islamic law and tradition, even going so far to avoid the title "caliph" and seeking approval for his status as *amir al-muslimin*, "commander of the Muslims," from the Abbasid caliph far away in Baghdad. He also, unlike Ibn Yasin, did not personally interpret and enforce Islamic law. Ibn Tashfin left that to the state-supported Islamic scholars and jurists.[612] The dominant position of these *fuqaha* (experts in Islamic jurisprudence) was one of two pillars of Almoravid rule; the other was primary position of the Sanhaja tribal confederation, within which the Lamtuna tribe in particular held the pride of place: "its warriors constituted the core of the army and occupied most of the important administrative posts."[613] At the urban level, the mayor of each major city was actually the chief *qadi*, or judge, appointed by the Almoravids.[614] All religious experts were from the Maliki interpretive school,[615] which had previously

---

[610] *Ibid.*, p. 82.
[611] Hodgson, *The Venture of Islam 2*, p. 269.
[612] Abun-Nasr, p. 83.
[613] *Ibid.*, p. 84.
[614] Messier, pp. 67, 68.
[615] See "Maliki," Wikipedia, accessed July 30, 2020.

ensconced itself in northwestern Africa, and they were so enamored of it that they utilized Maliki principals almost to the exclusion of the Qur'an and the hadiths.[616] (This would prove a point of contention, indeed weakness, when the Almohad challenge arose.) The Almoravid state was wealthy, in large measure, because it controlled trans-Saharan trade routes,[617] most profitably access to gold coming from medieval Ghana and Mali[618] and going to medieval, other Muslim polities and European ones, and even the Byzantine Empire. Overall, "when the Almoravid period is viewed from the standpoint of Morocco as a state and as an Islamic country, their achievements look formidable. When they entered Morocco it was split into petty tribal principalities…by the time they lost power to the Almohads, it had emerged as a unified country."[619] At their height, the Almoravids ruled not just all of modern Morocco and the Western Sahara, but also a large part of Mauritania, and even some of western Algeria; they also controlled over half of the Iberian peninsula. So as the 12th Christian/6th Islamic century dawned, Almoravid rule was extensive and seemed secure, certainly, in the Maghrib, showing no visible signs of decline. But their previous

---

[616] Abun-Nasr, p. 84.

[617] Messier, p. 69.

[618] "The Trans-Saharan Gold Trade (7th-14th Century)," *metmuseum.org,,* accessed July 30, 2020. West
African gold was the Old World's primary source of that precious metal prior to the European expansion into the New World and the exploitation of the gold (and silver) there.

[619] Abun-Nasr, p. 87.

patina of military invincibility had lost its sheen, thanks to defeats by the Christian warriors of Iberia,[620] and "their narrow dogmatism had alienated many of the learned religious leaders in their domains."[621] The Almohads would take full advantage of these chinks in Almoravid armor not just to challenge but, eventually, to overthrow that state.

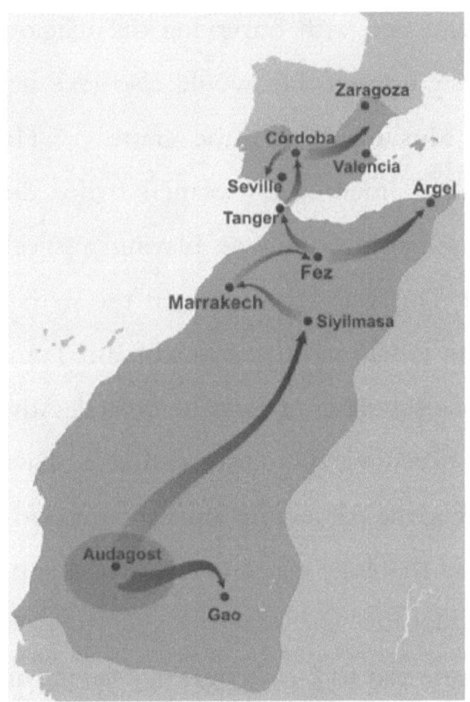

The Almoravid state at its greatest extent.[622]

---

620 See "Timeline of Muslim Presence in the Iberian Peninsula," especially the subsections "Political Fragmentation (1031-1130)" and "Decline and Submission to Christian Rule (1130-1481)," *Wikipedia*; accessed July 31, 2020.
621 Abun-Nasr, p. 86.
622 From "Almoravid dynasty," *Wikipedia*; accessed July 31, 2020.

The Almohads were established by Abu Abdallah Muhammad b. Tumart, born c. 1080 in what would now be southern Morocco. In his 20s he is said to have traveled to Islamic Spain, then to the Middle East, returning to the Maghrib in 1117. "In the years immediately after his return…Ibn Tumart acted not as the leader of a political conspiracy but as a religious reformer" who "would not be satisfied with observing the religious obligations of Islam punctiliously himself, but would also take it upon himself to summon other Muslims to do the same."[623] He wound up in Marrakesh, beating men and women who did not separate themselves and going after anyone playing musical instruments or drinking alcohol. This was in the time of the sixth Almoravid ruler, Ali b. Yusuf, who is said to have brought Ibn Tumart to the palace to debate religious scholars—whom he bested. Advised to have the cranky reformer executed, Ibn Yusuf demurred having him, instead, banished.[624] In this, the Almoravid amir chose poorly.

Almoravid theology was literalistic; but, curiously, it was not overly fundamentalistic. The state's Maliki scholars "accepted the passages which referred to God's hearing, seeing, and sitting on the throne literally. Ibn Tumart lined up on the side of earlier Islamic theologians who "rejected the literal interpretation of these passages, because it led to the assumption that the Divine Being had human characteristics and to undermining the belief in His immateriality

---

[623] Abun-Nasr, p. 87.
[624] *Ibid.*, p. 88.

and unity."[625] He condemned the Almoravids as *mujassimun*, "corporealists"—those who give Allah a body.[626] Over against their heresy he trumpeted *tawhid*, Allah's spiritual unity, and called those who followed him in this *al-Muwahhidun*—which, Westernized, became "Almohads." Ibn Tumart was thus less literalist than his enemies, in that sense; but in another, he was indeed more fundamentalist: he also attacked the establishment Maliki religious leaders for "equat[ing] the *shari`a* with the secondary works…of the Malikite school and…ignor[ing] reference to the Qur'an and the Prophetic traditions."[627] So the Almohads, the "allegorical mystics,"[628] proved more intolerant than their woodenly-literal enemies—for which the blame can be placed squarely on the eschatological dimension of Ibn Tumart's agenda. Yet he and his supporters also took the Almoravids to task for disregarding the fundamental texts of Islam. Perhaps it's accurate to say that both the Almoravids and their Almohad challengers practiced some degree of Islamic fundamentalism—just not the same brand.[629]

Ibn Tumart eventually fled south to the mountains to avoid an arrest order which Ibn Yusuf finally had issued. Shortly after he relocated to Tinmallal, only about 100 km from the Almoravid

---

[625] *Ibid.*

[626] See Norris, "Ibn Tumart and the Almoravids: 'The Evil Deeds of the Mujassimun….,'" *passim.*

[627] Abun-Nasr, p. 88.

[628] As I referred to them in my book *Holiest Wars*, p. 38.

[629] Nakita Valerio, "Tracing Almoravid and Almohad Differences," *thedrawingboardcanada.com*, February 29, 2016; accessed July 31, 2020.

capital,[630] deeming this a hijrah. About the same time he declared himself the Mahdi,[631] fulfilling an expectation that this figure would arrive in 500 AH/1107 AD.[632] He also meted out the death penalty for any of his followers who refused to acknowledge him as such.[633] "Before moving to Tinmallal Ibn Tumart was only a religious reformer; in Tinmallal he became the head of a rebellious religio-political movement directed at the Almoravids."[634] In 1128 he upped the violence ante with a massive *tamyiz*, or "purge," of thousands of skeptics, real or imagined, which demolished the tribes' power structure and replaced it with a hierarchical one with him, as the Mahdi, at the apex.[635] There were more than religious roots to this movement, however. There was an economic dimension: the Almoravids, especially in their urban areas, were quite wealthy and the Almohads wanted a larger piece of those pies; and the latter chafed under what they saw as the onerous taxation regime of the

---

[630] As per "Tinmel," *Wikipedia*; accessed August 2, 2020.

[631] This is the scholarly consensus, although García-Arenal, pp. 181, 182 has a different take: "As far as I have been able to see, there is no text in which Ibn Tumart explicitly claims to be…this Mahdi whose appearance is dictated by the manifest corruption of his times…. What Ibn Tumart does write is that 'the Mahdi came and God distinguished him by bestowing right guidance upon him and promised him he would change the habitual state of things….' Although Ibn Tumart does not say in a completely explicit way that he himself is the Mahdi, it is easy to see how inevitable and obvious the connection would have been for his followers and supporters." Clearly, the Almohads believed that Ibn Tumart was the Mahdi!

[632] García-Arenal, p. 167. Since Ibn Tumart had been born c. 1080, he could fit into this eschatological time frame.

[633] *Ibid.*, p. 171.

[634] Abun-Nasr, p. 89.

[635] García-Arenal, p. 171.

former. There was also a strong sociological element: the tribe was arguably every bit as important as religion in the Maghrib, and Ibn Tumart's agenda caught on mainly among the Masmuda, empowering them over against the Lamtuna-centered Almoravids. He broke their traditional power via the purge, however, and then reorganized the Almohad community "like a Berber tribal confederacy."[636] At the apex was the Mahdi; right below him were the first 10 tribal leaders who had sworn loyalty to him as such; the next layer consisted of 40 tribal representatives.[637] The Mahdist Almohad masses took their orders from this leadership. Finally, Ibn Tumart's personal charisma constituted a *sine qua non* for Almohad success.[638] While such is often religious, it is not automatically so. Personal magnetism operates just as much in the political realm, if history is any guide. But as noted previously in this work, Islam—especially in its pre-modern form—differentiated very little, if at all, between the sacred and secular realms. So charisma in one register easily bled over into the other, and this was certainly the case with the Almohad founder. "At least as he is portrayed heroically in the Almohad sources, Ibn Tumart himself was… 'architect' of the Almohad structure. The specific economic and historical conditions pertaining to the Masmuda tribes[639] provided the mortar with which

---

[636] Abun-Nasr, p. 89.

[637] *Ibid.*

[638] Fromherz, pp. 187, 188.

[639] Masmuda sub-tribes included the Hargha (Ibn Tumart's own one), Ganfisa, Gadmiwa, Hintata, Haskura and Hazraja. This is per "Ibn Tumart," *Wikipedia.*

to bind the tribal building blocks together…. Had any of these elements—the tribal building blocks, the charismatic architect and the economic mortar—been missing, no structure could have been built…. all these element…came together simultaneously to produce the right conditions for the rise of the Almohads."[640]

Both Ibn Tumart's movement and his war were predicated on the conviction that the Almoravids and all their subjects were "apostates who had to be annihilated wherever they were to be found."[641] Inflamed with that belief, and the conviction that the Awaited Mahdi led them, the Almohads finally left their mountain strongholds in early 1130 and, after defeating the surprised Almoravid forces near Aghmat, laid siege to Marrakesh, the Almoravid capital. The city held out until reinforcements arrived, and then in May Almoravid troops from within and without routed the Almohads at al-Buhayra. Ibn Tumart's forces suffered at least 12,000 casualties.[642] Just a few months later, Ibn Tumart would be dead. He shook loose the Mahdist coil either in August or September, 1130; but this was kept secret from the larger Almohad community for several years, until his deputy Abd al-Mu'min had led the armies to several defeats of the Almoravids. The new Almohad leader also had to violently put down revolts by a number of the Mahdi's followers when they learned he had died.[643] No later than

---

[640] Fromherz, p. 189.

[641] García-Arenal, p. 173.

[642] See Abun-Nasr, p. 90; also "Battle of al-Buhayra," *Wikipedia*, accessed August 1, 2020.

1133, Abd al-Mu'min "began the process of appropriating the Almohad movement for himself and replacing it with a model of dynastic power which differed greatly from the ideology of Ibn Tumart's preaching."[644] Abd al-Mu'min was, in a very real sense, the man who created the Almohad state. The people called him caliph, as Ibn Tumart's successor; but he used the title *amir al-mu`minin*, "commander of the faithful"—the first non-Arab to do so.[645] Between 1133 and 1147 he defeated the Almoravids and their Christian allies (on which more below), making all their domains Almohad. Two years after taking Marrakesh, in 1149, Abd al-Mu'min ordered his own purge, putting Ibn Tumart's to shame in terms of bloodshed. One Almohad historian wrote that 32,730 "suspicious individuals" were put to the sword—after which "there ceased to be any further differences of opinion."[646] As his state grew, it was initially empowered by dictating that there be no difference of opinion on Ibn Tumart having been the Mahdi, with religious scholars divided into these privileged Almohad ones who held to that belief, and those who possibly did not (but kept this to themselves) in smaller towns. The Almohads proper were also exempted from certain taxes, making them "a distinct and exclusive class of conquerors."[647] Abd al-Mu'min, however, broke with Ibn

---

[643] García-Arenal, p. 189.
[644] *Ibid.*
[645] Abun-Nasr, p. 94.
[646] García-Arenal, p. 190.
[647] Abun-Nasr, p. 94.

Tumart's partiality toward the Masmuda tribe by raising the status of his own, the Kumya—making Kumyan horse warriors the main Almohad cavalry, as well as his own personal bodyguard.[648] Ironically, much of the administration of the new empire fell to the former Almoravid Maliki jurists, which eventually contributed to the undermining of Mahdist belief as an ideological pillar. By the time of the third Almohad leader, Abd al-Mu'min's grandson, Abu Yusuf Ya`qub (r. 1184-1199), Mahdism had become an embarrassment. Ya`qub rejected the idea that Ibn Tumart had been the Mahdi, and "reprimanded the Almohad scholars who gave more prominence in their studies to Ibn Tumart's teachings than to the Qur'an and the Prophetic traditions...."[649] Within a few more decades, civil war would split the Almohad state. Idris al-Ma'mun (d. 1230) totally repudiated Almohad Mahdism, putting Maliki jurists back in charge of the religious establishment. By 1269 the Almohads were finished. But in their century or so of rule in north Africa, they had given "a concrete historical existence to the conception of the Maghrib as a distinct religio-cultural entity."[650] At its zenith, the Almohad state encompassed all of modern Morocco and Western Sahara, but was oriented more east-west than the Almoravid one had been. It also included much of Algeria, all of Tunisia, and part of Libya. At times the Almohads also ruled half of Iberia, as had the Almoravids.

---

[648] *Ibid.*
[649] *Ibid.*, p. 97.
[650] *Ibid.*, p. 101.

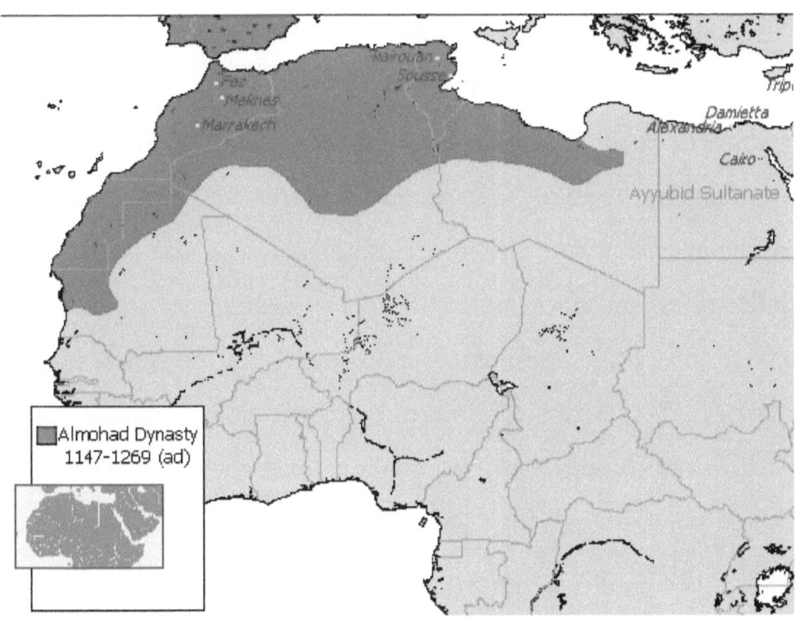

The Almohad Empire at its greatest extent.[651]

A number of Almoravid weaknesses were exploited by the Almohads.[652] First, the Maliki jurists whom the Almoravids had appointed as their religious enforcers were more opportunists than enthusiastic supporters, who watched out for their own interests more than the rulers. "Over-reliance on the[se] *fuqaha* eventually cost the Almoravids the support of local rulers who felt that they were passed over...."[653] Second, the Almoravids also arguably erred by focusing on jihad against non-Muslims; this worked in Iberia, against Christian, but limited their expansion and military options, vis-à-vis co-religionists in the Maghrib. Third, the Almohad threat on several

---

[651] "Almohad dynasty (1147-1269," *Wikimedia Commons*; accessed August 1, 2020.
[652] See Messier, pp. 73-75.
[653] *Ibid.*, p. 74.

fronts, coupled with the Christian one in Iberia, drained the Almoravid coffers and required them to raise taxes—but they had come to power partly by promising "no new taxes." Thus hoist by their own revenue petard, the Almoravids lost yet more support. Even more harmful was the fourth shortcoming: the Almoravid state had done a poor job of incorporating local notables (aristocrats) into their administration. Finally, the Almohads were dependent on their Sanhaja brothers from the Sahara to the south and east for reserves and for, if you will, ideological resupply, as well as the trade routes there for more prosaic reasons. The Almohads effectively interdicted these lines of transportation and communication, further weakening the Almoravid state.

The premise of this counter-example chapter is two-fold: 1) that, *mutatis mutandis*, the Almoravids can serve as an analog for the Ottomans and the Almohads as one of the challenges to the latter—or, perhaps more accurately, a combination of several thereof; and 2) whereas the Ottomans always succeeded against their challengers in that the state survived, the Almoravids failed miserably in that regard. In order to ascertain why that was, let us apply the same analytical lenses to the Almohad insurgency and the Almoravid counter-insurgency as we did in chapter three to the myriad opposition movements to the Ottomans and that Empire's responses. As was done in chapter three with the Ottomans, we will start with an analysis of the Almohad challenge and the Almoravid response in terms of causes and tactics; then we will examine those same phenomena in more strictly military terms.

Although the Almoravids were not experiencing any overt political instability in the first quarter of the 12th century, the Almohads, led by Ibn Tumart, did harbor religious grievances—which, again, were tantamount to political ones in that context. The Masmuda tribe and its subunits, which came to comprise the core of the Almohad movement, also certainly saw themselves as relatively deprived compared to the luxurious reign of the urban Almoravids—who just a few generations before had been nomads eking out an existence in the Sahara. And while religion—Islamic messianism, in particular—would come to define the struggle, it was at least as much rooted in ethnic-tribal rivalry, of Masmuda v. Sanhaja/Lamtuna. So in terms of why insurgents rebel against a state, the Almohads had a trifecta of reasons to do so. How did they do so? The course of Almohad resistance ran roughly like this.[654] After the hijrah to Tinmallal, the Almohads waged a guerrilla war in the High Atlas Mountains of central Morocco, making the transit to and from Sijilmasa, the "gateway of the trans-Saharan trade,"[655] quite difficult for the Almoravids. The state tried establishing counter-fortresses, as well as moving its commerce routes further east to circumvent Almohad raids.[656] Their attempt to take Marrakesh

---

[654] Largely drawn from Abun-Nasr, pp. 90-94.
[655] Per "Almohad Caliphate," *Wikipedia*.
[656] For a map of trans-Saharan trade routes, including these key areas of Almohad-Almoravid rivalry, see "Trans-saharan axes explored at different periods

thwarted in spring 1130, the Almohads contented themselves with dominating the High and Middle Atlas Mountain areas while simultaneously winning more (sub)tribes, including from the Sanhaja, to their banner and, as a result, swelling the ranks of their army. At this point the struggle was one of Almohad highlanders v. Almoravids lowlanders. In 1144 the Almohads engaged the Almoravids and their Christian allies, led by the Catalan Catholic Reverter I de La Guardia near Tlemcen (in the coastal plain of what is now northwestern Algeria). The Almohads won a crushing victory there after killing De La Guardia—ironically, the most competent Almoravid commander.[657] Shortly thereafter the Almohads took Oran (a major coastal city, to the east of Tlemcen), then Fez in 1146, before capturing Marrakesh the following year—effectively ending the Almoravid state. To make this point, the Almoravid palace and main mosque were razed, with the Kutubiyah Mosque built on the location of the latter.[658] Almohad expansion continued into Iberia, but especially the eastern Maghrib (Tunisia and Libya), aimed ostensibly at the Norman French territories there but more truly at the extending Almohad rule over the area's Muslims—in particular

---

between the 9th and the 17th c. A.D.," *1.bp.blogspot.com*; accessed August 2, 2020.

[657] See "Reverter de La Guardia," *Wikipedia*; accessed August 2, 2020. This "Catalan adventurer and military leader" had been a POW of the Almoravids for over a decade, when Ali b. Yusuf tapped him, perhaps in 1136, to take command of captured "Spanish" soldiers willing to fight the Almohads. They had great success until this defeat by the Almohads in 1144 who, in their Islamic zeal and anger, crucified De La Guardia's corpse.

[658] "Kutubiyya Mosque," *Wikipedia*; accessed August 2, 2020.

the Banu Hammad, who had allied with the Almoravids earlier. In 1152 the Almohads defeated the Hammadids, taking over that part of northeastern Algeria.[659] Abd al-Mu'min then called a halt to further military conquests in order to go back west and consolidate his rule. But he returned to the east in 1160 and expelled the Normans from their stronghold at Mahdiyah and Tripoli. The Almohad state would survive another century—but that is beyond the scope and point of this work.

As noted earlier, the Almohads initially possessed political/religious, economic and social motivations to fight against their Almoravid rulers. Almohad ideology was primarily religious—indeed, by modern standards, it would fall under the "religious extremism" category, being overtly apocalyptic and messianic, as well as violent. The movement also was one of ethnic differentiation, if not separatism *per se*, which ultimately aimed at regime change. The most important tactic was winning the support of the populace—or at least enough tribes to tip the odds in Almohad favor—while at the same time delegitimizing Almoravid rule. Ibn Tumart, and then Abd al-Mu'min, were both masters at this: the former in terms of crafting the message, the latter in carrying it out. In the 1130s the Almohads, as a highland insurgency, stayed out of the state's military reach and engaged in hit-and-run attacks. By the 1140s the Almohads made the quantitative and

<hr>

[659] "Hammadid dynasty," *Wikipedia*, accessed August 2, 2020.

qualitative leap from irregular to regular warfare, ultimately prevailing, because "[t]he jihad gave rise to the formation of large Caliphal armies led personally by the *imam*"[660]—at first Ibn Tumart, then Abd al-Mu'min. Almoravid counterinsurgency did consist of attempts to win—or at least retain the loyalty of—North African hearts and minds, but these failed in the face of the more powerful Almohad da'wah. The state did have at least one major search and destroy mission, although the rebels came to them: the Battle of Buhayra in 1130, when the Almohad insurgents besieging Marrakesh were severely defeated. But there is really no evidence of successful clear and hold operations by the Almoravids; once they started losing, the ruling group seemed to suffer simply a string of losses, unable to stave off defeat, until the end came in 1147.

What sorts of militaries were engaged in these medieval wars in the Maghrib and Iberia? Both the imperial states—Almoravids and Almohads—as well as the Iberian Muslim kingdoms fought in largely the same manner, and with largely the same weapons. The dominant weapons system was cavalry, generally light (unarmored, that is). Muslim light cavalry and infantry used composite bows and javelins. But the Almoravids and Almohads "also utilized an ancient Berber strategy using camel laagers[661] as a screen from which to launch attacks...and were still using stationary infantry phalanxes as

---

[660] Buresi, p. 164.

[661] A temporary fortification, usually made by "circling the wagons"—but, in this case, the camels. See "Wagon fort," *Wikipedia*, accessed August 2, 2020.

a defensive formation, supported by light infantry bowmen and javelineers. North African Berber troops...were also trained to manoeuvre silently to the sound of massed drums...."[662] By way of contrast, their Iberian Christian enemies—whether Aragonese, Castilian, Portuguese —"fought with a combined-arms tactical system which included unarticulated heavy infantry, light infantry bowmen and javelineers, northern European style heavy cavalry— and the new, Moorish-inspired light cavalry.[663] Christian troops were usually better armoured than their Muslim counterparts...wearing mail hauberks, separate mail coifs and metal helmets, and armed with maces, cavalry axes, sword and, if properly saddled, lances."[664]

Unlike with much of Ottoman history, especially that of the 19th and early 20th century, information on the medieval Almoravids and Almohads military history is much less detailed (where it exists at all). Therefore, analysis of Almohad guerrilla resistance, and Almoravid defense against it, needs be of a more general nature, and to a larger degree predicated on surmise, than that of chapter three. Nonetheless, doing so will enable the construction of at least the outline of an instructive counter-example to the Ottoman case.

The Almohads as guerrillas—which they were during the decade of the 1130s—made quite effective use of the terrain (High

---

[662] Brian Todd Carey, Joshua B Allfree, John Cairns, *Warfare in the Medieval World* (South Yorkshire, UK: Pen & Sword Books Ltd, 2006), pp. 102, 103.
[663] The Norman French from Sicily, whom the Almohads battled later in their expansionary phase, probably fought very much the same, with the possible exception of light cavalry contingents.
[664] Carey, *et al.*, p. 102.

Atlas Mountains) and operated from a secure, nearly-impregnable, base at Tinmallal. They also relied upon a very sympathetic population in and around that base. During this time frame, the Almohads engaged in raiding, and in both combat and logistic modes. They attacked any Almoravid forces which attempted to pursue them into the mountains; and they denied the state lines of communication, transportation and, most importantly, commerce connecting, in particular, the capital Marrakesh with the crucial Saharan trade entrepot of Sijilmasa.

Trans-Saharan trade routes, 1000-1500 AD.[665]

---

[665] From "File: Trans-Saharan routes early.svg," *Wikimedia*; accessed August 2, 2020.

The Almohads made a premature attempt at a combat persisting strategy when, buoyed by their victory over a small Almoravid force, they decided to try and take Marrakesh—only to be soundly defeated. For over a decade the Almohads then returned to a combat and logistical raiding approach, which not only prevented the Almoravids from decimating or perhaps eliminating their forces in a set battle; even more importantly, it allowed the eschatological guerrillas to win over more and more of the population, denuding the target regime of both legitimacy and manpower. By the early 1140s the Almohads felt powerful enough to switch to a combat persisting strategy: taking Almoravid towns, cities and territories by defeating them in more set-piece combat. This proved particularly effective in 1144, when the challengers defeated the forces, and killed the commander, of the Almoravids' powerful Christian mercenaries. Afterwards, the Almohads could engage in all four categories of guerrilla—or, by then, conventional—warfare: combat raids and persisting approaches (attacking Almoravid forces with destructive incursions and taking and holding territory), as well as logistic raiding and persisting (depriving the Almoravids of forts, supplies, weapons and men—as well as legitimacy). The Almohads extinguished the Almoravid state by 1147, then went on to apply these same methodologies to the Hammadids and Norman French in North Africa. They tried to do the same to the Iberian Christians, and indeed dealt them a huge defeat at the Battle of Alarcos in 1195.[666] But only 17 years later, the combined armies of the Reconquista returned the favor at the Battle of Las Navas de Tolosa,[667] which "the Christians won using a combined-arms effort, with heavy cavalry providing the offensive punch while infantry held fast against Muslim cavalry charges."[668] The Almohads would then be pushed out of Iberia over the next few decades—and, ultimately, eliminated in North Africa as well by 1269.

In the early days of fighting the Almohads, the Almoravids operated from secure base areas and so used defense with a combat strategy—usually with a low ratio of force to space. So when the Almoravids attempted to pursue the Almohads into the mountains and get at the latter's stronghold of Tinmallal, Ibn Tumart's forces could concentrate against, and interdict, them at key passes and chokeholds. This also showed the guerrillas' superior use of terrain. Almoravid attempts at a combat persisting strategy, exemplified by invading guerrillas' base area(s), were thus stymied. The one documented instance of the Almoravids having a high ratio of force to space, their routing of the Almohads before the walls of Marrakesh in 1130, shows how the state was capable of a successful defensive strategy. But the Almohads learned their lesson and withdrew into their mountain fastnesses for the rest of that decade, and so Almoravid attempts at a combat raiding strategy—counter-

---

[666] "Battle of Alarcos," *Wikipedia*; accessed August 2, 2020.
[667] See Carey, *et al.*, pp. 107-112.
[668] *Ibid.*, p. 112.

raids into guerrilla territory, which if successful might have had enormous political impact in terms of undermining Almohad fervor, especially if staged in tandem with the discontent that broke out upon learning of Ibn Tumart's death in 1132 or 1133—went for naught. Of course, no political (re)conciliation was possible between these two camps, considering the hatred for the Almoravids with which the Mahdi had imbued his followers. By the early 1140s, especially after 1144, the Almoravids were operating almost exclusively from vulnerable base areas, and probably almost always with a low ratio of force to space, especially compared to the Almohad armies which had been adding men for years. It is safe to assume Almohad armies in the tens of thousands, which would have almost certainly outnumbered the Almoravids.[669] In such circumstances, the Almoravids seem to have fallen upon a default strategy of simply holing up in their cities and hoping to outlast the besieging Almohads—to no avail. By the mid-1140s the Almoravids had become the caged hunted, not the hunters; and by 1147 they were extinct. The Almohads not only convinced their enemies to abandon its efforts to fight them; they eliminated them and took over all the former Almoravid domains. The Almohads had evolved (or, from the Almoravid perspective, transmogrified) from one

---

[669] Almost no sources provides numbers for Almoravid or Almohad forces when fighting each other. But we do have fairly reliable numbers for the Almohad army at the Battle of Las Navas de Tolosa: at least 30,000. "By Easter [1212 AD] an army of perhaps 30,000 [Christian] heavy cavalry and infantry prepared to march south to face a Moorish and Berber army that probably outnumbered them." So says Carey, *et al.*, p. 108.

man's idiosyncratic zeal, to an insurgency engaged in unconventional warfare, a guerrilla force, and then to a movement utilizing conventional warfare—and quite successfully.

The Almoravids resembled the Ottomans in some respect, but differed wildly in others. Both were extant Islamic states, enforcing (some degree of) Islamic law, ruling extensive territories, whose rulers grounded their legitimacy in, again, Islam. Both were of a certain ethno-linguistic group: the Almoravids Lamtuna and Guddala Berber, the Ottomans Turks—which differed from many of their subjects. Both were wealthy. But the Ottomans ruled a much grander empire; they openly claimed, and were largely accepted as deserving, the caliphate; and their state encompassed the Islamic heartlands, to include Mecca and Medina, not just peripheral territories. Also, Ottoman prestige was predicated, eventually, on the Empire's longevity. By the time of the final insurgencies vexing it, the state had been around for half a millennium. The entire lifespan of the Almoravid state was just over one century. Finally, the Ottomans, in any century, could bring much more military power to bear than the Almoravids could have even hoped to do. On the other side of the ledger, the Almohads combined elements of several Ottoman insurgencies. Ibn Tumart's charisma-based movement resembles those of the Sufi rebellions in the formative years of the Ottoman Empire, while his emphasis on the fundamental Islamic holy texts, over against any school's interpretation thereof, does seem rather like the Kadizadelis—if that latter group had raised the flag of armed rebellion, not simply inter-group violence. The Almohad fusing of religious doctrine with tribal loyalty smacks of the Zaydi Yemeni cause, although Ibn Tumart was no Shi`i.[670] The Almohads most obviously, however, bring to mind the last two anti-Ottoman movements covered earlier: the Wahhabis and the Sudanese Mahdists. The former's weaponized Islamic fundamentalism took much of the same trajectory as Ibn Tumart's; while the latter's Sunni eschatological zeal was, in fact, an updated version of his Mahdism, which saw its founder also pass from the scene before his agenda could be completely realized. Since the Wahhabis and the Sudanese Mahdists are the most like the Almohads, let us consider them vis-à-vis the Ottomans in comparison to the movement of Ibn Tumart and Abd al-Mu'min in relation to the Almoravids. Keep in mind that we are analyzing polities and opponents separated in time by some 750 years.

The Ottomans were immensely more powerful than the Almoravids—not just militarily, but politically as noted. Mecca and Medina were under their control, giving them supreme Islamic legitimacy. Furthermore, the Ottoman Sultans were acknowledged as the de facto leaders of Sunni Islam, and even as Caliphs—a position which they openly claimed by the time of Abdül Hamid II. The Ottoman state was a deep one, as well, having been erected on the

---

[670] "[T]he Almohad Imam, though impeccable, was not like the shi`ite Imam in having a revelatory function, but was more of a politico-religious leader to whom obedience and imitation were owed." García-Arenal, p. 179.

previous Eastern Roman one, and thus possessing ancient tradition even beyond the bounds of Islam. So the Ottomans could bring both enormous kinetic and ideological power to bear on any aspiring rivals. The Almoravids lacked recourse to such shock and law warfare. They also suffered from a number of weaknesses when confronted with the Almohad challenge:

- The aforementioned "narrow dogmatism"
- Shallow roots, their state having existed for less than a century
- Ethnic separatism, which alienated them from the populace
- Perception that their vast wealth was not benefitting the populace
- Perception of unjust taxation
- Power base in only one or two tribes
- Religious officials/administrators who did not work for the state's success
- Too deferential to the distant Abbasid caliph, thus undermining their authority
- Failure to take Ibn Tumart and his movement seriously—until too late
- Lack of decisiveness in dealing with an extremist, violent movement.

On the other side of the ledger, what were the strengths of the Almohad movement?

- Eschatological, Mahdist fervor
- Capable leadership: Ibn Tumart (charisma), Abd al-Mu'min (jihad, state-building)
- A "supra-tribal power structure,"[671] stemming from belief in Ibn Tumart as Mahdi

- Willingness to use extreme violence, not just against other Muslims but their own
- Claim to be on the side of those dispossessed by the Almoravids
- No hesitance in seizing the caliphal ring of power, so out-legitimizing the Almoravids.

As noted above, the two most salient anti-Ottoman movements were the Wahhabis and the Sudanese Mahdists. The former shared some characteristics with the Almohads: puritanical reforming zeal, questioning the ruling state's legitimacy, a strong tribal affiliation. But the latter are by far more relevant to any attempt to compare Ottoman and Almoravid success and failure. Muhammad Ahmad and Ibn Tumart both: claimed to the End Times Mahdi; operated as puritan reformers in the guise of frontier fundamentalists; not just questioned but openly attacked the ruling state's legitimacy; declared jihad on the extant establishment; and inspired movements that ultimately created Mahdist states. True, the Almohads ultimately overthrew the entire Almoravid state apparatus, whereas the Sudanese Mahdists only did so for one of the Ottoman territories. In this light, the Almohads and Sudanese Mahdists were both successful insurgencies, achieving stage three of Mahdist movements: forming a state, in the face of ultimately failed Almoravid and Ottoman COIN, respectively. But whereas Ibn Tumart/Abd al-Mu'min did so by converting the entire target polity

---

[671] *Ibid.*, p. 172.

to the new dispensation, the best that Muhammad Ahmad/Muhammd b. Abd Allah could do was to detach one southern tier province from the purview of the central state's secondary Egyptian rulers. Although the Ottoman state itself was never threatened by Sudanese Mahdism, its Egyptian province was. That it did not fall to the frontier fundamentalists from its southern border owed a great deal to the responses of the Istanbul-Cairo axis, which avoided the mistakes that the Almoravids had made vis-à-vis the Almohads. The Turkiyah government, most importantly, took Muhammad Ahmad seriously and worked to undermine his eschatological claims; fought him and his forces both kinetically and ideologically; and were not afraid to use force, or at least to step aside and let their British allies do so. Thus while the Mahdists of both the Sudan and the Maghrib succeeded, the former were at least contained in one outlying (albeit extensive) area and effectively quarantined off from the rest of the Empire. In that regard, the Ottomans fared far better than the Almoravids, whose apocalyptic menace proved existential, not simply exasperating.

CHAPTER FIVE—CONCLUSION

As explained in the opening chapter, this book has two primary purposes. The first is to examine how history's premier Islamic state, the Ottoman Empire, dealt with challenges similar to the modern, self-styled Islamic State. The information provided here, particularly the lengthy second and third chapters, has hopefully realized that *descriptive* goal. But early on I observed that a study such as this might be *prescriptive*, as well—that examining the Ottomans' COIN successes (as well as the Almoravids' massive failure) could potentially provide grist for the modern policy mill. I did so fully aware that "recognizing cultural factors and effectively implementing them are two different problems...."[672] I have always been an analyst—whether as a history professor, author, or during my five-year tenure working for US Special Operations Command—and never a policy-maker. I report and analyze, leaving it for others to decide what to do with the data. But if it is true that the "War on Terrorism" is in large measure a struggle against a worldwide Islamic insurgency—and clearly it is—then "counterinsurgency, not counterterrorism, may provide the best approach to the conflict."[673] And again, while COIN studies have a long pedigree, those that have examined the Ottoman Empire in this regard can be counted on one

---

[672] Morillo, p. 89.

[673] Kilcullen, p 166. He actually refers to "a global Islamist insurgency," but as I noted at some length in chapter one, that middle term is rubbish.

hand—indeed, on just one finger. (Such scrutiny of the Almoravids, in fact, heretofore has never been done.) At least one expert questions going back before the 20th century to look at COIN, maintaining that "while earlier campaigns still offer valuable tactical and operational lessons, they occurred under circumstances sufficiently different from those of today as to render their value as strategic examples highly questionable."[674] I, however, think exactly the converse is true: that the Ottoman, and, to a lesser degree, Almoravid, examples are valuable precisely because of their possible strategic lessons, even more so than in terms of tactics and operations. Terrorism is a form of insurgency and, alas, far too much of that today involves the world's second largest religion—a problem that cries out for "understanding cultural values of both insurgents and the civilian population in which the insurgents operate…."[675] The weapons and modes of insurgent, and counterinsurgent, combat are no longer defined by lever-action rifles and horse cavalry,[676] much less swords and spears. However, the ideas fueling Islamic insurgencies in the Ottoman Empire, and today, have changed very little—if at all.

There is, indeed, a global revolt rooted in a certain understanding of Islam, waged both peacefully and violently by

---

[674] Thomas R. Mockaitis, "Resolving Insurgencies" (Strategic Studies Institute, 2011), p. 6.

[675] Morillo, p. 89.

[676] The Ottomans, like many Western powers, used horse cavalry up to, and during, World War I. "Asakar-i Mansure-i Muhammadiye," *Wikipedia*; accessed August 13, 2020.

groups expressing largely the same beliefs (there is no deity but Allah, the Qur'an is his word and Muhammad is his messenger) while also aspiring to the same goals (more shari`ah; a new, legitimate caliphate; and ultimately, *insha'allah*, an Islamic planet). Across space and time, the Ottoman Empire faced down opponents with these same beliefs—which the Empire itself officially held, keep in mind, albeit in somewhat different form and perhaps less fanatically.[677] As for insurgent groups' goals, the Islamic world already had an Ottoman Sultan-Caliph who upheld Islamic law, although perhaps not to the degree preferred by Kadizadelis, Wahhabis or Mahdists, Sudanese or otherwise; and while he and his advisors may have dreamed of global hegemony before the 18th century, by the 19th and afterwards they were forced to settle for just maintaining the territory they already possessed—if that. Of course, the least bearable brand of opposition was the eschatological kind, as it not only offended Ottoman Islamic sensibilities by displaying pretentious arrogance, but also threatened to upset diplomatic apple carts, wherever it broke out. All of these are ideas and motivations operating on a strategic level, and thus in my estimation render the Ottoman (and Almoravid) struggle against them worthy of study; they may also offer us, and our allies, valuable insights into waging

---

[677] This was for two reasons: the Ottomans ruled a vast empire, even in its decline, with many non-Muslim subjects; and the predominant school of Ottoman jurisprudence was the Hanafi one, in which "freedom and flexibility of legal reasoning is the keynote of *istiḥsān*, or 'juristic preference....'" Coulson, *A History of Islamic Law*, p. 91.

COIN against enemies fighting under the banner of Islam. In this concluding chapter, then, I will focus on Ottoman (and Almoravid) strategy and even higher-level grand strategy in choosing why, how, where and when to fight insurgents; the operational and tactical has, I trust, been dealt with sufficiently in the preceding sections.

At the end of chapter three, I provided a brief overview of Ottoman COIN successes and failures. That needs to be further fleshed out. A modern metric in this regard provides for four scenarios: 1) insurgent wins 2) government wins 3) insurgencies devolving into terrorist or criminal groups, and 4) insurgencies being co-opted and (re)integrated into their society.[678] **Insurgent wins** include the Israeli Zionists wearing down the Brits, the Algerians finally ousting the French, and the Kosovars outlasting the Yugoslav Serbs. Insurgencies come out on top by making the occupying power appear illegitimate and/or its losing support at home for the conflict; receiving outside help; or gaining direct foreign power intervention (as in the latter example, with NATO intervening). **Government COIN victories** include the likes of the British in post-World War II Malaya, the Greeks in the same time frame, and Sri Lanka over the Tamil Tigers from the 1980s till 2009. Government wins tend to happen only under extremely favorable conditions, to include: when the insurgents are boxed into a geographically-isolated area, engaging in stupidly brutal and

---

[678] Mockaitis, "Resolving Insurgencies," *passim.*

exploitative operations, and are overly reliant on a single charismatic leader. **In the third instance, insurgents transmogrify into "extremists"/terrorists or simply criminals.** This happened with the Basque Euskadi ta Askatasuna, or ETA, organization, a core of which refused to take "yes" to most of its demands as an answer from Spain or France. Shining Path in Peru made the same mistakes—its heavy-handedness and unremitting Maoism,[679] plus the government's capture of leader Abimael Guzmán, destroyed its popularity and turned it into, now, a mere cocaine cartel. FARC (Fuerzas Armadas Revolucionarias de Colombia) took the same unwise path, also devolving into a drug operation. So insurgencies can actually competently counter, or even arguably defeat, government COIN operations but still "lose the peace." **Finally, armed anti-government movements can be incorporated (back) into the system and society,** and defanged. This is largely what happened with the paramilitary Irish Republican Army (IRA) via the more political Sinn Féin. Ditto for the Frento Farabundo Marti para la Liberación Nacional, the FMLN, which despite its Marxism was integrated into the administration in El Salvador following the USSR's collapse. Perhaps the most successful example of this category is that of Sierra Leone's Revolutionary United Front, RUF, which Freetown tamed by offering amnesty, political

---

[679] Even the Beatles, in 1968, knew what happened to those "carrying pictures of Chairman Mao." For the few who might not know the song, watch (and listen to!) "Revolution," *youtube.com*; accessed August 7, 2020.

representation for involved tribes, and bringing former guerrillas into the government. Overall,[680] a good case can be made that this final option—co-opting—is the best choice for defeating an insurgency, at least in modern times. But a clear government or insurgent win is rare, with more often the conflict simply grinding on for years. There is also a growing tendency, here in the 21st century, for insurgencies to transform into terrorism and/or criminal gangs. Once again, here are the posited scenarios.

For insurgents to win, they need to:

- Make the government illegitimate in the conflict area and hope it loses domestic support for the struggle
- Maintain resupply/safe havens (bases)
- Receive sufficient external support and/or direct intervention
- Degrade foreign support for the government.

The government, in order to come out on top must, in addition to using kinetic operations:

- Address root causes of the insurgency
- Box insurgents into a limited geographical area (if not already the case)
- Highlight insurgency brutality and exploitation
- Exploit (if relevant) dependence on single charismatic leader
- Cut off insurgents from foreign support

---

[680] Mockaitis, pp. 60-64.

- Receive some external support of their own, or at least convince the international community to remain neutral
- Finally, incorporate aspects of insurgent agenda, cadres into government.

How does this approach work when applied to pre- and early-modern Islamic insurgencies and the COIN responses to them?

The Ottoman government clearly defeated the Sufi challenges to its early reign. The Ottomans pursued three avenues to do so: they worked to cut off any external support which the Safavid Empire was providing to Sufis with Shi'i tendencies; they killed all-important charismatic leaders (Bedreddin, then later Shah Qulu) and so demoralized their followers; and, finally, in a surprisingly modern move, they incorporated some insurgents, such as the Bektaşis, into the imperial military and state administration. These movements had hoped to delegitimize the nascent House of Osman, but succeeded only temporarily at that. Just as damagingly, their havens proved insecure in the face of Ottoman military expeditions. And as noted, their foreign patron was attacked and its aid to these insurgents interdicted by the Ottoman state.

As for the Celalis, their armed discontent was receiving no external support (that we know of), and their leaders' sole approach was to undermine Ottoman rule in any Anatolian towns they commandeered, no doubt hoping against hope that the state might find them too much trouble to eliminate. Unfortunately for them, this proved not to be the case. Imperial troops isolated any Celali-dominated towns and, then—much as they had the earlier Sufi insurrectionists—co-opted at least one prominent leader into Ottoman administration by granting him a governorship. This was a wise course of action, considering that most Celali rank-and-file, as well as leaders, were former Ottoman military.

The Kadizadelis were, again, not so much insurgents as religious malcontents, but they did present much the same sort of challenge as an insurgency in terms of damaging the Ottoman state's religious credentials, and instigating urban violence. For the most part, the Ottomans countered this quasi-insurgency by addressing root causes and by turning the delegitimizing tables on the Kadizadelis: at times some of their clerics were even granted important positions in Istanbul, until their demands became too strident and excessive; then the state switched over to fatwas condemning their beliefs and practices, and eventually resorted to arrest and exile of the movement's leaders. These steps beat back the Kadizadeli hostile, but largely non-violent, takeover attempt.

The previous three opposition movements were, on a historical scale, short-lived, if in a sense explosive. The Druzes' intermittent insurgencies were more of a long-simmering problem for the Ottoman state—but one that could, and did, episodically boil over and necessitate imperial intervention to lower the temperature. But the Ottomans could never extinguish the Druze fire, so this conflict qualifies as one in which there was no clear win by either the insurgents or the government, for many years. The Druzes operated from their villages, which constituted safe havens—unless the Empire greatly increased its forces in their territories, as it intermittently did. These insurgents tended to regard the Ottomans as unwanted intruders, although they never actually branded them as illegitimate. But the Druzes did receive, at times, outside support, from the likes of Venice and Tuscany. Ottoman COIN in this long-standing conflict was multifaceted: ruthless kinetic military operations; interdicting foreign assistance by, for example, conquering the staging area of Cyprus; incorporation of Druze elders into local Ottoman administration; and capture and execution of charismatic (and effective) leaders, such as Fakhr al-Din—who had been appointed an Ottoman official before betraying the Empire. But another outside power, France, directly intervened and did more to put down the Druze insurgency than had the Ottomans. Even so, the Empire still held sway over most Druzes and might have solved the root causes of the insurgency, (over)taxation and Levantine sectarian strife, as they seemed on the verge of doing right before World War I. But the Empire would not long survive that conflict, and after it the Druze issue would become one for Western powers to deal with.

The Zaydi insurgency burned for one and a half centuries, with the Ottomans, who deemed Yemen a strategic asset worth fighting for, providing much of the fuel for that fire. The two chronologically-distinct periods of imperial occupation found the state using different COIN approaches there. In the first phase, the Shi`i tribes trumpeted the Ottomans lack of right to rule there, making it a mainstay of their insurgency; they also possessed multiple safe havens in the Yemeni highlands from which to stage attacks on the occupiers. Within less than a century, the Zaydi insurgents won by degrading the support of policy-makers in Istanbul for this distant Arabian enterprise. Ottoman COIN initially addressed at least some root causes of unrest by making deals with tribal shaykhs and sect leaders and committing to a *Pax Ottomanica*, and the obstreperous Zaydis were already confined to the high country. But venal and incompetent government officials gave the insurgents all the ammunition they needed to win this first round. When the Empire returned in the mid-19th century, it did not rely entirely on military force. There were concerted and sincere efforts to mollify, as well as pacify, the opposition—particularly, of course, the Zaydis: building infrastructure and schools, lowering taxes, even creating indigenous military units and bringing Yemenis into local government, etc. But the insurgents still would not acknowledge Ottoman ruling legitimacy there; government forces could never take all of their highland havens; and eventually outside powers (France, Italy) began providing material support in the form of weapons. So despite intense efforts at COIN, the Ottomans once again lost in Yemen.

Ottoman COIN against the Wahhabi Sa`udi insurgency was more indirect than direct, mostly carried out by its Egyptian proxy—

but the same metrics apply. The whole thrust of Wahhabi ideology was to degrade, indeed destroy, the Ottoman state's Islamic legitimacy in central and western Arabia. But in the early 19th century, this succeeded only among the Sa`ud tribe. Also, the insurgents were receiving no outside support, and it turned out that their central haven was not actually safe. Ottoman Egyptian forces militarily pursued a number of effective COIN strategies, as they: routed the insurgents; exploited their dependence on a single charismatic leader by capturing and decapitating him; boxed them into central Arabia and also sacked their home base; and highlighted insurgents' depredations (thus undermining their legitimacy) via clerical missives. So the government won the first round of COIN against the Wahhabi Sa`udis. But it was mostly a containment victory. The movement still survived and eventually triumphed over another Ottoman client state, that of the Rashidis. Once again the insurgents worked at undermining the Empire's religious and political right to rule in Arabia. This time they preserved a number of secure town-bases, and eventually received outside (British) diplomatic support. Ottoman COIN, by the eve of World War I, had failed. The Empire never adequately addressed the root causes of the insurgency: that the Turks were insufficiently Islamic and had no right to rule Arabs, in any event. These ideas precluded any incorporation into Istanbul's central administrative machinery, although by the end insurgent leaders were being granted governorships in Arabia. There were, again, denunciatory writings by

Ottomanophile religious leaders, but these did little to undermine staunch Wahhabi beliefs. And by the eve of World War I, the international community, notably the UK, was involved and decidedly sympathetic to the Wahhabi Sa`udi insurgency. Ultimately, Ottoman COIN in central Arabia came to naught—another imperial government loss.

As has been noted in another work, an insurgency built around a man claiming to be the Mahdi is, by definition in an Islamic context, the holiest war. That is what the Ottomans faced in late-19th century Sudan. Muhammad Ahmad's eschatological claim was a resounding intrinsic repudiation of Ottoman authority, and the breadth and depth of that belief—along with his followers' litany of military victories—created a number of Mahdist safe havens throughout the country. Also, the Turkiyah missed its early chance to confine the movement (to Aba Island, or even post-hijrah to Kordofan) or to arrest or kill its leader. Ottoman Egyptian officials, political and religious, tried to address this root cause, Mahdism, but as with the Wahhabis the fervor with which the Sudanese held to it belied Ottoman attempts at delegitimizing. Yes, the movement was dependent on a single charismatic leader—but by the time he died, the Mahdist insurgency had gone from victory to victory, and generated not just a state of its own but a belief system that would sustain it for over a decade. So the Ottoman COIN in Sudan, even with external military support coming from the British, proved incapable of defeating the Mahdists and retaining Sudan as part of

the Empire. The former insurgency, now a polity, would be defeated
13 years later—but then made part of the British, not Ottoman,
Empire.

Ottoman Army, 1900 [681]

So the Ottoman government clearly won against the early
Sufis, the Celalis and the Kadizadelis. One might make the case for
a qualified government victory against the Druzes, in that they never
totally broke away from Ottoman rule, nor convinced the Empire to

[681] "The Ottoman Imperial Army in 1900," *Wikipedia*; accessed August 10, 2020.

leave—World War I would do that. The insurgent Zaydis did win, in both time frames—after a very long time, although the Ottomans did not easily admit defeat. Both the Wahhabis and Sudanese Mahdists won, as well—although the Empire's COIN did arguably contain them, limiting the former to central Arabia (at least until World War I changed everything), and the latter to a large, but quite peripheral, province. The Ottoman state was also quite willing to defuse insurgent movements by bringing dissidents into local governance, if not into the central administration.   This worked with the Sufis, Celalis and, to a lesser extent, with the Kadizadelis. It worked less well with the Druzes and Zaydis, poorly with the Wahhabis, and not at all with the Sudanese Mahdists. What we do not really see with Ottoman insurgencies is any of them turning into terrorists or criminals.

As we know, Almoravid COIN against the Almohads failed. The latter's eschatological propaganda clearly rendered the state illegitimate and eroded its popular support.   The Almohad insurgents also maintained secure bases from the beginning, and the government was unable to keep them isolated in the mountain ones. It would seem that the Almohads might have been vulnerable to overdependence on Ibn Tumart, but for two reasons they proved not to be: Abd al-Mu'min and the inner circle kept his death secret for several years, forestalling defections; and that same leader proved enormously competent as a military leader and administrator, such that the loss of the founder made little difference in the short run.

And as would prove to be the case with the Sudanese Mahdists, the root cause of Almohadism was apocalyptic, and thus extremely difficult for non-Mahdists to invalidate—especially when they refuse to recognize the need to do so, until too late, which proved the Almoravids' mortal sin.

Can these lessons be applied, at all, to any of the many Islamic-based terrorist groups today? Yes, considering that many of them would (also) qualify as insurgencies. Terror tactics—beheading, blowing up restaurants, flying airplanes into buildings, to name but the most egregious—do not, in and of themselves, define terrorism *per se*. Those kinds of violence are simply tactics or tools. However, "insurgencies combine violence with political programs in pursuit of revolutionary purposes in a way that terrorism cannot duplicate. Terrorists may pursue political, even revolutionary, goals, but their violence replaces rather than complements a political program."[682] Each of these movements fighting the Ottomans did so with religious and political agendas. Brutality, or what we might call terrorist tactics, which they employed was usually in service of those aims—Zaydi killing of Ottoman prisoners, Sudanese Mahdist enslaving of non-Muslim POWs—and not simply wanton violence. Also, each one had substantial support among the populace, although some more than others. Scrutinizing, yet again, the 53

---

[682] Lieutenant Colonel Michael F. Morris, "Al-Qaeda as Insurgency," US Army War College Strategy Research Project, March 18, 2005, *usiraq.procon.org*, accessed August 9, 2020.

groups on the current US State Department's Foreign Terrorist Organization list,[683] I find that 51 of them, or 96%, are classifiable as insurgencies; that is, they all are fighting for some combination of goals which include establishing more (stringent) Islamic law, expelling unwanted occupiers (many fellow Muslims), and reestablishing an authoritative caliphate. The only two exceptions are Lashkar-i Jhangvi, a Sunni group in Pakistan and Afghanistan whose sole goal seems to be killing Shi`is; and the Iranian Republican Guards Corps, which as a state organ, of the Islamic Republic of Iran, cannot be defined as insurgent.[684] That said, which insurgencies in the Ottoman Empire are most similar to any of today's—and thus most likely to be instructive in terms of COIN? I would submit the Kadizadelis, Zaydis, Wahhabis and Sudanese Mahdists.

The Kadizadelis perhaps most resemble the non-jihadist wing of the modern global Islamic insurgency—groups such as Hizb al-Tahrir and Tablighi Jama`at, for example. The former is dedicated to increasing the piety of Islamic populations and, ultimately, reestablishing the caliphate.[685] The latter is a huge, South Asian-

---

[683] "Foreign Terrorist Organizations," *state.gov/foreign-terrorist-organizations/*; accessed August 10, 2020.

[684] Unless we view the IRI *in toto* as an insurgent nation-state against the entire global order, which is a defensible position but beyond the scope of this work.

[685] I have attended several of the "party of liberation's" American conferences and written on their agenda and activities. See my article "Gathering Clouds Here?," *washingtontimes.com*, August 2, 2009; accessed August 10, 2020. Also, see my essay "Hizb al-Tahrir: Still Coming to America in 2012," in *Sects, Lies, and the Caliphate*, pp. 181-190.

based Islamic revivalist movement which, unlike HT, is officially apolitical.[686] But the Kadizadelis also share characteristics with the modern Muslim Brotherhood which, despite the contentions of some that it is a terrorist group,[687] has actually renounced violent jihad.[688] These 17th century Ottoman religious agitators did also presage the Salafi-Wahhabi movement, insofar as they opposed Sufism and tried to influence the leadership to adhere to a more fundamentalist understanding of Islamic tenets. The bottom line is that the Kadizaelis did not advocate, much less engage in, jihad to change the extant regime. Like HT and TJ, and even to some degree the MB, Kadizadelism aimed to make the institutions, and thus the masses, more Islamic *sans* holy warfare.[689]

Today, leaders in both HT and the MB have expressed a desire to infiltrate and/or associate with Black Lives Matter and Antifa inside the United States, in order to advance the spread and power of their brand of Islam in this country.[690] Like Kadizadelis,

---

[686] See my entry "Tablighi Jamaat," *World Almanac of Islamism 2011*, put out by the American Foreign Policy Council (Lanham, MD: Rowman & Littlefield Publishers, Inc., 2011), pp. 866-873.

[687] Lukas Mikelionis, "Trumps Wants to Designate Muslim Brotherhood a Terror Group: Report," *foxnews.com*, April 30, 2019; also Veronica Kyrylenko, "Yes, the Muslim Brotherhood Is a Terrorist Organization," *americanthinker.com*, May 9, 2019. Both accessed August 10, 2020.

[688] "Muslim Brotherhood," n.d., *World Almanac of Islamism, almanac.afpc.org,* accessed August 10, 2020.

[689] HT hopes to do this by a top-down approach: if you (re)build the caliphate, they will come and be better Muslims. TJ takes a more grass-roots tactic: inculcate a more rigorous practice of Islam among Muslims, and eventually they will create more Islamic polities.

[690] See Stephen Johnson and Alison Bevege, " 'We Will Take Over:' Australian Leader of Extremist [sic] Islamic Group Says US Riots Are An 'Opportunity'

they hope to leverage urban violence as a means of getting what they want—while they also, it's worth noting, target Christians and Jews.[691] The Ottomans countered the Kadizadeli threat mainly by ideological refutation, and by exiling their leaders. Of course, they could do the former with authority, as the preeminent Islamic state of their time. The US is a secular republic but with a huge Christian majority; thus in both registers it lacks the Islamic cachet to delegitimize advocates for shari`ah or the caliphate.[692] One idea, drawn from the Ottoman v. Kadizadeli conflict, would be for more moderate/less literalist Islamic leaders to speak out, and write, against those Muslims who wish to Islamize our system. Two such thinkers come to mind: Dr. Zuhdi Jasser and Fethullah Gülen. Jasser has been a prominent Sunni critic of political Islam and its adherents, but as medical doctor, and not an Islamic scholar or cleric, his influence among Muslims themselves is questionable.[693] Gülen is a prominent, and powerful, Turkish cleric who since 1999 has lived in Pennsylvania.[694]

For Muslims To Seize Global Leadership and Impose Sharia Law," *dailymail.co.uk*, June 7, 2020, as well as Christina Lin, "Muslim Brotherhood, Antifa, and Hybrid Warfare to Destabilize America?," *blogs.timesofisrael.com*, July 20, 2020; both accessed August 10, 2020.

[691] Daniel Greenfield, " 'God Is Dead:' Leftist Rioters Vandalize Churches and Synagogues," *frontpagemag.com*, June 4, 2020; accessed August 10, 2020.

[692] Of course, American law does draw the line at those who wish to upend our system of government entirely, and replace it with another—or at least it did before the street violence of summer 2020 commenced.

[693] See my article "Zuhdi Jasser, M.D.: Islam's Luther—or its Don Quixote?," *hnn.us*, April 19, 2010; accessed August 10, 2020.

[694] See Claire Berlinski, "Who Is Fethullah Gülen?," *city-journal.org*, Autumn 2012, and Jillian Kester-D'Amours, "ANALYSIS: Dissecting Turkey's Gulen-Erdogan Relationship," *middleeasteye.net*, July 25, 2016; both accessed August 10, 2020.

A neo-Sufi, he runs the global charter school network named after him and advocates "jihad of the mind," not that of the sword. He and Turkish President Erdoğan were once allies, working to make staunchly secular Turkey more Islamic. But the Turkish President blamed him for the 2016 coup attempt there, and the two are now bitter enemies. Gülen is not an American citizen, and has been so reclusive since coming to the US that he would probably be unwilling to critique fundamentalist Muslims in the US.[695] It is thus the case that a medical doctor and a foreign mystic are the best options the US might have of ideologically countering domestic fundamentalist Islamic movements. Of course, if ideological counters fail, there's always the exile option—which the Ottomans took. But unlike in that Empire, citizens in the US have Constitutional rights, which would make expulsion rather problematic.

What about abroad, where such movements are a clear and present danger—not theoretical? Delegitimizing modern Kadizadelism should, at least in theory, be much easier for an Islamic polity than for the Great Satan. A number of Muslim-majority countries have banned HT, notably Egypt, Turkey and Pakistan.[696] Likewise, the MB is listed as a terrorist organization by

---

[695] He did write an article for "The Washington Post" on September 21, 2001, in which he stated that "a real Muslim cannot be a terrorist." But that link no longer works. Information can be found here: "Fethullah Gulen Condemns 9-11 Terrorist Attacks," *guleninthenews.blogspot.com*, September 1, 2011; accessed August 10, 2020.

[696] See "Hizb ut-Tahrir," *Wikipedia*; accessed August 11, 2020.

at least five Islamic nations: Syria, Egypt, Sa`udi Arabia, Bahrain and the United Arab Emirates.[697] But in some Islamic circles that is a badge of honor, not a scarlet letter. The biggest problem is that none of those countries commands the Islamic stature that the Ottoman Empire did, with a leader convincingly, to many Muslims, claiming the caliphate, as well as control of Mecca and Medina. Muslims are, compared to Ottoman times, scattered, divided and leaderless. Egypt has al-Azhar Mosque (and University), the Grand Imam of which is deemed by many the highest authority in Sunni Islam.[698] But in some of its rulings, al-Azhar has displayed sympathy, if not complete agreement, with Islamic fundamentalists.[699] The same is largely true of the Kingdom of Sa`udi Arabia, which is in large measure built on Wahhabism—and thus unable, or unwilling, to repudiate that brand of Islam.[700] From the perspective of many Islamic leaders and establishments, notably Riyadh's, the problem with groups like HT and the MB is not so much their staunch Sunni Islam as that their political agendas would push extant rulers—particularly the house of Sa`ud—out of power. (On the other side of the ideological fence, ironically, TJ has been banned in the Kingdom because it is *too* peaceful, having renounced militant jihad.[701]) But Kadizadeli-style

---

[697] Per "Muslim Brotherhood," *Wikipedia*; accessed August 11, 2020.

[698] "Grand Imam of al-Azhar," *Wikipedia*; accessed August 11, 2020.

[699] Maher Gabra, "The Ideological Extremism of al-Azhar," *The Washington Institute for Near East Policy*, March 3, 2016; accessed August 11, 2020.

[700] Recent moves purportedly in that direction may be a mirage, according to Ola Salem and Abdullah Alaoudh, "Mohammad bin Salman's Fake Anti-Extremist Campaign," *foreignpolicy.com*, June 13, 2019; accessed August 11, 2020.

threats are mainly ones of ideas, and can be combatted in that register; not just with with condemnatory fatwas, as in Ottoman times, but with disparaging Friday *khutbah*s (sermons), and possibly even social media emasculation, as well. Additionally, in the longer term, the inculcation of a less fundamentalist brand of Islam, often Sufi-tinged, is worth pursuing[702]--emulating the Ottomans, whose state-supported Sufism proved at least a partial antidote to Islamic literalism.

What if the challenge is not just rhetorical, however? As noted earlier in this work, the Kadizadelis were proto-Wahhabis. The two groups shared much the same Islamic fundamentalist ideology, but the former never rose up against the state; while the latter weaponized Sunni zealotry and eventually established, when allied to the house of Sa`ud, the modern Kingdom. Wahhabism is thus, today, the official ideology of a state. But its close no-state counterpart, Salafism, empowers many (if not most) of those 51 insurgent-terrorist groups—most notably al-Qa`idah and ISIS, both of which detest the Sa`udis more than any other rulers.[703] The Wahhabi Sa`udi state thus, quite ironically, finds itself in much the

---

[701] "Tablighi Jamaat," *World Almanac of Islamism*, p. 868.

[702] Zoe Zuidema, "Moroccan Islam: An Effort to Fight Radicalism," *moroccoworldnews.com*, July 17, 2017; accessed August 11, 2020.

[703] Although the ones in Pakistan, Afghanistan, India and Bangladesh may draw their direct line of descent from the 19th century Deobandi movement, a Salafism which is distinct from, but very similar to, Arab Wahhabism. See Ira M. Lapidus, *A History of Islamic Societies* (Cambridge: Cambridge University Press, 1988), pp. 725, 726.

same position vis-à-vis Islamic fundamentalist insurgencies as did the Ottoman Empire when their ancestors were waging war on the Sultan. Of course, Wahhabi-Salafi style Islamic fundamentalists are a challenge to many other Muslim rulers, as well. In fact, these movements represent the most common threat to extant Muslim governments. Some of the most prominent are: the various and sundry ISIS branches in Syria/Iraq, Sinai, Bangladesh, Khorasan (Afghanistan), the Philippines, West Africa and the Maghrib; AQ in the Arabian Peninsula, India, Islamic Maghrib and Syria (al-Nusrah Front); Boko Haram and Ansaru in Nigeria and environs; and the several incarnations of Ansar al-Shari`ah in Libya and Tunisia. The specific COIN approach to each of these by will differ, depending on regional and local circumstances. But distilling from the Ottoman experience, at a minimum a government, to have any chance of prevailing, must be willing to: take the kinetic fight to its enemies, especially in denying, if not destroying, insurgent bases; interdict any outside support for the movement; capture or kill charismatic leaders, especially competent ones; and delegitimize insurgent ideas and approaches as unIslamic. This final tack, to succeed, would likely require admitting the Islamic textual basis of at least some of the insurgents' criticisms, as well as the undeniable validity of jihad in the religion.[704] This would amount to a virtual, if not real, co-opting of the movement: rather than bringing insurgent leaders into

---

[704] Unlike the approach of Shaykh al-Yaqoubi, discussed in the first chapter of this book.

government administration, the state would instead grant the movement some degree of religious legitimacy. However, as Ottoman clerics did their enemies, the insurgents could nonetheless be rebuked for arrogantly claiming to understand Islam better than the learned authorities, for ignoring the consensus of Islamic tradition, and of course for perpetrating violence against fellow Muslims. While such censure would not be sufficient to extinguish a fundamentalist insurgency, it would certainly be necessary.

It's not difficult to find a modern analog for the Zaydi insurgents in the Ottoman Empire. The Zaydi Houthis are still fighting in and around Yemen. But the extensive Ottoman experience there is practically ignored by modern mavens. A Brookings Institute analysis of the current war in southwestern Arabia merely says, in passing, that the Zaydis "fought against both the Ottomans and the Wahhabis in the 18th and 19th centuries."[705] That's it. An allegedly in-depth examination from Ohio State University doesn't even mention the 159 years the Ottomans spent occupying that country, instead skipping from the 9th century AD to the 1960s.[706] Beginning in 2011, in the wake of the "Arab Spring," Yemen's political unity began dissolving. The Zaydi Houthis rose up in rebellion against the Sunni rulers, feeling—with some

---

[705] Bruce Riedel, "Who Are the Houthis, and Why Are We at War with Them?," *brookings.edu*, December 18, 2017; accessed August 11, 2020.

[706] Asher Orkaby, "Yemen: A Civil War Centuries in the Making," in *Origins: Current Events in Historical Perspective*, Volume 12, Issue 8, *origins.osu.edu* (May 2019); accessed August 11, 2020.

justification—that they were doing little to protect them against attacks by AQ and, later, ISIS. This erupted into full-scale civil war, with a transnational dimension: Iran has been accused of assisting its Shi`i cousins, while KSA has attacked Zaydi positions from the air, assisted by other Arab nations and, perhaps, American intelligence. As of summer 2020, the Houthi group Ansar Allah controls about half the country, mainly the traditional Zaydi highlands. But it also occupies San`a. Competing factions of the former government hold sway in Aden and the extreme south. AQAP (al-Qa`idah in the Arabian Peninsula) and ISIS-Yemen Province dominate some areas in the east.[707] Once again, KSA find itself in a similar position to its former master, the Ottoman Empire, bogged down in a Yemeni war. In other parallels to the previous Ottoman occupations, the Zaydis are also fighting Sunni Islamic fundamentalists from outside Yemen—but in this case, AQAP and ISIS, rather than Wahhabis; and an outside power is running weapons to the Shi`i insurgents— but instead of Italy, this time it's Iran.[708] If there's one thing the outside Sunni belligerents—mainly KSA and the UAE, who are driving the issue—should learn from the long and bitter Ottoman experience there, it's this: even if you are willing to commit to inserting substantial ground forces which will remain for decades, as

---

[707] See "Yemeni Crisis (2011-Present)," and "Saudi Arabian-led Intervention in Yemen," both *Wikipedia*, as well as "Yemen Crisis: Why Is There a War?," *bbc.com*, June 19, 2020; all accessed August 11, 2020.

[708] "Pompeo Says U.S. Seized Iranians Weapons on Way to Houthi Rebels in Yemen," *usnews.com*, July 8, 2020; accessed August 11, 2020.

well as to a massive and enormously expensive nation-building program—you still probably won't defeat the Zaydis. And there is precious little evidence that the other Arab nations have the stomach, or will risk their pocketbooks, in a neo-Ottoman approach to the Yemen dilemma. The Zaydi Houthis make up as much as half the population, they have ruled the country on-and-off for a millennium, and they have legitimate grievances over against oppressive Sunni fundamentalists, whether indigenously Yemeni or foreigners. Zaydi Houthis may shout slogans promising death to the U.S. and Israel, but these are more to make their Iranian patrons happy than a serious conviction. If the world's foremost Islamic empire could not subdue Yemen's recalcitrant Shi`is, what hope does KSA have, even with much shorter supply lines? Very little. Then there's the negative example of Egypt's ill-fated foray into Yemen in the 1960s, which turned into Cairo's Vietnam. The Zaydis simply want to be left alone to rule their rump highland state. Let them. The Ottomans eventually learned the folly of trying to take over and modernize Yemen. We and our allies might learn from their example.

Mahdists are a qualitatively different challenge to existing Islamic states.[709] While such eschatological insurgencies as those created and led by Ibn Tumart and Muhammad Ahmad had similar grievances and shared a frontier fundamentalist Islamic ethos, the

---

[709] A number of the most important such movements in history are covered in my 2005 work *Holiest Wars*.

same might be said of any number of situations in the Islamic world over the past almost 15 centuries. Yet Mahdist movements arose in only some of them.[710] Thus what has been said about Christian messianic movements holds true for the Islamic kind, as well. "One cannot predict the advent of millenarianism any more than one can predict tornados. All one can do is observe that, when certain conditions overtake certain individuals with certain mythologies or theological expectations, certain outcomes commonly, but not inevitably, ensue."[711] When they do manifest, Mahdis are quite problematic. They, and their followers, are fanatical. A Mahdi's subjective experiences, used to substantiate his claims, are by definition irrefutable. Anyone with hubris enough to hold such a view of himself is also, by definition, narcissistic—which can easily translate, for the faithful, into convincing charisma. Both the Almoravid and Ottoman examples show that a potential Mahdist whirlwind must be deflated before it spins out of control. Ibn Yusuf should have listened to his advisors and arrested, probably executed, Ibn Tumart. Had that happened, there would never have been an Almohad insurgency, and the Almoravids likely would have survived for much longer. Ottoman COIN against the Sudanese Mahdists is

---

[710] As covered earlier in this book, the Ottomans faced a number of other, less powerful movements led by self-proclaimed Mahdis: Shah Qulu, Nur Ali Khalifah, Shah Wali, several anonymous Naqshbandis, Sayyid Abd Allah, Faqih Sa'id and Ali al-Idrisi. There were also two Jewish messianic challenges: those of Sabbatai Sevi and Shukri Kuhayil.

[711] Dale C. Allison, *Jesus of Nazareth: Millenarian Prophet* (Minneapolis: Fortress Press, 1998), p. 82.

more instructive. When someone says he's the Mahdi, take it seriously enough, early on, to bring him in for interrogation—if not for incarceration, and perhaps even execution. If that's not done, and the movement gets off the ground, send sufficient forces to stop it in its tracks—don't give Mahdists a chance to win over government forces, because that will just increase their eschatological status. Once Mahdism is developed and growing, an Islamic polity will need to have the religious establishment issue fatwas undercutting its leader and beliefs. Any Islamic state's leadership would no doubt be tempted to simply dismiss a Mahdist claimant as delusional or clinically insane. But the problem with doing that is the depth and breadth of belief in the Mahdi in the modern Islamic world:

Belief in Mahdi's Imminent Return

% who expect Mahdi to return in their lifetime

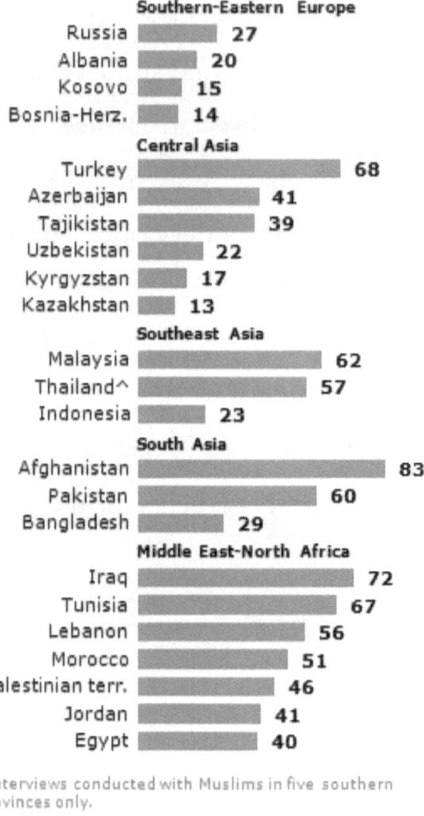

Belief in Mahdi's Imminent Return[712]

It's easy to dismiss the late 19th century Sudanese masses as gullible, superstitious peasants. But then how to explain those large percentages in modern Turkey, Malaysia, Iraq or the Palestinian

[712] "Chapter Three: Articles of Faith," *The World's Muslims: Unity and Diversity*, *pewforum.org*, August 9, 2012; accessed August 11, 2020.

territories who expect the Mahdi to appear soon? The Sa`udis were seriously threatened by a Mahdist insurgency in 1979, which occupied the main mosque in Mecca for several weeks before being eliminated—so much so that the government had its senior Wahhabi clerics issue fatwas stating why the "Mahdi" was a pretender.[713]   Since then dozens of movements claiming to be preparing the way for the Mahdi, or to led by him already, have surfaced in the Islamic world.[714] ISIS from 2014-2019 was openly eschatological,[715] naming its official magazine *Dabiq*—after the hadith-predicted site of the Islamic "Armageddon," in northern Syria[716]—although never proclaiming its "caliph" the Mahdi. In late 2019 a chief military advisor to Turkish President Erdoğan stated publicly that "his organization, which is fully funded and supported by the Turkish government, has been working to pave the way for the long-awaited mahdi...for whom the entire Muslim world is waiting."[717] Just a few weeks later, the advisor was forced to resign[718]--probably not because of this being an "extremist" belief, but

---

[713] Per Trofimov, *The Siege of Mecca*, pp. 99ff, 238ff.

[714] See my book *Ten Years' Captivation with the Mahdi's Camps*, pp. 161-191 in particular.

[715] *Ibid.*, pp. 33-67.

[716] "Chapter: the Conquest of Constantinople, the Emergence of the Dajjal and the Descent of `Eisa [sic] bin Mariam," *The Book of Tribulations and Portents of the Last Hour, sunnah.com*, accessed August 11, 2020.

[717] Levent Kenez, "Erdoğan's Chief Advisor: We Are Working to Open the Way for the Mahdi, the Redeemer of Islam," *nordicmonitor.com*, December 28, 2019; accessed August 11, 2020.

[718] "Military Adviser to Turkey's Erdoğan Resigns after Mahdi Remarks," *ahvalnews.com*, January 8, 2020; accessed August 11, 2020.

because he openly stated what the Turkish leadership did not want revealed yet. And of course the entire existence of the Islamic Republic of Iran is predicated on the future coming of their Mahdi, the returned 12th Imam (a descendant of Muhammad through Ali).[719]

As the most direct heir of the Ottoman Empire, the Turkish state might be expected to be the most amenable to lessons learned from its predecessor polity. It certainly faces similar threats, if a government report from last year on Islamic threats to Turkey is any indication.[720] The Diyanet, Turkey's supreme religious authority (which replaced the Ottoman Ministry of Sharia in the 1920s),[721] issued it. The document surveys "Islamist [sic] groups" that might prove problematic, or even dangerous, to the Turkish state, and classifies them "according to their Islamic traditions." Here are the categories:

- Those which adhere to "the Islam of the Quran" and downplay the Hadiths "as a burden." This movement is known as Qur'anism.[722]

---

[719] Iran's theological and political proclivities are also outside the scope of this book. But for cogent commentary on such see, again, *Ten Years' Captivation with the Mahdi's Camps*, pp. 103-160. Some of that discusses my trip to Iran in 2008—as does this article of mine: "The Importance of being Mahdist," *washingtonexaminer.com*, September 8, 2008; accessed August 12, 2020.

[720] Dicle Eşiyok, "Secret Diyanet Report Gauges Threat Posed by Turkey's Islamists," *ahvalnews.com*, July 10, 2019; accessed August 11, 2020.

[721] "[The] Diyanet has inherited the historical legacy of the Ottoman Empire regarding state-religion relations…." Ahmet Erdi Öztürk, "Transformation of the Turkish Diyanet Both at Home and Abroad: Three Stages," *European Journal of Turkish Studies, journals.openedition.org*, Volume 27 (2018); accessed August 12, 2020.

[722] See "Quranism," *Wikipedia*; accessed August 12, 2020.

- Salafism, especially those who pledge allegiance to ISIS.
- Mahdist movements "that use Messianic rhetoric," to include the recently-arrested Turkish Mahdist Adnan Oktar, aka "Harun Yahya."[723]
- "Traditionalists" who harbor beliefs such as "women who wear trousers are destined for hell." This even includes some Islamic preachers who support President Erdoğan.
- The shadowy Call and Brotherhood Foundation,[724] which is a Turkish version of the MB. This grouping also includes HT. Both these groups are non-jihadist. But this category also includes Turkish Hizbullah, a militant Kurdish Sunni group which is opposed to the secular-Marxist PKK (Ankara's inveterate enemy).[725]
- Groups that follow the teachings of Said Nursi (d. 1960), a late Ottoman and early Turkish Republic Sufi teacher. Fetullah Gülen, as well as Adnan Oktar, fall into this category.
- Naqshbandi Sufis "who have filled the void left by the Gülen movement's divorce from the AKP" (Adalet va Kalkınma Partisi, or Justice and Development Party" of Erdoğan). In particular the Turkish religious authorities are suspicious of the Süleymancılar,[726] a branch of

---

[723] On Turkish Mahdism, including Oktar, see my blogpost "The Sultan v. the Mahdi," *occidentaljihadist.com*, July 13, 2018; also *Ten Years' Captivation with the Mahdi's Camps*, pp. 235-241.

[724] Precious little information is available online on this organization. Here is its business listing at the page of the "Union of NGOs of the Islamic World:" "Call and Brotherhood Foundation," *idsb.org*, accessed August 12, 2020.

[725] See "Turkish Hezbollah," *Wikipedia*, August 12, 2020. Turkey has been accused of assisting TH against the PKK.

[726] According to "Süleymancılar" and an article on its founder, "Süleyman Hilmi Tunahan," both *Wikipedia*, both accessed August 12, 2020.

the Naqshbandi order which, despite running Islamic schools, mostly abroad, on behalf of the government is now accused of "ties to foreign intelligence organisations." [727]

Six of these seven hearken back to factions vexing the Ottoman state: Kadizadelis were the proto-Salafis of 17th century Istanbul; Islamic messianists were exemplified by, but not limited to, the followers of Muhammad Ahmad; consigning allegedly immodest women to hellfire was then the Wahhabi specialty; and Sufis served as either a blessing or a curse to the Ottomans—although in modern Turkey they are deemed mostly the latter, unless they are performing for tourists.[728] Transnational groups, like MB splinter ones and HT, are lumped together by Ankara today likely because of their foreign provenance and transnational nature, as well as their implicit (and sometimes explicit) criticism of the Turkish Republican system.[729] As such, they had no close analogs in Ottoman times, although as

---

[727] All the directly quoted material in this list comes from the Eşiyok article.

[728] This is a reference to the "whirling dervishes" of the Mevlevi order. For an overview of modern Turkish orders, see "Sufism in Turkey," *rlp.hds.harvard.edu*, n.d.; accessed August 13, 2020.

[729] AKP Turkey's relationship with the MB is complicated. Erdoğan seems to support it, and there is a Turkish MB-like group, Millî Görüş ("National Vision"), much larger than the Call and Brotherhood Foundation, which appears to be modeled on the MB. Turkey "sees the rise to power of (Sunni) Islamic movements as an opportunity for the Justice and Development party to rise as a leader of…the post-revolutionary Arab world." This may overstate the yearning for Turkish influence in that region, however, as well as understate how much the Ottomans as still seen as imperialists. Quote is from Mohammed Abdel Kader, "Turkey's Relationship with the Muslim Brotherhood," *english.alarabiya.net*, October 14, 2013. See also "Millî Görüş," *Wikipedia*. Both accessed August 13, 2020.

noted, above, their eschewing of jihad, and operations mainly in the ideological realm, do echo the Kadizadelis. Turkish Hizbullah is the odd man out in this grouping—why the Diyanet places this militant Kurdish insurgency in with Call and Brotherhood and HT is strange. Religion aside, TH actually looks rather like the Zaydi resistance to the Empire: an ethnolinguistic group chafing under Turkish "occupation." Only contemporary Qur'anists had no real equivalent in the Empire. In terms of threat level, none of these modern movements poses anything approaching an existential political, much less military, threat to the Turkish Republic. The Diyanet, following the Erdoğan administration, does seem to think that the Süleymancılar might be a political hazard, in the same way that the Gülenists (allegedly) proved to be during the abortive 2016 military coup. As for the others, Ankara is as capable of dealing with any of them as was Istanbul; they are nuisances more than actual perils.

Between 1416 and 1916 the Ottoman state dealt with a legion of insurgencies. This book has examined seven of them, both for their historical importance and for potential insights into the current global COIN struggle against Islamic insurgencies. Here are the primary lessons to be gleaned from the Ottomans' wars against their mutinous Muslim factions:

- There is very little that is new under the sun, as far as challengers go. Religion—specifically, some brand of Islam—was a major motivation for six of the seven movements vexing the Ottomans, although other factors (political, socioeconomic, cultural) were also present. So it remains today, for the vast majority of the world's insurgent-terrorist groups.

- Mahdism was perhaps the most potent, and prevalent, type of insurgency—epitomized by that of Muhammad Ahmad, but also encompassing eight other such movements[730] (and, of course, Ibn Tumart's against the Almoravids). But opposition to foreign occupation, exemplified by the Zaydis' virtual forever war against Istanbul, proved the most stubborn. The former still exists, but has not weaponized since 1979—although it no doubt will again. The latter still vexes, in the form of AQ, ISIS, Jemaah Islamiyah,[731] Jaysh al-Adl,[732] and many others—most notably the PKK,[733] in its ongoing struggle with what it terms Turkish occupation.

- Forcing Westernization down subjects' throats is a dicey prospect. The Tanzimat clearly infuriated the Zaydis; British-backed Ottoman interdiction of the Islam-approved slave trade incensed many Sudanese; and Turkish consorting with infidel Christian Europeans helped alienate the Wahhabis. The US might learn something from this about our forever war in Afghanistan. If an Islamic state pushing Western-style reforms causes problems, what hope does a Western

---

[730] Again: Shah Qulu, Nur Ali Khalifah, Shah Wali, two Naqshbandi shaykhs, Sayyid Abd Allah, Faqih Sa'id, Ali al-Idrisi.

[731] Which is fighting the Islamic government of Indonesia to establish a fundamentalist state. See "Jemaah Islamiyah," *Wikipedia*, accessed August 13, 2020.

[732] A Sunni Baluch group fighting the government of Iran in the southeast of that country, per "Jaish al-Adl," *Wikipedia*, accessed August 13, 2020.

[733] "Kurdistan Workers Party," *Wikipedia*, accessed August 13, 2020.

secular republic, which is nonetheless perceived as a Christian power, have of making such work?

- It is possible to both punish and learn from dissent.[734] The Ottomans did this in a religious sense with Bedreddin, seeking his wisdom before executing him. But they also did so in a more utilitarian manner with Bektaşi Sufis, Celalis, Kadizadelis, Druzes and Zaydis by seeking their input into governance (although some was eventually rejected). No such learning was possible with Wahhabis or Mahdists, whose anti-state polemical zeal and activities were simply impossible to assimilate. Today this would mean excluding the Taliban from any future Afghani government, and continuing the ban on Gülenists from Turkey's; but it might also require Hamas being brought into the negotiation equation with Israel, or talking to the Zaydi Houthis, not simply bombing them.

- COIN was as much ideological as kinetic warfare. The Ottomans were resolutely Islamic, every bit as much as their insurgents (and more so than the heterodox Zaydis or heretical Druzes). But their establishment Hanafi interpretive school of Islamic law was more flexible than the others—particularly the Hanbali one, whence the Wahhabis came.[735] Despite claims from some quarters that Erdoğan's Turkey is a "rogue state" that aims to bring back Ottoman domination of the Middle East,[736] the reality is that for all its recent geopolitical

---

[734] Again, this is from Barkey, p. 174.

[735] The Hanbalis were "the supreme exponents of an anti-rationalist attitude in [Islamic] law…." Coulson, p. 89.

[736] As, for example, by Yochanan Visser, "ANALYSIS: Turkey Has Become a Rogue State," *israelnationalnews.com*, February 8, 2020; accessed August 13, 2020.

intractability, Turkey remains a NATO member, the most Westernized majority-Muslim nation, and the dominant Sunni power in the Middle East and, actually, the world. Its Hanafism, coupled with its ties to the West, means that Turkey remains the most moderate Islamic influence—and thus the one with the most potential to delegitimize Islamic terrorists.

- The Ottomans deployed both *steel* and *hunger* in their COIN against insurgents. But against those arising from within mainstream Sunnism—Kadizadelis, Wahhabis, Sudanese Mahdists—and thus constituting the most powerful ideological threats, the Empire also used *ink*; that is, Ottoman religious leaders penned fatwas, and other written works, undercutting their Islamic critics. Again, this is where Turkey can play a key role in international affairs; its Ottoman legacy may rankle some, especially Arabs. But that same legacy also gives the Turks prestige that no other modern Islamic country can match—and thus the capacity to wield not just steel and hunger, but ink imprimaturs, in the service of moderate Islam.

The world is still going through the most recent phase of terrorism—that of a religious (mainly Islamic) nature.[737] As

---

[737] This is part of the famous classification by David C. Rapaport, "The Four Waves of Rebel Terror and September 11," *Anthropoetics: The Journal of Generative Anthropology*, Volume VIII, Number 1 (Spring/Summer 2002); accessed August 13, 2020. The waves or phases of terrorism are: anarchist, 1880s-1920s; anti-colonial, 1920-60s; New Left, 1960s-1990s; and Religious, mainly Islamic, since 1979. Of course, Islamic terrorism-as-insurgency long predates 1979, as this book has shown. Still, Rapoport's paradigm is so influential that it must be mentioned.

explained, since modern Islamic terrorism is practically coterminous with insurgency, the study of how history's foremost Islamic state waged COIN, across space and time, is not just noteworthy, but instructive. As has been written in a very similar context: "analysis of the Arab as a counterinsurgent, and the draconian methods usually involved, is not a call for emulation by the West but simply a portrayal aimed to foster a deeper understanding of the whole gamut of waging counterinsurgent war...."[738] In this work, the Arabs have often been insurgents, the Ottoman Turks always the counterinsurgents. True, we aren't the Ottomans, and neither are our Middle Eastern and Islamic world allies. But for 500 years that paramount Islamic state survived its enemies, both foreign and domestic. Mahmud II had his Abd Allah bin Sa`ud, Abdül Hamid II his Muhammad Ahmad—perhaps modern Muslim, and Western, leaders may profit from their example.

---

[738] DeAtkine, "The Arab as Insurgent and Counterinsurgent," in Rubin, ed., *Conflict and Insurgency in the Contemporary Middle East*, p. 40.

www.ingramcontent.com/pod-product-compliance
Lightning Source LLC
Chambersburg PA
CBHW021242060726
47590CB00005B/1867